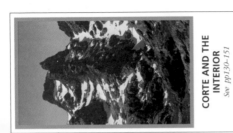

**CORTE AND THE INTERIOR**
*See pp130–151*

**AJACCIO AND THE WEST COAST**

Ajaccio

*Iles Sanguinaires*

**BONIFACIO AND THE SOUTH**

Bonifacio

*Ile Cavallo*

*Iles Lavezzi*

**BONIFACIO AND THE SOUTH**
*See pp106–129*

0 kilometres          15

0 miles          15

# EYEWITNESS TRAVEL
# CORSICA

LONDON, NEW YORK,
MELBOURNE, MUNICH AND DELHI
www.dk.com

PRODUCED BY Fabio Ratti Editoria Srl, Milan, Italy

PROJECT EDITOR Donatella Ceriani

ART EDITOR Oriana Bianchetti

EDITORS Marina Beretta, Angela Magrì

DESIGNER Elisabetta Mancini

CONTRIBUTORS Fabrizio Ardito, Cristina Gambaro, Angela Magrì

PHOTOGRAPHERS Fabrizio Ardito, Adriano Bacchella,
Cristina Gambaro, Lucio Rossi, Marco Stoppato

CARTOGRAPHERS Grafema Cartografia Srl, Novara

ILLUSTRATORS Modi Artistici, Anna Mucciarelli, Tiziano Perotto

ENGLISH TRANSLATION Richard Pierce

Dorling Kindersley Limited
EDITORS Sylvia and David Tombesi-Walton
(Sands Publishing Solutions); Lauren Robertson
CONSULTANT David Abram
SENIOR DTP DESIGNER Jason Little
PRODUCTION Melanie Dowland

Reproduced by Fabio Ratti Editoria Srl, Milan
and in Singapore by Colourscan
Printed and bound in China by L. Rex Printing Co. Ltd

First American Edition 2003
10 11 12 13 10 9 8 7 6 5 4 3 2 1

Published in the United States by DK Publishing,
375 Hudson Street, New York, New York 10014

**Reprinted with revisions 2006, 2008, 2010**

Published in Great Britain by Dorling Kindersley Limited

A CATALOG RECORD FOR THIS BOOK IS AVAILABLE FROM THE LIBRARY OF CONGRESS

ISSN 1542-1554
ISBN 978-0-75666-158-8

THROUGHOUT THIS BOOK, FLOORS ARE REFERRED TO IN ACCORDANCE WITH
EUROPEAN USAGE, I.E. THE "FIRST FLOOR" IS THE FLOOR ABOVE GROUND LEVEL.

*Front cover main image: Red granite cliffs of the Réserve Naturelle de Scandola*

MIX
From responsible
sources
FSC™C018179

---

**The information in this DK Eyewitness
Travel Guide is checked regularly.**
Every effort has been made to ensure that this book is as up-to-date
as possible at the time of going to press. Some details, however,
such as telephone numbers, opening hours, prices, gallery hanging
arrangements and travel information are liable to change. The
publishers cannot accept responsibility for any consequences arising
from the use of this book, nor for any material on third party
websites, and cannot guarantee that any website address in this
book will be a suitable source of travel information. We value the
views and suggestions of our readers very highly. Please write to:
Publisher, DK Eyewitness Travel Guides, Dorling Kindersley,
80 Strand, London, WC2R 0RL, Great Britain.

◁ **The white limestone cliffs at Bonifacio, with the famous Grain de Sable**

# CONTENTS

**The Romanesque church of
San Michele de Murato**

**Laricio pines in the beautiful
Forêt d'Aïtone**

A crystal-clear sea and white rocks in a cove in front of Îles Lavezzi

Cheese and charcuterie – two of the many specialities of Corsica

SPORTS AND OUTDOOR
ACTIVITIES **188**

# SURVIVAL GUIDE

PRACTICAL
INFORMATION **196**

TRAVEL
INFORMATION **204**

GENERAL INDEX
**208**

# CORSICA
AREA BY AREA

A typical maquis plant,
*Euphorbia dendroides*, in bloom

# TRAVELLERS'
NEEDS

Snow-capped mountains near
Monte Cinto

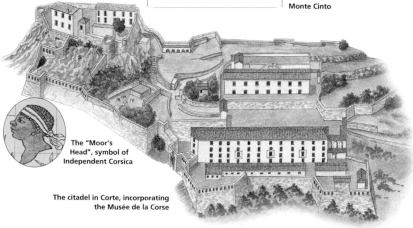

The "Moor's
Head", symbol of
Independent Corsica

The citadel in Corte, incorporating
the Musée de la Corse

# HOW TO USE THIS GUIDE

This guide helps visitors to get the most out of their stay in Corsica by providing detailed descriptions, practical information and expert advice. *Introducing Corsica* sets the island in its geographical, historical and cultural context. *Corsica Area by Area* describes the main sights in detail, with maps, photographs and illustrations. *Travellers' Needs* offers recommendations on hotels, restaurants, local food, bars, shopping, sports and entertainment, while the *Survival Guide* provides useful information on safety, health, transport and local currency.

## CORSICA AREA BY AREA

Corsica has been divided into four main areas, each coded with a coloured thumb tab *(see the front flap and inside front cover)*. The sights described in the regions are plotted and numbered on a *Regional Map*. The key to symbols and a *Road Map* can be found on the back flap and inside back cover.

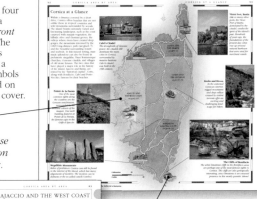

**1 Corsica at a Glance**
*This presents the island divided into four areas, whose colours correspond to those on the colour-coded thumb tabs.*

**The drawings** illustrate the main sights in each area.

**2 Introduction**
*The history, landscape and character of each area are described here, showing how the region has developed over time and what it has to offer visitors.*

**The area colour code** is in the top margin of each page.

**A locator map** shows the colour of each area in relation to the island of Corsica for quick reference.

**3 Regional Map**
*This gives an illustrated overview of the area. All the sights covered in the chapter are numbered and there is useful information on getting around by car and public transport.*

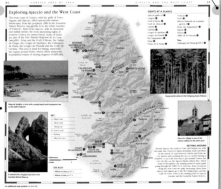

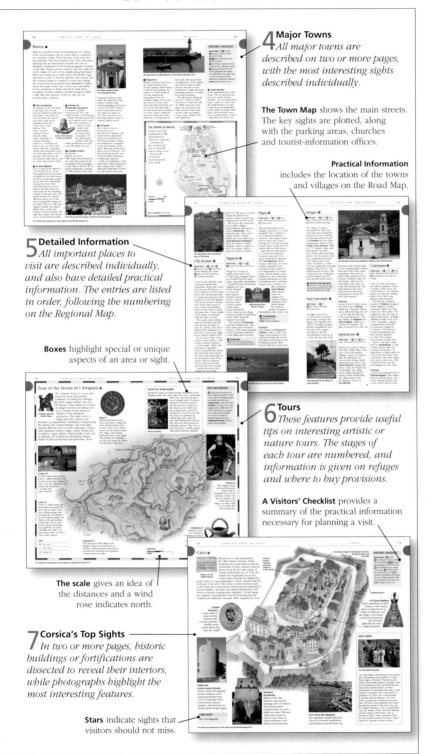

**4 Major Towns**
All major towns are described on two or more pages, with the most interesting sights described individually.

**The Town Map** shows the main streets. The key sights are plotted, along with the parking areas, churches and tourist-information offices.

**Practical Information** includes the location of the towns and villages on the Road Map.

**5 Detailed Information**
All important places to visit are described individually, and also have detailed practical information. The entries are listed in order, following the numbering on the Regional Map.

**Boxes** highlight special or unique aspects of an area or sight.

**6 Tours**
These features provide useful tips on interesting artistic or nature tours. The stages of each tour are numbered, and information is given on refuges and where to buy provisions.

**A Visitors' Checklist** provides a summary of the practical information necessary for planning a visit.

**The scale** gives an idea of the distances and a wind rose indicates north.

**7 Corsica's Top Sights**
In two or more pages, historic buildings or fortifications are dissected to reveal their interiors, while photographs highlight the most interesting features.

**Stars** indicate sights that visitors should not miss.

# INTRODUCING
# CORSICA

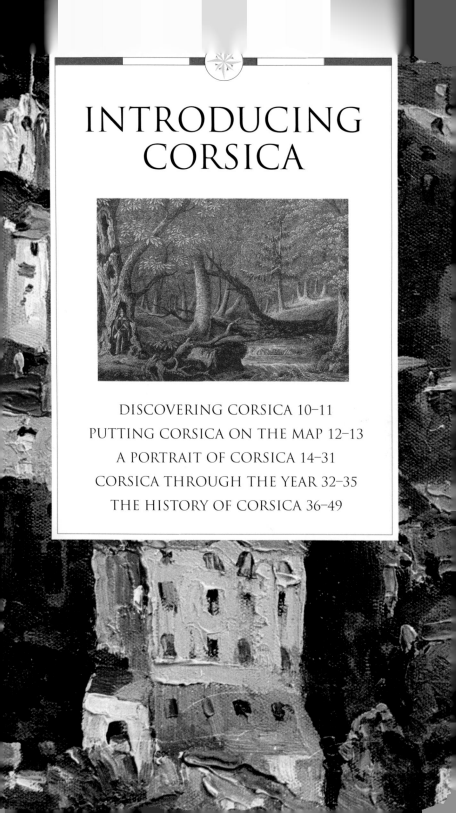

# DISCOVERING CORSICA

Corsica, which has been part of France since 1768, is a herb-filled, mountainous island lying off the north coast of Italy. The fourth-largest Mediterranean island, its cracked and dusty roads, laid-back coastal towns, Genoese citadels and hilltop villages attract return visitors time and again. The rugged countryside offers plenty

**Mouflon mountain goat**

of scope for outdoor activities – from hiking, mountain biking, horse riding and rock climbing, to canoeing, rafting and paragliding – and there are as many as 2,000 species of flora to admire. The best beaches are on the west coast and there are watersports for everyone. Divers can even explore underwater limestone caves in the south.

## BASTIA AND THE NORTH

- **Walking the Sentier des Douaniers coastal footpath**
- **Charismatic Bastia**
- **Wide beaches at Calvi**
- **Hand-crafted goods**

The northeast peninsula of this region stretches up towards Genoa in Italy, from where its former rulers came to build their towns and watch towers. At the tip of Corsica's northern region is the **Sentier des Douaniers** *(see pp68–9)*, a coastal footpath offering wonderful views and walks among the aromatic maquis of juniper, asphodel and rosemary. Corsica's northern edge is dotted with fishing villages and yacht harbours, such as pretty **St-Florent** *(see p70)*, where the chic and the beautiful go shopping and sit out late at night.

On the east coast is **Bastia** *(see pp58–63)*, the island's second-largest city. A slightly decayed, commercial town its charms are often overlooked. Search out pastel-coloured streets, a fine natural harbour and old quarter with its crumbling Genoese remains and you may be pleasantly surprised. The Citadel is also a grand place for a stroll. Don't miss the flamingos in the **Etang de Biguglia**, south of the city.

The best beaches in the region are to be found on the north coast, at **L'Île Rousse** *(see p74)* and **Calvi** *(see pp78–80)*, which has another Genoese citadel and is one of the most attractive resorts on the island. Sip aperitifs on smart Quai Landry while the sun sets and luxury yachts drop anchor before you.

Behind the two towns is the **Strada di l'Artigiani** *(see pp76–7)*, the artisans' route, where you can find typically Corsican souvenirs, such as handmade ceramics, glass and musical instruments, as well as delicious wine, honey and cheese.

**One of the many white sandy beaches around Calvi**

## AJACCIO AND THE WEST COAST

- **The pristine Réserve Naturelle de Scandola**
- **Historic Ajaccio: Napoleon's birthplace**
- **Porticcio – top beach resort**

Great beaches and exhilarating hiking can be found along this craggy coastline, which is one of the most diverse stretches on the island. Here, rocks rise up between sandy shores, inlets and coves, some of which are so remote they can be reached only by boat or on foot. A major highlight is the **Réserve Naturelle de Scandola** *(see pp104–5)*, a UNESCO World Heritage site, where both the dramatic volcanic cliffs and the pristine sea are protected for the benefit of ospreys, shearwaters and 450 species

**A panoramic view of Bastia's old town from the harbour**

◁ **A Corsican village depicted by Xiaoyang Galas in her oil painting** *Sea, Sun and Village*

The ancient capital Corte, in the island's interior

of algae. Hike inland, too, along the well-marked tracks in the **Calanques de Piana** *(see pp100–1)*, where colourful rocks have been blasted into imaginative shapes by the wind.

Corsica's capital and largest town is located towards the south of this region: **Ajaccio** *(see pp86–91)* is compact enough to explore with ease. It is a pleasure to wander the tightly-packed streets of the old centre or along the wide avenues of the modern city. Visit the house where Napoleon Bonaparte was born to learn more about the town's most famous son. Then, climb aboard the Petit

An aerial view of the Réserve Naturelle de Scandola

Train for a tour of the coast.

Just south of Ajaccio, **Porticcio** *(see p93)* is one of the island's most popular resorts and features a long sandy beach and ample facilities for watersports fans.

## BONIFACIO AND THE SOUTH

- **Parc Marin de Bonifacio: a divers' paradise**
- **Amazing prehistoric remains**
- **The spectacular Aiguilles de Bavella**

Sitting on high cliffs, the south is the heart of ancient Corsica. At the southernmost tip of the island lies **Bonifacio** *(see pp110–17)*, a sturdy old town with a bastion overlooking the breezy marina.

Marine life is preserved in the **Parc Marin de Bonifacio** *(see p113)*. This whole high-cliffed southern coast, with its dramatic rocky outcrops and nearby islands, is a classic Mediterranean destination, offering great waters for divers, as well as the popular resorts of **Propriano** *(see p128)* and **Porto-Vecchio** *(see p120)*.

Inland, there are echoes of prehistory, with menhirs, caves and other Neolithic traces. Sites are most easily reached from the town of **Sartène** *(see p126)*; from here, you can also tour the **Megaliths of Cauria** *(see p127)*, where around 500 sites have been unearthed. The famous anthropomorphic menhirs of **Filitosa** *(see p129)* are another unmissable sight.

There are good hiking opportunities among the ragged teeth of the **Aiguilles de Bavella** *(see pp122–3)*. The road going over its high pass is one of the most

spectacular on the island. Keep an eye out for mouflon mountain goats, and savour the air perfumed with herbs and flowers.

## CORTE AND THE INTERIOR

- **Corsica's ancient capital**
- **Great hiking terrain**
- **Country chapels and Greek and Roman remains**

High, rugged and not always easily accessible, the wild and beautiful interior is where to find Corsica's soul. In the middle of it all, surrounded by mountain peaks, is **Corte** *(see pp134–7)*, the island's ancient capital, fortified by a citadel. The island's university was founded here by Corsica's liberator, Pascal Paoli, and a sense of proud nationalism pervades the city.

From here, hikers depart for mountains, valleys and gorges, for this is also the heart of the **Parc Naturel Régional de la Corse** *(see p99)*, which covers nearly two-thirds of the island. Visit in spring when the maquis *(see p73)* comes ablaze with pink and yellow blossom.

From Corte you can also seek out the delightful chapels in **Bozio** *(see pp138–9)* and **Castagniccia** *(see pp146–7)*, while down on the flat east coast are the ruins of **Aléria** *(see p144)*, a former Greek settlement, where the Romans began their conquest of the island.

A grouper, a common sight while diving near Bonifacio

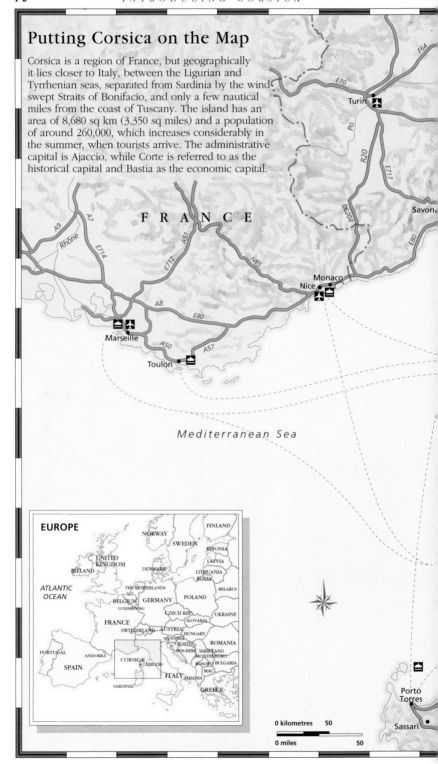

# Putting Corsica on the Map

Corsica is a region of France, but geographically it lies closer to Italy, between the Ligurian and Tyrrhenian seas, separated from Sardinia by the wind-swept Straits of Bonifacio, and only a few nautical miles from the coast of Tuscany. The island has an area of 8,680 sq km (3,350 sq miles) and a population of around 260,000, which increases considerably in the summer, when tourists arrive. The administrative capital is Ajaccio, while Corte is referred to as the historical capital and Bastia as the economic capital.

FRANCE

Turin

Savona

Monaco
Nice

Marseille

Toulon

*Mediterranean Sea*

**EUROPE**

FINLAND
NORWAY
SWEDEN
ESTONIA
UNITED KINGDOM
LATVIA
IRELAND
DENMARK
LITHUANIA
RUSSIA
ATLANTIC OCEAN
THE NETHERLANDS
BELARUS
BELGIUM GERMANY
POLAND
LUXEMBOURG
CZECH REP.
UKRAINE
FRANCE
SWITZERLAND
AUSTRIA
SLOVAKIA
SLOVENIA
HUNGARY
CROATIA
ROMANIA
PORTUGAL
ANDORRA
BOS-HERZ
SERBIA AND MONTENEGRO
KOSOVO
BULGARIA
CORSICA
Ajaccio
MAC.
SPAIN
ITALY
ALBANIA
SARDINIA
GREECE

Porto
Torres

Sassari

0 kilometres    50

0 miles         50

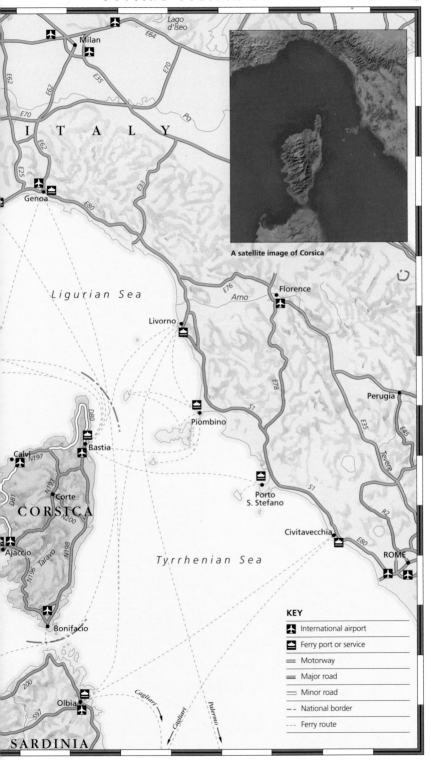

**A satellite image of Corsica**

Lago d'Iseo

Milan

*ITALY*

Genoa

*Ligurian Sea*

Livorno

Florence

*Arno*

Piombino

Perugia

Calvi

Bastia

Corte

**CORSICA**

Ajaccio

Porto S. Stefano

*Tyrrhenian Sea*

Civitavecchia

**ROME**

Bonifacio

Olbia

*Cagliari*

*Cagliari*

*Palermo*

**SARDINIA**

**KEY**

🛧 International airport

⛴ Ferry port or service

═ Motorway

═ Major road

═ Minor road

-- National border

--- Ferry route

# A PORTRAIT OF CORSICA

*The light-reflecting granite rocks, the dense, dark forests, the sandy coves, the expansive panoramas of Cap Corse or the compressed Bozio valley – Corsica is an enigmatic island with many and varied facets. Despite its large number of visitors, the island remains a wild and fascinating place.*

A long, slow continental drift moved Corsica from the coast of Provence to its present position, in the northernmost waters of the Tyrrhenian Sea, with the Côte d'Azur and the Tuscan archipelago only a stone's throw away. A central chain of tall mountains culminating in Monte Cinto (2,706 m/8,878 ft) descends from Calvi, in the northwest, towards Porto-Vecchio, in the southeast corner of the island, separating it into two distinct regions. Pisan and Genoan rulers called the northeastern part *Diqua dei monti* ("Hither the mountains") while the for them inaccessible, untamed southwestern part was known as *Dila dei monti* ("Beyond

**A brotherhood member**

the mountains"). Geologically, the divide separates the schist regions to the east from the predominantly granite areas descending towards the west coast. The exceptions to this rule are the extraordinary landscapes along the coasts of the Scandola Nature Reserve, the result of ancient volcanic eruptions, and the bright limestone rich in fossils on the cliffs of the south coast, especially around Bonifacio. Inland, mountains, gorges and torrents make Corsica a hiker's paradise. "Imagine a world still in the midst of chaos, a tempest of mountains separating narrow gorges in which torrents flow," wrote the French author Guy de Maupassant.

A fishmonger's stall at the Ajaccio marina

◁ The crowded Vieux Port of Bastia, with the characteristic façade of the church of St-Jean-Baptiste

**Traditional Corsican products**

He continues "No plains, but rather immense waves of granite and colossal undulations of earth covered with maquis or tall chestnut and pine forests." Much of Corsica's fascination is due to this lush interior cut through by wild torrents, a sign that it receives a heavier rainfall than the other Mediterranean islands. Corsica also has a splendid sea that is much admired by travellers from all over the world. This means, of course, that the coastline is often crowded, but it is still possible to find secluded coves, only accessible by foot or boat.

**A local handmade marionette**

### AN AGE-OLD CULTURE

Archaeologists say that the first humans arrived in Corsica around 9,000 years ago, probably after dangerous, but short, sea journeys from the Tuscan coast. The first Corsicans owed their survival to the breeding of livestock and hunting, which later gave rise to their own unique

**Sheep on their way to a pasture – an age-old Corsican scene**

megalithic culture. The best examples of this can be found in the southwest region of the island: the menhirs of Filitosa, the dolmens at Sartène and the *castelli* at Cucuruzzu and Capula. Agricultural products were introduced by Greek colonists and then spread when the Romans conquered the island and made the principal city, Aléria, their capital. With the grim and chaotic Middle Ages came invaders, pirates, preachers and, above all, merchants. A bone of contention between the agile ships of Pisa and Genoa, Corsica became a Genoese colony in the 13th century and was to remain so, amid revolts and battles, up to the 18th century.

### THE "CORSICAN NATION"

The Corsicans were fierce opponents already of the Roman legions and have always felt they were a separate people with their own language (still a hallmark of the "Corsican nation") and ancient traditions. The downfall of Genoese power paved the way for the French and, at the same time, for the brief but crucial period of independence, linked to the figure of Pascal Paoli, the "Father of the Nation" *(see pp46–7).* Renowned as the birthplace of Napoleon Bonaparte – who was born in Ajaccio on 15 August 1769 – Corsica has been part of France for over two centuries.

The Corsicans' continued demands for independence from France are a sign of their national pride, which is rooted in the distant past. Although there is still an ardent yearning for the "Corsican nation", support for the violent paramilitary groups so active in the 1970s is no longer very strong. Since the

Starting a sailing trip from a Corsican beach

Ajaccio and Bastia. Apart from Corte, the interior is sparsley inhabited – a fact that makes it appealing to the many visitors who come here to experience wilderness, leaving behind the hustle and bustle of modern life. Paradoxically, what leads to a diminishing population and lack of conventional work opportunities, is in some way still beneficial since it attracts tourists.

Luckily tourism, despite being a major source of income, has not been allowed to take over the island, not even along the coasts. So far, the natural environment and local traditions have been respected, thanks to projects such as the Parc Régional de la Corse *(see p99)*, and there are no sprawling highrise resorts on the island.

Matignon Agreement, finally reached in 2001, France has been investing heavily in both economy and infrastructure on the island, a fact that perhaps has made total autonomy less tempting. The wish for cultural independence and identity, however, is still deeply felt, with manifestations centred at the University of Corte, and through an abundance of websites relating to the island's language, history and traditions *(see also pp30–31)*.

Corsicans are generally quite traditional, and family comes first – a reflection of the old clan values *(see p31)*. Women might no longer be the cause of vendettas, but the attitude towards them is very conservative and, compared to northern Europe, equality is a very remote goal. On the other hand, no one receives more respect than a Corsican mother.

The locals' reputation of aloofness or suspiciousness towards strangers is not altogether an exaggeration, but visitors who show respect and admiration for this captivating island will be welcome and treated with Mediterranean warmth.

### THE PEOPLE AND THE LAND

There are only about 260,000 Corsicans on the island; three times as many work in mainland France. During the winter, as less jobs are available in the tourism sector, many leave for temporary work on the continent. The majority of the population live along the coast, mostly near the main towns such as

One of Corsica's many beaches

# Corsica's Landscape and Fauna

Corsica is essentially a tall, craggy peak descending to the sea, with valleys furrowed by mountain torrents and small plains around the river estuaries. As well as the coastline and the sea, the mountains also offer spectacular natural scenery, with summits over 2,500 m (8,200 ft) high and the large Corsican pine forests that cover the central zone of the island. Many rivers, mostly along the east coast, create coastal lakes called *étangs* near their outlets. There is an abundance of flora, with almost 3,000 species of plants, 80 of which are endemic, providing a marvellous carpet of Mediterranean maquis *(see p73)*.

A river along the route to the Col de Bavella

## THE COASTLINE

The maquis undergrowth dominates the coastline up to the first hill ranges. In the eastern plain around Porto-Vecchio and in the peninsula of Cap Corse there are cork oaks and holm oaks. In the inhabited coastal areas, the century plants (Mexican agave), palm trees, prickly pears and aloes create an exotic atmosphere. The large umbrella pine woods are particularly thick around Porto-Vecchio and Calvi.

**The aloe** *is a succulent plant with spinous leaves that, from January to April, has lovely red or yellow tubular flowers that bloom in thick clusters.*

**Myrtle** *is a fragrant evergreen shrub that thrives in sunny areas. Its lovely white flowers bloom in spring, while the berries mature in the autumn.*

## THE HILLS

Maquis shrubs cover the first hill ranges and are present up to 1,000 m (3,300 ft). Olive trees grow to an altitude of 600 m (2,000 ft). At a lower level, vineyards cover the seaward slopes of Cap Corse, the Nebbio area, and the eastern and southern coastal plains. The numerous citrus-fruit orchards boast fine oranges, lemons, mandarins, limes and clementines. There are also many eucalyptus trees, introduced in 1868 to drain the swampy coasts and eradicate malaria.

**Woodpeckers** *live in the woods of Corsica. Visitors may hear their characteristic pecking and glimpse their bright plumage among the pine and cork oak trees.*

**Olive trees** *are among the trees that live longest, becoming gnarled with time. Olives are harvested by hanging large nets under each tree.*

## WILDLIFE

As well as the wild boar and the rarely seen mouflon, which is the symbol of the island, the Corsican deer has also recently returned to the area, thanks to a reintroduction project. The rocky coasts are the habitat of such marine birds as seagulls, ospreys and cormorants. In the maquis, the Hermann's tortoise can be found, which is

**Tyrrhenian wall lizard**

closely related to a species now extinct on the European continent. There are no vipers in Corsica, but there are two endemic species of lizard, the Tyrrhenian wall lizard and the Bedriaga's wall lizard, as well as the harmless Aesculapian snake. The sea is rich in fish, including groupers and breams, and also provides tasty molluscs and crustaceans.

**A family of boars, common in Corsica**

## THE FORESTS

The central zone of the island is an immense forest, except for the valley floors and the areas destroyed by fire. At an altitude of 500–800 m (1,600–2,600 ft) there are chestnut trees, planted by the Genoese. Chestnuts were a staple in the diet of the mountain population. Further up, at 700–1,500 m (2,300–5,000 ft), are the conifers, with the marvellous Valdu-Niellu, Aïtone and Vizzavona forests, dominated by giant Laricio pines.

**Mushrooms** *thrive in the damp underbrush of the forests, at the foot of conifers and beech trees. They are gathered from late summer onwards.*

**Chestnuts** *mature in early autumn. As the prickly burs fall to the ground, they break, showing the nuts inside. September and October are the ideal times for hikes among the chestnut orchards.*

## THE MOUNTAINS

Covered by snow from autumn to late spring, the mountains in Corsica are tall and solitary, inhabited only by a few shepherds. At 1,500 m (5,000 ft), the woods give way to alders, junipers and barberries. Higher up, just before the rocky peaks, are the grassy mountain pastures. The tallest peaks are Monte Cinto (2,706 m/8,878 ft), Monte Rotondo (2,622 m/8,602 ft), Monte Padro (2,393 m/7,851 ft) and Monte d'Oro (2,389 m/7,838 ft).

**The golden eagle** *is a formidable raptor that lives on the tallest peaks. It can catch large prey, such as lambs, in its powerful talons.*

**The juniper** *is one of the characteristic and most fragrant plants of the high mountain zones. It can be recognized by its silver-green needles and almost black berries.*

# The Corsican Coastline

**Maritime pine cones**

From the small isolated bays among granite rocks on the west coast, to the long sandy beaches between Bastia and Bonifacio that are ideal for family holidays, Corsica is a paradise for sunbathers. The island's 1,000 km (620 miles) of coastline offer visitors the chance to lie in the sun from May to October, and it is possible to find secluded spots even in July and August. Except for the major beaches near towns such as Calvi, Porto-Vecchio and Ajaccio, most have no lifeguards, so it is advisable to be cautious when bathing, especially when the wind is strong and the sea is rough.

*From St-Florent to L'Île Rousse, small bays with fine sand alternate with cliffs covered in maquis.*

*From Calvi to Ajaccio, steep cliffs line the coast and many beaches can be reached only by sea. Landing is not possible along the red cliffs of the Scandola Nature Reserve.*

| 0 kilometres | 25 |
| 0 miles | 15 |

*Golfe d'Ajaccio has many beaches and rocky areas. The Pointe de la Parata peninsula extends into the sea towards the Îles Sanguinaires, where the sea is crystal clear.*

*The white cliffs along the southern coast around Bonifacio are among the best known in Corsica. Some of the large rocks even have a name, such as the famous Grain de Sable ("grain of sand"), seen here in the background.*

L'Île Rou
② Calvi
Figarella
Tartagine
D81B
L'Asco
Fango
D81
Golo
D84
Porto ③
Liamone
D81
Liamone
Cruzini
Gravona
Ajaccio
Prunelli
Porticcio ④
Taravo
Propriano
Sartène
N196
Tonnara

*Along the Cap Corse,*
*high cliffs frame many*
*bays with picturesque*
*little harbours, such as*
*this one at Centuri.*

*The coast south of Bastia*
*is known for its coastal lakes,*
*which are called étangs.*
*These form interesting*
*marshy zones at the river*
*mouths, such as the Étang*
*de Biguglia, seen above.*

*South of Porto-Vecchio,*
*the coastline becomes less steep and*
*has magnificent coves with incredibly*
*crystal-clear water and fine sand.*
*Rondinara bay, seen here from above,*
*is one of the best examples of these.*

## CORSICA'S TEN BEST BEACHES

**The most inaccessible ①**
Saleccia beach *(see p72)*, one of Corsica's most arresting white-sand bays, is accessible only by boat or via an 11-km (7-mile) rutted track.

**The most fashionable ②**
Shallow, crystal-clear water and a charming harbour: Calvi beach, with fine bathing facilities, is one of the liveliest in Corsica.

**The best for diving ③**
Surrounded by a eucalyptus grove, the beach at Porto is the best starting point for those who want to explore the west coast's sea floor.

**The most urban ④**
The beaches at Porticcio, opposite Ajaccio, have white sand and good facilities and are frequented by the locals. The best known is La Viva.

**The best for kite-surfing and windsurfing ⑤**
Tonnara beach, at the end of the deep Golfe de Figari, is a favourite with kite- and windsurfers because there is always a stiff breeze.

**The most sheltered ⑥**
The small coves of the Îles Lavezzi, bordered by rocks sculpted by the sand and wind, can be reached by boat from Bonifacio.

**The most tropical ⑦**
A shell-shaped cove with brilliant turquoise water and white sand, the beach at Rondinara also has a camp site and a restaurant.

**The best for watersports ⑧**
The beach at Santa Giulia, a tranquil sandy bay bordered by dunes and pine trees, is equipped for all aquatic sports, such as windsurfing, canoeing and sailing.

**The most photogenic ⑨**
With its white sand, pink cliffs, dunes, pines and a lovely blue sea, the beach at Palombaggia, south of Porto-Vecchio, is perhaps the most spectacular.

**The most family-friendly ⑩**
Of the long, sandy beaches fit for families, the best is at Aléria, on the east coast.

# GR20: Stages 1–5

Crossing Corsica from northwest to southeast, the GR20 (Grande Randonnée 20) is 200 km (124 miles) long. The path runs at an average altitude of 1,000–2,000 m (3,300–6,600 ft), linking Calenzana, in the Balagne region, with Conca, in the Porto-Vecchio hinterland. Every year several thousand hikers try this tour, which is only for those in very good condition. The GR20 is divided into 15 stages, and the hikes last from 8am–5pm on terrain with altitude differences as much as 800 m (2,600 ft). Stages 1 to 5 have spectacular but difficult stretches, the most notorious being Cirque de la Solitude, a route fitted with fixed ladders, chains and cables.

**CALVI**

**D151**

**Calenzana**, a tiny village in the Balagne region, is where the GR20 begins. The first stage has a steep ascent and is quite challenging.

CAPO
U DEN

2,032
(6,667

Ortu di u Piobbu

**Stage 1**
Start: *Calenzana (275 m/902 ft)*
Finish: *Ortu di u Piobbu*
*refuge (1,570 m/5,151 ft)*
Length: *10 km (6 miles)*
Degree of difficulty: *hard*
Average duration: *7 hours*
Maximum altitude:
*1,570 m (5,151 ft)*
Stopover: *Ortu di u Piobbu*
*refuge (bed space for 30)*

*CIRQUE DE BONIFATU*

Carozzu

**The Sentier de Spasimata** *is a path that skirts the slopes of the Cirque de Bonifatu. It is famous for the restored footbridge suspended over a torrent.*

**Stage 2**
Start: *Ortu di u Piobbu refuge (1,570 m/5,151 ft)*
Finish: *Carozzu refuge (1,270 m/4,167 ft)*
Length: *8 km (5 miles)*
Degree of difficulty: *hard*
Average duration: *6 1/2 hours*
Maximum altitude: *1,950 m (6,400 ft)*
Stopover: *Carozzu refuge (bed space for 24)*

*CIRQUE DE LA SOLITUDE*

**The refuges** *along the route are small stone constructions built in the local mountain architectural style, so that they blend in well with the natural setting. The Carozzu refuge is immersed in the surrounding vegetation; other refuges are in open meadows.*

**The alpine asphodel** *is a species of plant that blooms between late May and June.*

**Stage 5**
Start: *Bergeries de Ballone*
*(1,440 m/4,724 ft)*
Finish: *Castel de Verghio*
*(1,404 m/4,606 ft)*
Length: *13 km (8 miles)*
Degree of difficulty: *average*
Average duration: *7 hours*
Maximum altitude: *2,000 m (6,562 ft)*
Stopover: *Castel de Verghio*
*hotel (29 rooms and restaurant)*

Col de
Verghio

Castel de Verghio

D84

EVISA

## WARNING

The GR20 route takes about 14 days to complete, hiking an average of seven hours a day. As such, it is recommended only for persons in good physical condition, with some experience in hiking and climbing. Hikers must be equipped with mountain boots, waterproof jackets, fleece wear, sun hats and first-aid kits. In the summer, food is available at some refuges, but it is safest to bring your own provisions. You can restock (on food and drink) at points where the trail descends to road level.

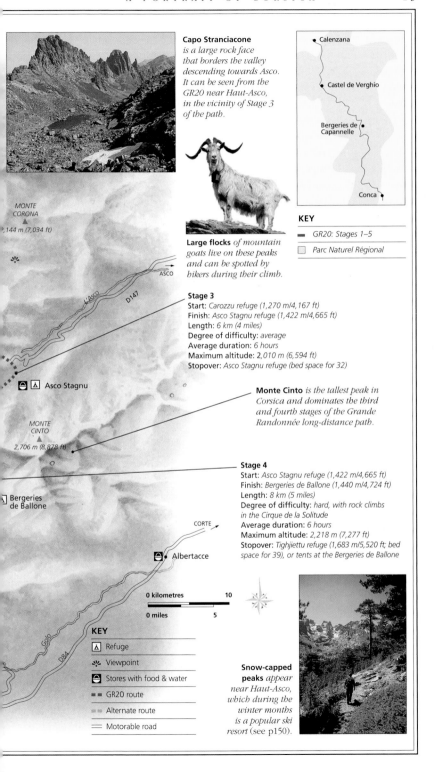

**Capo Stranciacone**
*is a large rock face
that borders the valley
descending towards Asco.
It can be seen from the
GR20 near Haut-Asco,
in the vicinity of Stage 3
of the path.*

**Large flocks** *of mountain
goats live on these peaks
and can be spotted by
hikers during their climb.*

Calenzana

Castel de Verghio

Bergeries de
Capannelle

Conca

**KEY**

GR20: Stages 1–5

Parc Naturel Régional

**Stage 3**
Start: *Carozzu refuge (1,270 m/4,167 ft)*
Finish: *Asco Stagnu refuge (1,422 m/4,665 ft)*
Length: *6 km (4 miles)*
Degree of difficulty: *average*
Average duration: *6 hours*
Maximum altitude: *2,010 m (6,594 ft)*
Stopover: *Asco Stagnu refuge (bed space for 32)*

**Monte Cinto** *is the tallest peak in
Corsica and dominates the third
and fourth stages of the Grande
Randonnée long-distance path.*

**Stage 4**
Start: *Asco Stagnu refuge (1,422 m/4,665 ft)*
Finish: *Bergeries de Ballone (1,440 m/4,724 ft)*
Length: *8 km (5 miles)*
Degree of difficulty: *hard, with rock climbs
in the Cirque de la Solitude*
Average duration: *6 hours*
Maximum altitude: *2,218 m (7,277 ft)*
Stopover: *Tighjiettu refuge (1,683 m/5,520 ft; bed
space for 39), or tents at the Bergeries de Ballone*

MONTE
CORONA
2,144 m (7,034 ft)

ASCO

L'ASCO

D147

Asco Stagnu

MONTE
CINTO
2,706 m (8,878 ft)

Bergeries
de Ballone

CORTE

Albertacce

GR20

D84

0 kilometres          10

0 miles          5

**KEY**

Refuge

Viewpoint

Stores with food & water

GR20 route

Alternate route

Motorable road

**Snow-capped
peaks** *appear
near Haut-Asco,
which during the
winter months
is a popular ski
resort (see p150).*

# GR20: Stages 6-10

Stage 7 of the GR20 offers the best views but is one of the toughest stretches. It does not climb any peaks, but it crosses the GR20's highest pass, the Brêche de Castillo, at 2,225 m (7,300 ft). The easiest part is the eighth stage, a shaded route without steep slopes.

ALBERTACCE

Col de Verghio

Golo

D84

Castel de Verghio

D84

EVISA

FORÊT DE VALDU-NIELLU

Lac de Nino

Tavignano

Manganu

Soccia

Orto

VICO

Guagno

*At the Col de Verghio the view opens on to a pass crossed by a motorable road. This is the edge of the Valdu-Niellu woods. A little further up are the alpine meadows and rocky zones.*

**Lac de Nino** *(Lake Nino) is a glacial lake that feeds the Tavignano river. It forms a marshy area called Pozzine ("the wells") that from above looks like lace work.*

### Stage 6
Start: *Castel de Verghio (1,404 m/4,606 ft)*
Finish: *Manganu refuge (1,601 m/5,253 ft)*
Length: *14 km (9 miles)*
Degree of difficulty: *average*
Average duration: *5 1/2 hours*
Maximum altitude: *1,760 m (5,774 ft)*
Stopover: *Manganu refuge (bed space for 31)*

## KEY

| | |
|---|---|
| 🛖 | Refuge |
| ☆ | Viewpoint |
| 🏠 | Stores with food & water |
| ▪▪ | GR20 route |
| ▪▪ | Alternate route |
| ═ | Motorable road |
| ▪▪ | Other paths |

**Lac de Capitello** *is surrounded by rocky scenery. The Punta dei Sette Laghi (Seven Lakes Peak) is so named because it affords an excellent view of a series of glacial lakes.*

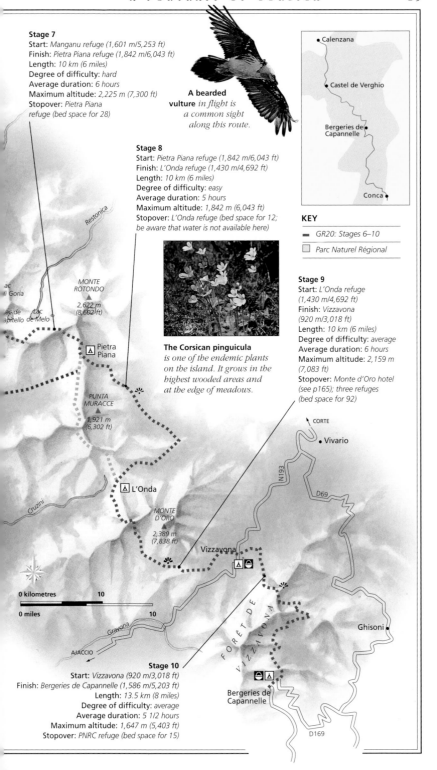

**Stage 7**
Start: *Manganu refuge (1,601 m/5,253 ft)*
Finish: *Pietra Piana refuge (1,842 m/6,043 ft)*
Length: *10 km (6 miles)*
Degree of difficulty: *hard*
Average duration: *6 hours*
Maximum altitude: *2,225 m (7,300 ft)*
Stopover: *Pietra Piana refuge (bed space for 28)*

**A bearded vulture** *in flight is a common sight along this route.*

**Stage 8**
Start: *Pietra Piana refuge (1,842 m/6,043 ft)*
Finish: *L'Onda refuge (1,430 m/4,692 ft)*
Length: *10 km (6 miles)*
Degree of difficulty: *easy*
Average duration: *5 hours*
Maximum altitude: *1,842 m (6,043 ft)*
Stopover: *L'Onda refuge (bed space for 12; be aware that water is not available here)*

Calenzana
Castel de Verghio
Bergeries de Capannelle
Conca

**KEY**

GR20: Stages 6–10
Parc Naturel Régional

**Stage 9**
Start: *L'Onda refuge (1,430 m/4,692 ft)*
Finish: *Vizzavona (920 m/3,018 ft)*
Length: *10 km (6 miles)*
Degree of difficulty: *average*
Average duration: *6 hours*
Maximum altitude: *2,159 m (7,083 ft)*
Stopover: *Monte d'Oro hotel (see p165); three refuges (bed space for 92)*

MONTE ROTONDO
2,622 m (8,602 ft)
ac di Goria
ac de tac apitello de Melo
Restonica
Pietra Piana
PUNTA MURACCE
1,921 m (6,302 ft)
Cruzini
L'Onda
MONTE D'ORO
2,389 m (7,838 ft)

**The Corsican pinguicula** *is one of the endemic plants on the island. It grows in the highest wooded areas and at the edge of meadows.*

CORTE
Vivario
N193
D69
Vizzavona

AJACCIO
Gravona
0 kilometres 10
0 miles 10

FORÊT DE VIZZAVONA
Ghisoni

**Stage 10**
Start: *Vizzavona (920 m/3,018 ft)*
Finish: *Bergeries de Capannelle (1,586 m/5,203 ft)*
Length: *13.5 km (8 miles)*
Degree of difficulty: *average*
Average duration: *5 1/2 hours*
Maximum altitude: *1,647 m (5,403 ft)*
Stopover: *PNRC refuge (bed space for 15)*

Bergeries de Capannelle
D169

# GR20: Stages 11–15

The last stages of the GR20 path offer no respite to those who have come this far without descending to the valley. Almost all stages have difficult stretches but make up for this with spectacular views, especially in the Aiguilles de Bavella area. Two weeks should be enough to walk the entire GR20, finishing at Conca.

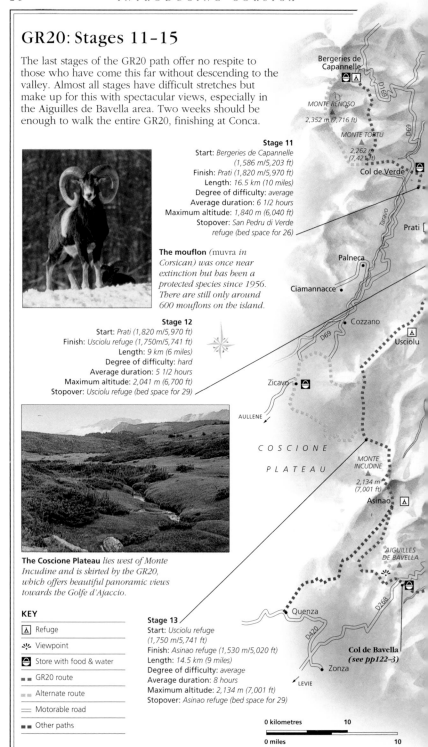

### Stage 11
Start: *Bergeries de Capannelle (1,586 m/5,203 ft)*
Finish: *Prati (1,820 m/5,970 ft)*
Length: *16.5 km (10 miles)*
Degree of difficulty: *average*
Average duration: *6 1/2 hours*
Maximum altitude: *1,840 m (6,040 ft)*
Stopover: *San Pedru di Verde refuge (bed space for 26)*

**The mouflon** (muvra *in Corsican) was once near extinction but has been a protected species since 1956. There are still only around 600 mouflons on the island.*

### Stage 12
Start: *Prati (1,820 m/5,970 ft)*
Finish: *Usciolu refuge (1,750 m/5,741 ft)*
Length: *9 km (6 miles)*
Degree of difficulty: *hard*
Average duration: *5 1/2 hours*
Maximum altitude: *2,041 m (6,700 ft)*
Stopover: *Usciolu refuge (bed space for 29)*

**The Coscione Plateau** *lies west of Monte Incudine and is skirted by the GR20, which offers beautiful panoramic views towards the Golfe d'Ajaccio.*

### Stage 13
Start: *Usciolu refuge (1,750 m/5,741 ft)*
Finish: *Asinao refuge (1,530 m/5,020 ft)*
Length: *14.5 km (9 miles)*
Degree of difficulty: *average*
Average duration: *8 hours*
Maximum altitude: *2,134 m (7,001 ft)*
Stopover: *Asinao refuge (bed space for 29)*

## KEY

| 🔺 | Refuge |
| ⚡ | Viewpoint |
| 🔲 | Store with food & water |
| ▪▪ | GR20 route |
| ▪▪ | Alternate route |
| ═ | Motorable road |
| ▪▪ | Other paths |

Map labels:
Bergeries de Capannelle
MONTE RENOSO 2,352 m (7,716 ft)
MONTE TORTU 2,262 m (7,421 ft)
Col de Verde
Prati
Palneca
Ciamannacce
Cozzano
Usciolu
Zicavo
AULLENE
COSCIONE PLATEAU
MONTE INCUDINE 2,134 m (7,001 ft)
Asinao
AIGUILLES DE BAVELLA
Quenza
Col de Bavella *(see pp122–3)*
Zonza
LEVIE
D169, D69, Tavaro, D420, D268

0 kilometres    10
0 miles    10

soni
→ GHISONACCIA
Fium'Orbo

The kite *is commonly seen in the Parc Naturel Régional (Regional Park). Kites can be recognized by their distinctive forked tail.*

- Calenzana
- Castel de Verghio
- Bergeries de Capannelle
- Conca

**KEY**

▬ *GR20: Stages 11–15*

☐ *Parc Naturel Régional*

**The martagon lily**
*is one of the most spectacular alpine bulbous plants, with large flowers that are easy to recognize because of their warm orange colour.*

**Stage 14**
Start: *Asinao refuge (1,530 m/5,020 ft)*
Finish: *Paliri refuge (1,040 m/3,412 ft)*
Length: *13 km (8 miles)*
Degree of difficulty: *hard*
Average duration: *7 hours*
Maximum altitude: *1,530 m (5,020 ft)*
Stopover: *Paliri refuge (bed space for 20)*

Asinao

**Punta Paliri** *dominates the Bavella forest and rises up behind the Bavella refuge, which is the last high-altitude stage in the GR20 route before it descends back to "civilization".*

## THE "SEA AND MOUNTAINS" AND "SEA TO SEA" PATHS

**A hiker halfway between the mountains and the sea**

The GR20 is not the only long hiking route in Corsica. There are two *Mare e Monti* (between sea and mountains) paths: the first links Calenzana to Cargèse in ten easy stages and the second goes from Porticcio to Propriano in five stages overlooking the sea. There are also three *Mare a Mare* (from sea to sea) paths: the northern one stretches from Moriani to Cargèse in 12 stages, the central one from Ghisonaccia to Porticcio in seven stages, and the southern path goes from Porto-Vecchio to Propriano in five stages. These paths are relatively easy to walk, although in the central zone they intersect with the GR20. *Gîtes d'étape* (hikers' hostels) along these routes offer half-board stopovers. See also page 188.

SOLENZARA
Solenzara

Ⓐ Paliri

PUNTA D'ORTU
▲
695 m (2,280 ft)

• Conca

↓ PORTO-VECCHIO

**Stage 15**
Start: *Paliri refuge (1,055 m/3,461 ft)*
Finish: *Conca (252 m/827 ft)*
Length: *12 km (7 miles)*
Degree of difficulty: *average*
Average duration: *5 hours*
Maximum altitude: *1,055 m (3,461 ft)*
Stopover: *Gîte La Tonnelle (bed space for 30)*

# Architecture in Corsica

The various peoples that have ruled Corsica have left their imprint in the cities and around the island. The Pisans built the Romanesque churches, while the Genoese built almost all the splendid Baroque ones as well as the defensive structures indispensable for an island: the watchtowers along the coastline and the citadels. In the field of domestic architecture, the mortuary chapels, which were often constructed along the sides of roads, are particularly interesting. They were a mark of distinction of the rich families, especially those that had made their fortunes abroad.

**Polychrome marble on the façade of a Romanesque church**

## ROMANESQUE

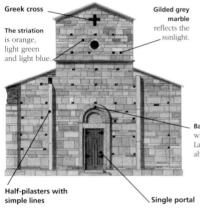

**Greek cross**

**The striation** is orange, light green and light blue.

**Gilded grey marble** reflects the sunlight.

**Half-pilasters with simple lines**

**Bas-relief** with the Lamb of God above the portal.

**Single portal**

Corsica has some splendid examples of Romanesque church architecture, mostly dating from the late 11th century onwards, during Pisan rule. These churches often have an aisle-less nave with a semicircular apse, while the façade is decorated with blind arches and panels that continue along the sides. Polychrome marble is also a characteristic feature.

**La Canonica Church** (see p148) *has extremely simple lines and an interior with two aisles. The only other church with this feature is Santa Maria Assunta at St-Florent (see p70).*

## BAROQUE

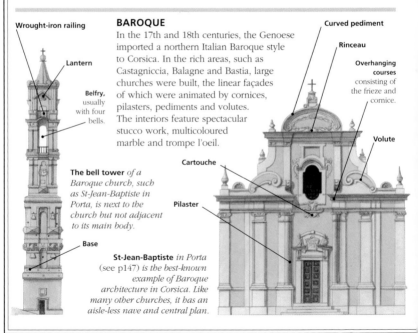

**Wrought-iron railing**

**Lantern**

**Belfry,** usually with four bells.

**The bell tower** *of a Baroque church, such as St-Jean-Baptiste in Porta, is next to the church but not adjacent to its main body.*

**Base**

**St-Jean-Baptiste** *in Porta (see p147) is the best-known example of Baroque architecture in Corsica. Like many other churches, it has an aisle-less nave and central plan.*

**Cartouche**

**Pilaster**

In the 17th and 18th centuries, the Genoese imported a northern Italian Baroque style to Corsica. In the rich areas, such as Castagniccia, Balagne and Bastia, large churches were built, the linear façades of which were animated by cornices, pilasters, pediments and volutes. The interiors feature spectacular stucco work, multicoloured marble and trompe l'oeil.

**Curved pediment**

**Rinceau**

**Overhanging courses** consisting of the frieze and cornice.

**Volute**

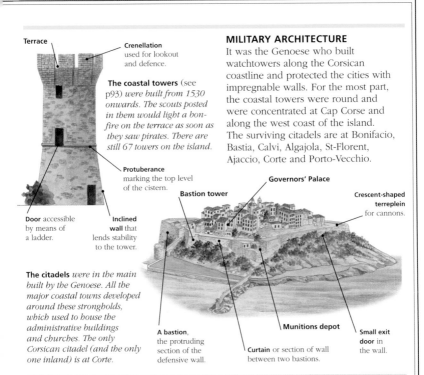

**Terrace**

**Crenellation**
used for lookout
and defence.

**The coastal towers** (see
p93) *were built from 1530
onwards. The scouts posted
in them would light a bon-
fire on the terrace as soon as
they saw pirates. There are
still 67 towers on the island.*

**Protuberance**
marking the top level
of the cistern.

**Door** accessible
by means of
a ladder.

**Inclined
wall** that
lends stability
to the tower.

**The citadels** *were in the main
built by the Genoese. All the
major coastal towns developed
around these strongholds,
which used to house the
administrative buildings
and churches. The only
Corsican citadel (and the only
one inland) is at Corte.*

**A bastion,**
the protruding
section of the
defensive wall.

## MILITARY ARCHITECTURE
It was the Genoese who built
watchtowers along the Corsican
coastline and protected the cities with
impregnable walls. For the most part,
the coastal towers were round and
were concentrated at Cap Corse and
along the west coast of the island.
The surviving citadels are at Bonifacio,
Bastia, Calvi, Algajola, St-Florent,
Ajaccio, Corte and Porto-Vecchio.

**Governors' Palace**

**Bastion tower**

**Crescent-shaped
terreplein**
for cannons.

**Munitions depot**

**Small exit
door** in
the wall.

**Curtain** or section of wall
between two bastions.

## CEMETERY ARCHITECTURE
A hallmark of the rich families
in the north of the island are the
mortuary chapels, which are true
mausoleums built on private land,
often at the side of minor roads.
They reflect different styles, from
the small Classical Roman temple
to Baroque and Neo-Classical
styles, and Byzantine architecture.

**The Neo-Classic
catafalque** *has the simple
lines of this 18th-century
style. The pilasters and
tympanum are inspired
by ancient temples, while
the dome, often crowned
by the statue of a saint or
the Virgin Mary, is in the
Christian tradition.*

**Statue
of the
Virgin**

**Decorative element** in the
shape of a vase adorned with
a flame, typical of Classical
architecture.

**Ornament**
resembling a
piece of leather
with rolled edges.

**Lunette** consisting
of a fixed glass panel.

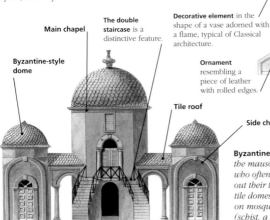

**Main chapel**

**The double
staircase** is a
distinctive feature.

**Byzantine-style
dome**

**Tile roof**

**Side chapel**

**Byzantine taste** *is often visible in
the mausoleums of merchant families,
who often travelled widely to carry
out their trade. The superimposed
tile domes were inspired by those
on mosques, although the material
(schist, a local slate) is less precious.*

# Language, Literature, Music and Traditions

Corsica is a bilingual region, and all road signs are written in Corsican and French. The Corsican language is similar to Italian and is still spoken and written everywhere, though less by young people. The island's literary tradition is mostly oral, based on legends that were handed down during cold winter months around the hearth, or in the songs describing the salient events in the lives of the locals. The ancient melodies are now being performed by music groups that sing in the local language and are also famous outside of Corsica.

Local costume

An allegory of Corsica in an 18th-century print

Page from an old encyclopedia with the entry "Corsica"

## THE CORSICAN LANGUAGE

In the northeast, the Corsican language *(Corsu)* is soft and musical, with an inflection and many words that are similar to Tuscan dialects. It is harsher and more crisp in the southwest, bearing influences of neighbouring Sardinia. The "double d" is used a lot in the southwest. For example, the word for "beautiful" in Bastia is *bellu*, while in Ajaccio it becomes *beddu*.

The Corsican language derived from Latin and, over the centuries, has been influenced by the various populations that ruled the island, mainly Tuscan – and not only because of Pisan dominion. In fact, Genoa,

which ruled Corsica for five centuries, used Tuscan as the official and written language. The few Genoese words that have remained exist mostly in maritime and technical terminology. Influences also came from southern Italy, especially Calabria and Sardinia, and from French, which determined the spread of generic terms such as *cammi di ferru*, or railway, *(chemin de fer* in French).

The French language was first used in Corsica in 1769, when the island was annexed by France. It began to spread in the late 19th century, with the introduction of compulsory education.

Two ancient "foreign" dialects have remained on the island, but are disappearing due to the predominance of French. In Bonifacio, the Ligurian dialect of the 13th-century Genoese colonists can still be heard, while at Cargèse, Greek, imported by refugees from the Peloponnese in the 17th and 18th centuries, is virtually extinct. As for books, all the texts printed before the 18th century are in Italian. After that time, French became widespread, even though Italian was still used.

Recognized as a regional language in 1974, Corsican

is now enjoying a revival thanks to the courses at the University of Corsica *(see p137)*, where a vast data bank on the language has been created. Although most children on the island learn Corsican at home, the language is also taught at school, and many schools offer bilingual education.

Many associations and periodicals have also promoted Corsican, and there are several radio stations broadcasting in Corsican. The first newspaper in Corsican, *A Tramuntana*, was published in 1896, followed by others, especially in the period between the two World Wars.

The phrasebook on page 222 gives some examples of Corsican words.

## CORSICAN LITERATURE

Corsican has always been a spoken language and the local literary production was passed on orally, expressed as stories *(stabatoghji)* and legends *(fole)* that were handed down from generation to generation. Then there were poems and songs that narrated life experiences: the *lamentu* for a death or a departure, and the *voceri*, the cries

Honoré de Balzac (1799–1850)

of black-clad women for a violent death.

Written literature made its appearance around the 17th century, with the establishment of the first literary circles, most of which were linked to liberation movements. The literature of this period dealt mainly with history and politics. Only at the end of the 19th century were the first poems, short stories and novels published in the Corsican language.

Between the World Wars, *A Muvra* became the newspaper of the Partitu Corsu d'Azione (Corsican Action Party), the main independence-movement party.

In the 19th century, many prominent French authors wrote works inspired by the island: Honoré de Balzac's *The Vendetta*; Guy de Maupassant's *The Corsican Bandit*, *A Vendetta* and *Histoire Corse*; and Alexandre Dumas' *Corsican Brothers*.

Among contemporary authors, Angelo Rinaldi paints a ruthless portrait of his home town, Bastia, in the novels *La Dernière Fête de l'Empire* and *Les Roses de Pline*, and Marie Susini deals with the Corsican family and provinciality in novels such as *L'Île sans Rivage* and *La Renfermée*. Sisters Hélène and Jeanne Bresciani, both authors in their own right, together wrote *2, rue de la Marine*, a poetic account of coming to terms with the death of their father, reflected through Corsican culture.

## MUSIC

Songs are undoubtedly the best expression of Corsican musicality. An excellent example of this discipline is the *paghjella*,

*Cetera, a 16-string cittern*

a traditional polyphonic song for three male voices that may have been imported from the Balearic Islands and is still sung during mass and other religious ceremonies in some towns and villages. Each voice has a specific function: the first, a tenor, provides the melodic and tonal base; the second, which is lower, provides the background; and the third, the highest, adds improvised embellishments. According to tradition, the singers must all be dressed in black. All Corsican songs express an emotion, a state of mind, or retell a joyful or painful event. In the past, they were used to hand down traditions orally.

A particularly sorrowful song, the *voceru*, is sung by women dressed in black on the occasion of a wake: they weep and sing while rocking their bodies back and forth to mourn the deceased. A more playful genre is the *chjama e rispondi*, a form of choral competition in which two contestants improvise insults in verse.

Instruments in Corsica are traditionally wind-based, and typical of a pastoral society: flutes and fifes made of wood or animal horns (*a ciallamella, u liscarolu, a caramusa, u fischju*). Jew's harps (*ghjerbula*) and castanets (*chjoche*) are also used, as well as violins and guitars. Some instruments have recently been revived – for example, the 16-string *cetera*, a sort of cittern; the *pifane*, a goat horn used in the past by local shepherds; and the *pirula*, another wind instrument.

Some local groups – such as I Muvrini, A Filetta, Canta U Populu Corsu and Donasulana – have specialized in polyphonic music and have become famous on and off the island.

---

### LOCAL TRADITIONS

Almost all Corsicans are Catholic and the local traditions that have been preserved are mostly of a religious nature. The most fascinating are the processions held during Easter Week, for example in Bonifacio, Calvi, Sartène and Erbalunga. Local saints' days are well celebrated in the cities and villages, as are ceremonies for the dead, accompanied by solemn processions to the cemeteries or to the unusual and impressive mortuary chapels *(see p29)* along the roads of Cap Corse and the west coast. However, the best-known "custom" in Corsica is the vendetta, which was common practice up to the mid-19th century. The physical distance and perceived indifference of Genoese justice led Corsican families to take the law into their own hands and seek revenge for offences. Rivalry for love, the division of a plot of land or any other dispute, even the most futile, could trigger a chain of murders – or even wars – that would carry on for generations. The

feud would end only if the parish priest managed to broker an agreement between the families. Avengers going into hiding in the maquis were known as *bandits d'honneur* ("bandits of honour") to differentiate them from common highway robbers.

**Scene of a vendetta between Corsican clans in a period print**

# CORSICA THROUGH THE YEAR

The best months to visit Corsica are May, June and September: the climate is mild, the prices are lower, and the beaches are not crowded. In addition, the risk of fires is low. In the summer, the island is filled with tourists and it is more difficult to find convenient and comfortable accommodation. Hikers and cyclists especially should avoid

**Mural at Solenzara**

July and August because of the heat. From November to April, Corsica comes to a halt, and only a few hotels are open in the cities and main tourist locations along the coast. In these colder months, transport connections with the island are reduced to a minimum, and the sea can be quite rough.

Rockrose and lavender in bloom in the spring months

## SPRING

The blossoming maquis fills the air with its sweet scent. This begins in March with rosemary and lavender and continues in April with the pink and white rockrose flowers that cover entire areas. In mid-May, myrtle begins to blossom. The air is mild and visitors can enjoy a swim in the clear waters. At high altitudes, the snow may last until June and some paths and roads are closed.

## MARCH

**Our Lady of Mercy Feast** *(18 Mar)*, Ajaccio, with a procession and solemn mass.
**Bastia Film Festival** *(Mar)*. A celebration of international film production.

**Olive Festival** *(mid-Mar)*, Santa Lucia di Tallano.
**Greek Orthodox Procession** *(Easter Mon)*, Cargèse. Traditional ceremonies and songs among the Greek community.
**Procession de la Cerca** *(Maundy Thu, Good Fri)*, Erbalunga. This 21-km (13-mile) procession begins at 7am and goes through all the towns in the Brando region. At 8pm there is the *Granitula* procession, with hooded penitents.
**Good Friday Procession**, Bonifacio. The five city confraternities carry wooden sculptures and walk to the church of Ste-Marie-Majeure to worship the relics of the Holy Cross.
**Good Friday Procession**, Sartène. At 9:30pm, in the city illuminated by candles, there is the *Catenacciu* (Great Penitent) procession.

## APRIL

**Salon de la Bande Dessinée** *(early Apr)*, Bastia. Comic books and strips.
**Brocciu Day** *(date depending on cheese production)*, Piana. Festival dedicated to *brocciu* (traditional sheep's-milk cheese).

## MAY

**May 1 Fair**, Ucciani. Trade show of Corsican handicrafts.
**Festimare** *(early May)*, L'Île Rousse. A sea festival for young people.
**Ste-Restitude's Feast Day** *(late May)*, Calenzana. Pilgrimage, procession.
**Île Danse** *(late May)*, Ajaccio. Dance festival with leading European companies.
**Régates Impériales** *(late May)*, Ajaccio. A regatta on old sailing boats in the Gulf of Ajaccio.

The Orthodox Easter procession at Cargèse

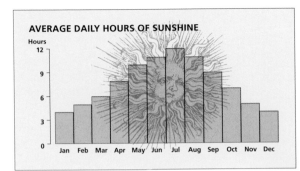

## AVERAGE DAILY HOURS OF SUNSHINE

Hours

12 — 9 — 6 — 3 — 0

Jan Feb Mar Apr May Jun Jul Aug Sep Oct Nov Dec

### Sunshine Hours

*Corsica is well-known as a sunny island, even in autumn and spring, when the weather is still mild due to the many daily hours of sunshine. Along the coast, the warm sun makes swimming possible even into the early autumn.*

## SUMMER

During the summer, the number of visitors to Corsica triples. The hotels, residences and camp sites are all booked up and charge high-season rates. The beaches are constantly packed with bathers, and the harbours are filled with sailing boats and motorboats. At this time the island also offers many festivals to enjoy.

## JUNE

**St Erasmus's Feast Day** *(2 Jun)*, Ajaccio, Bastia, Calvi. The feast day of the patron saint of fishermen includes a procession in the sea.
**Cavall'in Festa** *(early Jun)*, Corte. Horse festival with parades in period costumes, shows, contests, exhibitions and displays.
**Rencontre d'Art Contemporain** *(Jun–Sep)*, Calvi. Exhibition of contemporary art held in the citadel.
**La Nuit du Conte** *(Jun)*, Vero. Celebrations for the arrival of summer.
**Fête de St-Jean** *(24 Jun)*, Bastia. A traditional celebration held in honour of St John.
**Jazz Festival** *(last week of Jun)*, Calvi. Concerts and jam sessions along the quayside.
**Nautival** *(end of Jun)*, Macinaggio. Sea festival with stalls, performances, fish tastings and a procession.

## JULY

**La Relève de la Garde** *(every Thu throughout Jul)*, Ajaccio. Changing of the Guard ceremony, in costume.
**Wine Fair** *(first weekend of Jul)*, Luri.
**La Relève des Gouverneurs** *(11 July)*, Bastia. Commemoration of an historical event with a procession in the citadel.
**Book Fair** *(Jul)*, L'Île Rousse. Corsican books and authors.
**Music in the Village** *(Jul)*, Corbara. Concerts and shows.
**Calvi on the Rocks** *(Jul)*, Calvi. Rock and dance music.
**Estivoce** *(early Jul)*, Pigna. Corsican polyphonic music: folk music, medieval religious songs, theatre.
**Blues Festival "Nuits du Blues"** *(first two weeks of Jul)*, Ajaccio. National and international musicians, exhibitions and films.
**Olive Festival** *(first weekend after 14 Jul)*, Montegrosso. Trade show featuring olive oil produced in the Balagne area.
**Festival Jacques Luciani** *(mid-Jul)*, Corte. Festival of folk dances.
**Guitar Nights** *(third week of Jul)*, Patrimonio. Folk, jazz and gypsy musicians.
**Mediterranean Trophy** *(last ten days of Jul)*. Starting from Bastia, this regatta stops at Ajaccio, Maddalena and Elba.
**Les Estivales** *(Jul–Sep)*, Ajaccio. A traditional music festival also featuring dance performances.

**Participants in the Mediterranean Trophy regatta**

## AUGUST

**Film Festival** *(late Jul–early Aug)*, Lama. Featuring showings of European films, as well as Q&A meetings with directors.
**Ballu in Corti** *(Aug)*, Corte. Traditional dance with violin accompaniment.
**Music Festival** *(first week of Aug)*, Erbalunga. Outdoor concerts.
**Notre Dame des Neiges** *(8 Aug)*, Bavella. Religious procession.
**Celebrations in Honour of Napoleon** *(mid-Aug)*, Ajaccio. Ceremonies for the birth of Napoleon Bonaparte. Exhibitions and parades in period costumes.
**Calvi Allegria** *(mid-Aug)*, Calvi. Sound-and-light spectacle narrating the history of Calvi's citadel.
**Porto Latino** *(mid-Aug)*, St-Florent. Lively festival of Latin-American music.
**St Bartholomew Procession** *(24 Aug)*, held in Bonifacio.

**The Guitar Nights festival**

## AVERAGE MONTHLY RAINFALL

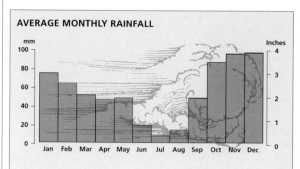

| mm | | | | | | | | | | | | Inches |
|---|---|---|---|---|---|---|---|---|---|---|---|---|
| 100 | | | | | | | | | | | | 4 |
| 80 | | | | | | | | | | | | 3 |
| 60 | | | | | | | | | | | | |
| 40 | | | | | | | | | | | | 2 |
| 20 | | | | | | | | | | | | 1 |
| 0 | Jan Feb Mar Apr May Jun Jul Aug Sep Oct Nov Dec | | | | | | | | | | | 0 |

**Rainfall**
*Autumn and winter are the wettest periods of the year in Corsica, with intense rainfall that may last several days. At the end of the summer there are often violent thunderstorms, but it is still the driest season on the island.*

## AUTUMN

The sky is clear, the climate is mild, and until October the temperature of the sea is warm enough for bathing. On the coastline, the maquis begins to blossom again after the summer drought, and the strawberries and black myrtle berries ripen. In the valleys and mountains, the trees take on the colours of the autumn. In the chestnut-grove regions, Castagniccia and Evisa, the earth is carpeted with prickly chestnut burs, and the first rainfall encourages mushrooms to grow.

## SEPTEMBER

**Settembrinu di Tavagna** *(end of Aug–early Sep)*, Tavagna. Festival of international music –

including Cuban, Corsican, African and Romany.
**Procession of the Virgin Mary** *(7–10 Sep)*, Casamaccioli. This celebration of the Virgin Mary is the oldest pilgrimage on the island.
**8 September Procession**, Lavasina. A torch-lit procession and midnight mass.
**Fête de Notre Dame** *(8 Sep)*, Bonifacio. The Festival of the Virgin Mary, during which a special dish of stuffed aubergines (eggplant) is prepared and eaten.
**European Diving Film Festival** *(early Sep)*, different location each year. Festival of films on underwater diving by leading directors in this genre.
**Porto-Vecchio Fair** *(second week of Sep)*, Porto-Vecchio. This annual trade fair features a complete range of Corsican handicrafts.

The Procession of the Virgin Mary at Casamaccioli

**Polyphonic Music Week** *(3rd week of Sep)*, Calvi. Traditional Corsican music.
**International Cup** *(Sep)*. A regatta starting from Marseille, on the French mainland, and stopping at Calvi and Propriano.
**Mele in Festa** *(Sep)*, Murzo. A festival to celebrate honey, a Corsican speciality.

One of the public events honouring Napoleon Bonaparte at Ajaccio *(see p33)*

## AVERAGE MONTHLY TEMPERATURE

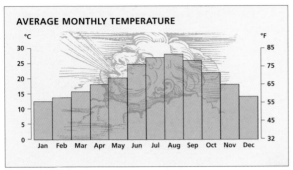

**Temperature**
*Thanks to the sea, the temperature along the coast is mild even in winter, the annual average being 15° C (59° F). Inland, however, the winter is harsh, with heavy snowfall and frequent frost, while the summers are cool, even if the sun is very hot.*

## OCTOBER

**Rally de France** *(late Sep–early Oct)*. Great auto-rally champions compete on the winding roads of Corsica – one of the most interesting stages of this race.
**Les Musicales de Bastia** *(Oct)*, Bastia. Jazz, dance, theatre and music.
**Le Tour de Corse à la Voile** *(late Oct)*. Regatta with start and finish at Bonifacio.
**Festiventu** *(last week of Oct)*, Calvi. A festival of model-aeroplane contests and hot-air balloon flights.

## NOVEMBER

**Chestnut Festival** *(Nov)*, Evisa. Harvest celebrations.
**Mediterranean Cultures Film Festival "Arte Mare"** *(Nov)*, Bastia. Film productions, art and literature from Mediterranean countries.
**Journées de la Pomme** *(first weekend of Nov)*, Bastelica. Apple festival. Preserves, juices and dried fruits can be sampled and purchased. Also available are charcuterie and handicrafts.

## WINTER

The weather becomes colder, partly due to the mistral wind. The mountain tops are covered with snow and the ski-lift facilities are sporadically in operation. At Christmas Corsican cities

are decorated with holiday illuminations, and in Ajaccio games are organized and stalls display their wares. At this time of the year, many hotels and restaurants are closed, and accommodation can be difficult to find outside the cities and main tourist localities.

However, this can be a very pleasant season; the coastline is green, the streets are lined with flowers, the maquis vegetation retains its foliage, and on sunny days it is possible to forget that it is winter.

In December, the olives are gathered and taken to the presses, and in February the almond trees begin to blossom, allowing for the first taste of spring.

## DECEMBER

**Chestnut Festival** *(early Dec)*, Bocognano. A popular festival featuring dishes and desserts made from chestnut flour.
**Animation de Noël** *(Dec)*, Ajaccio. Christmas entertainment in the streets of the capital: bingo contests, games and gig rides.

## JANUARY

**Chestnuts, harvested in late autumn**

**Italian Film Festival** *(late Jan)*, Bastia. Popular festival featuring screenings of Italian films, themed by director and/or actor, exhibitions, conferences, and Italian cuisine.

**The polyphonic music group A Filetta performing at a festival**

**St Anthony Procession** *(first Sun after 17 Jan)*, Corbara and Aregno. Procession in honour of St Anthony.

## FEBRUARY

**A Tumbera** *(second week of Feb)*, Renno. This festival is organized around a type of Corsican pig and offers competitions and food stalls.

### PUBLIC HOLIDAYS
**New Year's Day** (1 Jan)
**Easter Sunday and Monday** (Mar or Apr)
**Labour Day** (1 May)
**1945 Victory Day** (8 May)
**Ascension Day** (40 days after Easter)
**Pentecost Sunday and Monday** (mid-May–mid-Jun)
**Bastille Day** (14 Jul)
**Assumption Day** (15 Aug)
**All Saints' Day** (1 Nov)
**Armistice Day** (11 Nov)
**Christmas Day** (25 Dec)

# THE HISTORY OF CORSICA

*S*ituated near the Tuscan and Provençal coasts, Corsica has been occupied, colonized and fought over for millennia. Its history and culture are the results of the convergence of different civilizations, from the Carthaginians and Romans to the Pisans, Genoese and French. These experiences have given rise to the unique identity of the Corsican nation.

The rock massif that includes the island of Corsica reached its present position in the Tyrrhenian Sea about 18 million years ago.

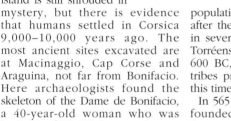

**Drinking vessel in the shape of a horse's head (480 BC)**

The exact date of the arrival of people on the island is still shrouded in mystery, but there is evidence that humans settled in Corsica 9,000–10,000 years ago. The most ancient sites excavated are at Macinaggio, Cap Corse and Araguina, not far from Bonifacio. Here archaeologists found the skeleton of the Dame de Bonifacio, a 40-year-old woman who was buried in 6570 BC; her remains are now kept in the Levie museum.

In the 6th millennium BC, Corsica experienced a considerable influx of migrant populations. The Neolithic inhabitants of this period bred livestock and practised weaving. This growth in population was followed by ever-increasing trade. The mid-4th millennium was the age of megalithic monuments *(see p129)*, the most impressive ruins of ancient Corsica *(see pp38–9)*. During this period, the Corsicans traded mostly with

people on the Italian coast: digs have brought to light Etruscan vases and other items from Magna Graecia.

Around 1500 BC, with the advent of the Bronze Age, the south of Corsica was invaded by a population known as the Torréens, after the towers *(torri)* they erected in several parts of the island. The Torréens ruled the south until about 600 BC, when infighting between tribes prompted another migration, this time to Sardinia.

In 565 BC, colonists from Phocaea founded the city of Alalia. After Etruscan and Carthaginian rule, the city was conquered by the Romans when Scipio's legions landed in 259 BC and renamed Aléria. During the Pax Romana, the city was developed, first by Caesar and then by the emperors Hadrian, Caracalla and Diocletian. It became the capital of the province of Corsica and remained so until the Barbarian invasions in AD 455. In 100 BC, the Roman general and consul Marius founded the colony of Mariana, just south of present-day Bastia.

## TIMELINE

| 10,000 BC | 5000 | 1000 | 500 | 300 | 100 |
|---|---|---|---|---|---|
| **8000 BC** Humans settle in Corsica | **1500 BC** Torréens from Asia Minor invade southeastern plains | **565 BC** Foundation of Alalia (later named Aléria) by colonists from Phocaea | **100 BC** Marius founds the colony of Mariana<br>**280 BC** Carthaginian conquest | | |
| **6570 BC** Date of the burial of the Dame de Bonifacio | | *Ancient axe head kept in the Levie museum* | | **259 BC** Beginning of Roman conquest | |
| **3500–1000 BC** Period of Corsican megalithic monuments | | | | **4th–3rd centuries BC** Etruscans and Syracusans in Corsica | |

◁ **"Father of the Nation" Pascal Paoli, portrayed by Richard Cosway**

# From Megaliths to Romans

**Attic crater,
5th century BC**

Ancient Corsica was an island whose prehistoric populations were extremely dynamic. The most active period of these ancestral cultures began in the Neolithic era, roughly 6000 BC, an epoch when cardial ware was produced. During this time, these populations became more settled, lived on livestock raising, and began to build their dwellings with dry walls, often fortifying them. Towards the end of this period, the megalithic monuments (see p129) first appeared. There soon followed invasions, first by the Torréens and then by the Phocaeans and the Etruscans. Lastly, the Romans settled in Alalia, founded by the Phocaeans, renaming it Aléria. Their hegemony extended over most of the island, remaining until the Barbarian invasions.

**Anthropomorphic menhirs,**
*with facial features and
sometimes warriors'
weapons, are unique to
Corsican culture.*

**The alignments
of menhirs** *are
a distinguishing
element of
Neolithic Corsican
culture. Many of
the arrangements
were probably
connected to
prehistoric
religious rituals.*

**Filitosa** has one of the most important alignments of anthropomorphic menhirs on the island (see p129).

• Filitosa

## THE REMAINS OF THE PAST

Most of the menhir alignments and dolmens that are still standing date from the period between the 2nd and 1st millennia BC. They are mainly located in southwest Corsica, while fortified castles can be found on the hills in the eastern sector. The most important Roman ruins lie at the site of Aléria, where the original plan of this ancient city can still be seen.

Cauria

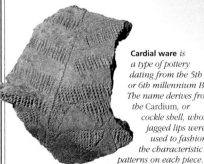

**Cardial ware** *is
a type of pottery
dating from the 5th
or 6th millennium BC.
The name derives from
the* Cardium, *or
cockle shell, whose
jagged lips were
used to fashion
the characteristic
patterns on each piece.*

**The Cauria plateau** has many of the best-preserved menhirs and dolmens, which miraculously avoided destruction by the Christians. Stantari, Pagliaju, Renaggiu and Fontanaccia are the sites to visit (see p127).

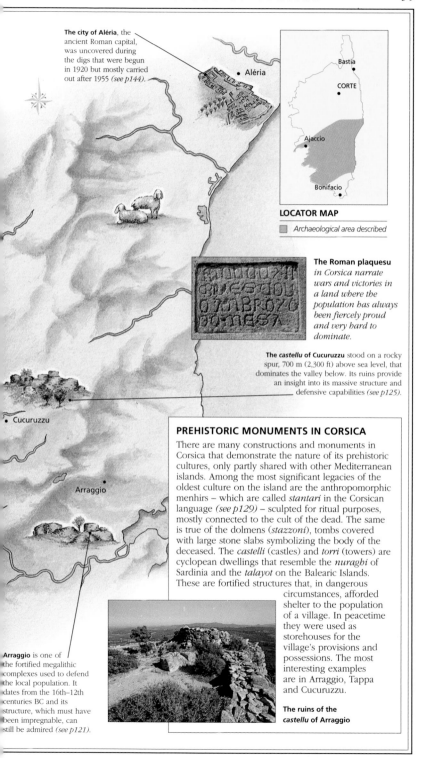

**The city of Aléria**, the ancient Roman capital, was uncovered during the digs that were begun in 1920 but mostly carried out after 1955 *(see p144)*.

• Aléria

**LOCATOR MAP**

Archaeological area described

**The Roman plaquesu** *in Corsica narrate wars and victories in a land where the population has always been fiercely proud and very hard to dominate.*

**The *castellu* of Cucuruzzu** stood on a rocky spur, 700 m (2,300 ft) above sea level, that dominates the valley below. Its ruins provide an insight into its massive structure and defensive capabilities *(see p125)*.

• Cucuruzzu

Arraggio

**Arraggio** is one of the fortified megalithic complexes used to defend the local population. It dates from the 16th–12th centuries BC and its structure, which must have been impregnable, can still be admired *(see p121)*.

## PREHISTORIC MONUMENTS IN CORSICA

There are many constructions and monuments in Corsica that demonstrate the nature of its prehistoric cultures, only partly shared with other Mediterranean islands. Among the most significant legacies of the oldest culture on the island are the anthropomorphic menhirs – which are called *stantari* in the Corsican language *(see p129)* – sculpted for ritual purposes, mostly connected to the cult of the dead. The same is true of the dolmens (*stazzoni*), tombs covered with large stone slabs symbolizing the body of the deceased. The *castelli* (castles) and *torri* (towers) are cyclopean dwellings that resemble the *nuraghi* of Sardinia and the *talayot* on the Balearic Islands. These are fortified structures that, in dangerous circumstances, afforded shelter to the population of a village. In peacetime they were used as storehouses for the village's provisions and possessions. The most interesting examples are in Arraggio, Tappa and Cucuruzzu.

**The ruins of the *castellu* of Arraggio**

## BARBARIAN INVASIONS

The fall of the Roman Empire had immediate repercussions for the island, which was soon overrun by Barbarian populations. The Vandals landed in Corsica in AD 455 and were probably the cause of the final abandonment of Aléria. After conquering the North African coastline, the Vandals sent bishops from the conquered cities into exile in Corsica. This was probably a key factor in the evangelization of the island, which had begun a century earlier. In 534 the Byzantines, under Emperor Justinian, took over, but the island remained at the mercy of repeated Barbaric invasions, including those of the Lombards and the Saracens. The Lombards ruled until 774, when they were defeated by the Franks, who had initially been called to support the papacy in Rome against the Lombard threat. The Frankish king, Pepin the Short, donated Corsica to Pope Stephen, a deal that was confirmed by his son Charlemagne 20 years later.

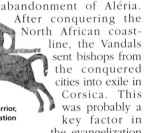

A Vandal warrior, shield decoration

However, a new threat was looming on the horizon for the inhabitants of Corsica. The Arab expansion across the Mediterranean was extensive during this period. A series of landings along the entire coastline of Corsica, particularly in the fertile region of Balagne, was so overwhelming that a 15th-century chronicler, Giovanni della Grossa, talked of a mass conversion to Islam.

The many Carolingian expeditions did very little to lessen the pressure of the Saracens, and many Corsicans fled from the island to settle on the nearby Italian coast. Historians mention a flourishing Corsican community in the Roman port of Ostia, the town of Pope Formosus (891–896), who had been born in the Corsican town of Porto.

A 16th-century painting depicting the Arab invasion of Corsica

## FEUDALISM IN THE MIDDLE AGES

After the year 1000, the influence of the mainland increased, and feudalism developed in Corsica with a structure similar to that prevailing throughout Europe. On the island, however, this political configuration was strongly influenced by the power of the various clans that fought among themselves. These feuds led to the division of the territory into two geographical areas: the *Deça des Monts*, the northeastern half of the island, which was more developed and receptive to trade; and the *Delà des Monts*, the pastoral and "backwards" southwestern sector. Internal struggles prevented the island from strengthening its military force, so the papacy was forced to request that the republics of Pisa and Genoa should step in to defeat the Arabs and bring stability to the island of Corsica.

## TIMELINE

| | | | |
|---|---|---|---|
| **3rd–5th centuries** Evangelization of Corsica | **5th and 6th centuries** Vandals and Ostrogoths invade | | |

*Carolingian coin*

| AD 200 | 400 | 600 | 800 |
|---|---|---|---|

**420** Aléria falls to the Vandals

*Benedictine monks*

**755** Probable donation of Corsica to the pope by Pepin the Short

Pisan Romanesque bas-relief, San Quilico, Cambia *(see 146)*

such as the beautiful churches of La Canonica and San Michele de Murato, and the development of Cap Corse, where the Pisans created vineyards, small ports and emporia.

## EARLY GENOESE RULE

After defeating Pisa, the Republic of Genoa worked swiftly to consolidate its grip on the island by laying out a series of defensive systems along the coastline

## THE PISAN PERIOD

In 1077, the Church granted Corsican rule to Bishop Landolfe of Pisa, thus initiating the period of Pisan domination. There were interesting cultural developments during this time, but it was troubled from a political standpoint. The rivalry with Genoa was at first handled well, thanks to the Holy See, but soon degenerated so much that, in 1133, Pope Innocent II had to divide the island's six bishoprics between Pisa (Ajaccio, Aléria and Sagone) and Genoa (Accia, Mariana and Nebbio).

By 1187, the Genoese, who were becoming increasingly powerful in the Mediterranean, took possession of the harbour of Bonifacio and, in 1268, founded Calvi. The Genoese took control of Corsica in 1284 with the naval battle of Meloria *(see pp42–3)* near the Tuscan coast.

and creating an administrative structure. However, this proved to be a difficult task. Genoese rule was opposed by some of the local lords, in particular those in Cinarca, who were still faithful to Pisa. With the aim of setting up a Corsican government ruled by the towns (perhaps in the wake of the rise of the Italian city republics), the lords stirred up popular insurrections. In addition, there were repeated attacks by other European nations, often with the backing of the Church. For example, in 1297, Pope Boniface

Boniface VIII (1294–1303)

VIII, asserting the rights of the Holy See in the Mediterranean, granted Corsican and Sardinian rule to the Aragonese kings, who sided with the Cinarca lords and remained a thorn in the side of the Genoese republic until the French took over in the mid-18th century.

There are many traces of Pisan rule on the island, including Romanesque architecture,

Relief at La Canonica, a church built in the Pisan period

*The citadel of Bonifacio*

**1195** Genoese colony is established in Bonifacio

**1297** Boniface VIII gives Corsica in fee to kingdom of Aragon

| 1000 | 1100 | 1200 |
|---|---|---|

**1077** Pope Gregory VII grants Corsica to Pisa

**1133** Pope Innocent II divides bishoprics between Pisa and Genoa

**1268** The Genoese found Calvi

**891–896** Papacy of Formosus, born in Porto

**6 August 1284** Battle of Meloria

# The Battle of Meloria

**The coat of arms of Pisa**

In the course of its history, Corsica was subject to the rule of two Italian maritime republics, Pisa and Genoa. The event that marked the passage from one ruler to the other was the Battle of Meloria (1284). Both republics had previously helped to free the Mediterranean from the Saracens and the pirates that had been plaguing the region, after which they vied for control of Corsica. In 1077, Pope Gregory VII granted Corsican rule to Landolfe, the bishop of Pisa. This led to an increase in friction: skirmishes, confrontations and treaties became the norm, until the battle. During the first two centuries of Genoese rule, the island continued to be torn by war, pirate attacks and vendettas. Only in the late 1500s did Genoa manage to impose some kind of order.

**The coat of arms** *of the Republic of Pisa displays a ship that is also found on the Leaning Tower in Campo dei Miracoli. It is one of the many iconographic symbols of the city's maritime supremacy.*

**Oberto Doria**

**The commander** Albertino Morosini was, with Ugolino della Gherardesca and Andreotto Saraceno, the head of the Pisan fleet, which was helpless against the two Genoese fleets.

**The Saracens** *set fire to the towns and massacred the inhabitants or made them their slaves. Pisa in particular was devoted to freeing the island from this scourge.*

**The Pisan fleet** comprised 72 galleys and its defeat was total: 5,000 Pisans died and 11,000 were taken to Genoa in chains.

## THE FATE OF COUNT UGOLINO

After the defeat of Meloria, Ugolino della Gherardesca gave castles and land to the enemy to avoid a siege by the Florentines and Luccans, who were allies of Genoa and therefore enemies of Pisa. Accused of betrayal, he was imprisoned with his sons and grandsons in a tower, where he died. Dante considered him a traitor to his country, and in the *Divine Comedy* had him put in Hell, a curse that accompanied the count for centuries: "Ah, Pisa, scandal to the people / of the beauteous land where the 'yes' is heard, / since thy neighbours are slow to punish thee / let the Caprara and Gorgona move."

**Illustration of the** *Divine Comedy*

**Benedetto Zaccaria** *led a second group of Genoese ships that arrived by surprise at Meloria at a later stage in the battle, when the Pisans felt they were almost out of danger. His intervention was a key factor in the Ligurian republic's victory.*

**The chains** *of the anchors of the Pisan ships were impounded by the Genoese at the end of the battle. Considered a sort of war booty, they were on exhibit in Genoa as a sign of the city's supremacy. Only in the 19th century were they given back to Pisa, where they hang under the loggia of the Camposanto.*

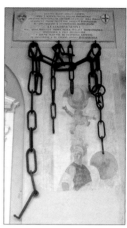

**The cliffs of Meloria** are about 7 km (4 miles) off the coast of Livorno, facing Corsica.

**Meloria** was the scene of an earlier battle, in 1241, in which the Pisans, aided by the emperor Frederick II, defeated the Genoese.

**The wealth** *of Genoa, which stemmed from commercial trading, made it a political power that dominated the Mediterranean for a long time.*

## IN THE THICK OF THE BATTLE

In August 1284, a Genoese fleet led by Oberto Doria sailed into the waters opposite Porto Pisano. Startled by this move, the Pisans attacked from the cliffs of Meloria. The battle was violent and the outcome uncertain, until the arrival of a second group of Genoese galleys, which caught their enemies by surprise and decided the outcome of the fight. Giovanni David's *The Battle of Meloria* (left) hangs in the Palazzo Ducale in Genoa.

**The Genoese fleet** consisted of 93 galleys.

**The Genoese galleys** *were fast ships, suitable for both cargo transport and naval battles. Largely because of these vessels and their commanders, Genoa prospered and became a power able to defeat its enemies and rivals.*

**The Genoese fleet near the coast of Corsica on a print kept at the Musée de la Corse**

## THE END OF THE MIDDLE AGES

The 14th century was a troubled time for Corsica. In 1348, the population was decimated by the Black Death, and difficult living conditions triggered a series of revolts among the islanders. On the one hand, there were the landowners who were keen to maintain the feudal system, and on the other there were the commoners, who wanted to get rid of the aristocrats.

One of the members of the feudal faction was Arrigo della Rocca, who in 1376 asked the Aragonese to come to his aid. The commoners also boasted legendary figures, such as Sambucuccio d'Alando, a peasant whose famous exploits shook the foundations of local feudalism. The common people established the *Terres des Communes*, a confederation of villages favouring the common use of local land, in opposition to the feudal powers.

*Sambucuccio d'Alando*

## GENOESE POLICY

Occasionally, the Genoese Republic gave control of the island over to private organizations that, as well as administering it, also safeguarded Genoa's interests. The first such commercial company to have this assignment was the Maona, in 1378, but it soon went bankrupt, prompting some of the nobles to ask the Aragonese throne for help. One of these nobles was Vincentello d'Istria, a soldier, estate owner and pirate who, in 1420, led a Spanish fleet of 400 ships to the island. Bonifacio resisted, but almost all of Corsica fell into Vincentello's hands. A few years later, Genoa had an opportunity to subdue the feudal landowners but did not make the most of it. The Genoese chose instead to ignore the *Terres des Communes*' request to protect the interests of the people. This refusal only increased the gap between the coastal town populations and those in the interior; it was the latter who were to cause the biggest problems in the future.

## THE BANK OF ST GEORGE

In 1453, Genoa delegated control of Corsica to the Bank of St George, whose power was sanctioned by the *Capitula Corsorum*, the statute of the Genoese government of the island.

## TIMELINE

**1348** The plague decimates the island population

**1376** Arrigo della Rocca asks the Aragonese to support the rebellion

**1453** *Capitula Corsorum*: Corsica governed by the Bank of St George

| 1300 | 1350 | 1400 | 1450 | 1500 |
|---|---|---|---|---|

*Victims of the plague*

**1378** Corsica governed by the Maona organization

**1358** Revolt of Sambucuccio d'Alando

**1420** Revolt of Vincentello d'Istria, who founds Corte

**1498** Sampiero Corso is born in Bastelica

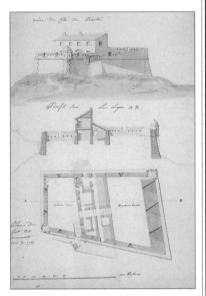

This Genoese bank ruled Corsica with special powers. It had the right to collect taxes, mint coins and to administer justice, and it had its own army. The bank's activities were many and varied, and were controlled by a series of basic guidelines. One of its primary objectives was to guarantee political control of the land by curbing the powers of the feudal lords. In addition to this, the Genoese promised to make the coastal plains productive in the hope of overcoming the scourge of malaria.

**Royal Corsican artillery (1740)**

## SAMPIERO AND THE END OF GENOA

Born in 1498 in a hamlet near Bastelica, Sampiero Corso was one of the many islanders forced by poverty and tradition to enlist as a mercenary in the French Army. In 1553, after the momentous clash between France and Spain, the French decided to land on Corsica to gain a solid foothold in the Mediterranean. Sampiero Corso also took part in the French expedition, which was backed by the ships of the renowned pirate Dragut.

The Genoese strongholds fell one after the other – Bastia, St-Florent, Corte, and even the impregnable Bonifacio – until a peace treaty obliged the French to withdraw. Sampiero refused, however, and continued his struggle against the Genoese, even going so far as to ask various European courts to come to his aid. In 1563, a few months after landing once again in Corsica with the hope of stoking the fire of popular rebellion, Sampiero was assassinated. Genoese rule was reinstated in 1569, and for the next 200 years the island swung between insurrections on the one hand and normal colonial administration on the other. Genoa's power was in decline, however, and widespread dissatisfaction smouldered among the Corsicans. In the early 18th century, a series of revolts led first to independence for the island, and then to annexation by France. The only traces of the troubled Genoese rule that future islanders would note would be the chain of coastal towers and some cities with massive walls – the citadels.

**Monserrato Fort, in Bastia, in a 1761 drawing**

Sampiero Corso

**1640–70** Religious revival

**1676** Foundation of a Greek colony at Sagone

**1729** Revolt of Corte and peasants

1550     1600     1650     1700     1750

**1569** Genoa reconquers Corsica

**1553** Sampiero Corso's landing with a French expedition

*The citadel of Corte*

**1755–69** Pascal Paoli's government

# Revolt and Independence

One key event triggered the Corsicans' fight for independence – the imposition of new taxes by the Genoese rulers in 1729. Many Corsicans refused to pay the taxes and several years of revolts followed. In 1735 in Corte, the Corsicans first drafted a constitution for an independent sovereign state. The following year, Corsica elected a king, Baron Theodor von Neuhof, but he abandoned the throne after only eight months. In 1745, Jean-Pierre Gaffori became the leader of a major insurrection, followed by the 30-year-old Pascal Paoli in 1755. Paoli succeeded in establishing a constitutional state, founded the University of Corte, and created an army. For 14 years the island was independent, but on 8 May 1769, Paoli lost the battle of Ponte-Novo, and French rule began.

**Theodor von Neuhof**, *a German baron who had taken up the island's cause, was elected king by the Corsicans in 1736 but was forced to flee only a few months later.*

**Jean-Pierre Gaffori** *was one of the leaders of the 1745–55 revolts and was a member of the triumvirate during that period. He was assassinated in a street in Corte in 1753.*

**The hills of Castagniccia**

**French army**

**Faustina**, *Gaffori's wife, also took part in the clashes. She is portrayed in the bas-reliefs on the pedestal of the monument to her husband in Corte (see p134).*

**A combatant** *for Corsican independence wrote in a letter: "General, I entrust my old father to your care, as in two hours I shall be among those who have died for their country."*

## THE END OF A DREAM

On 8 May 1769, near the bridge at Ponte-Novo, the nationalist Corsican troops led by Pascal Paoli suffered a decisive defeat at the hands of the French army. This event brought to an end 14 years of independence, the only period to date during which the island was free from domination by other peoples or nations.

**The Moor's Head**
*has been the symbol of Independent Corsica for three centuries. Used by the Aragonese kings to celebrate the victory over the Moors in the 13th century, it was ceded to local clan leaders, taken up by Neuhof and then adopted by Paoli.*

## JAMES BOSWELL AND CORSICA

The British author James Boswell went to Corsica in 1765 and published his travel journal, *Account of Corsica*, in England three years later, thus spreading the image of Pascal Paoli's democratic government throughout Europe. During the period of the French Revolution, the still-fresh memory of French intervention on the island made the revolutionary politician Comte de Mirabeau express his "regret and sorrow" for having helped to suppress the freedom of such a proud people.

**Two thousand Corsican patriots** led by Paoli took part in the battle.

**Ponte-Novo** was named after a new stone bridge built by the Genoese over the Golo river.

**The French army surrounding the Corsicans on the bridge**

**Pascal Paoli** *was not only a fine military strategist, he was also an educated, enlightened and cultured man. He drafted the only constitution that Corsica ever had and founded the University of Corte, which was reopened in 1981 (see p137).*

**The bridge** was a typical Genoese construction, much like those that can still be found on the island.

**The Golo river**

## TIMELINE

| 1720 | 1730 | 1740 | 1750 | 1760 |
|---|---|---|---|---|
| | **1735** Declaration of Independence | **1755** Pascal Paoli is elected General of the Nation | **8 May 1769** Corsicans defeated at Ponte-Novo | |
| **1729** First revolt against Genoa; start of the War of Independence | **1748** Second French intervention | **1765** The University of Corte opened | | |
| **1733** Second revolt headed by Hyacinthe Paoli, Pascal's father | **1745** Third revolt led by Jean-Pierre Gaffori | **1753** French troops leave the island | **1762** The Moor's Head becomes the national symbol | |
| **1738** France intervenes on request by the Genoese | | | | |

### FRENCH DOMINION

During Corsica's years of revolt and brief period of independence, France had kept a close eye on the island, intervening on the side of Genoa against the Corsicans. In 1768, the weakened Genoese ceded the island to France, but French rule only started after a final attempt of resistance at the Battle of Ponte-Novo in 1769 *(see pp46–47)*. Corsica was now governed by a provincial administrator and a military governor, one of whose duties was to repress popular revolts, which from then on were labelled as banditry.

*Napoleon Crossing the St Bernard Pass,*
*Jacques-Louis David, 1800*

Corsica was divided into provinces, each of which had its own law court. The cities gradually lost the privileges conferred on them by the Genoese, and efforts were made to establish clear-cut limits between private property and the municipalities.

Supporters of French rule were granted a series of benefits, including land, which stirred discontent among the people. Corsican nationalism was by no means dead, as proved by a rebellion that broke out in Niolo in 1774 and by the constant support given to General Paoli during his exile by the French. At the first signs of revolutionary activity in France, Corsicans made it quite clear that they would not be mere spectators to these events. There were differences, however, between the demands made by the French and those of the Corsicans. The latter were not interested in the struggle against the noble class, but fought for equal rights for French people and Corsicans. In 1790, the people disarmed the garrison in Bastia and political exiles such as Paoli could return to the island.

Sentenced to death by radical French revolutionaries, the Jacobins, Paoli appealed to the English for help. Their intervention led to the birth of the Anglo-Corsican kingdom (1794–96), with Sir George Elliott as viceroy. The sidelined Paoli left for London, where he died in 1807. In 1796 French troops were sent out to retake the island. They were led by a young Corsican-born officer – Napoleon Bonaparte. He would always have close ties with his motherland, and Ajaccio in particular *(see p87)*.

### THE 19TH AND 20TH CENTURIES

After Napoleon's fall in 1815, the 19th century in Corsica was fairly calm, and the presence of France took on ever-increasing importance. The decrease in banditry and vendettas, alongside a relatively stable economic and political scene, lent a certain credibility to French rule.

Efforts were made to create a middle class that would support and promote the island's growth. One of the most successful initiatives was the development of an infrastructure on the island, which vastly

## TIMELINE

*Napoleonic crest*

**1790** Paoli returns from exile

**1830** First maritime service to Corsica established

**1894** Inauguration Ajaccio–Bastia railway

| 1775 | 1800 | 1825 | 1850 | 1875 |
|------|------|------|------|------|

**1769** Birth of Napoleon Bonaparte in Ajaccio

**1794–96** Anglo-Corsican kingdom

**1827** Opening of Ajaccio–Bastia road

**1855–70** Repression of banditry and blood feuds

**Corsican emigrants waiting to embark**

improved communications. The Ajaccio–Bastia road was constructed in 1827 and the railway in 1894, and a permanent ferry service was established in 1830. All this led to an unprecedented population increase, from 150,000 people in 1790 to 300,000 in 1890. There was a parallel development in agriculture, even in the hills and mountain areas inland, and the centralized administration tried to curb the free circulation of transhumance shepherds. Around the mid-19th century a liberal Corsican middle class was on the rise.

However, a short time later, during the Industrial Revolution, Corsica was affected by decline. The mainly rural and, in comparison, non-modernized society could not compete with agricultural products from the mainland and the French colonies. Despite improvements in living standards, dire poverty once again afflicted the island, forcing thousands of Corsicans to emigrate. Corsica paid a high toll in World War I (20,000 dead), then lost an average of 5–6,000 people annually to emigration. In

**A Corsican Nationalist Party rally**

1942, Italian troops occupied Corsica. After the rise of a strong Resistance movement known as the "Maquis", Corsica was the first French *département* to be liberated, in 1943.

### THE INDEPENDENCE MOVEMENT
At the end of World War II, the many Corsicans who had gone abroad were repatriated, and in the 1960s there was a new presence in the elections, the Front Régionaliste Corse (FRC). In 1973, the FRC, together with the Action Régionaliste Corse (ARC), demanded autonomy for Corsica, a decentralized government and protection for Corsican land against tourist developments. In 1975, a series of demonstrations ended in the shooting of two police officers. Following this, the Front de Libération Nationale de la Corse (FLNC) was founded, which committed many acts of terrorism.

While the independence movement rapidly gained popularity, the island was again divided into two *départements*, Haute-Corse and Corse-du-Sud. In 1981, the University of Corte was reopened. The process of establishing a federal statute for Corsica began in 1991. The 1990s saw a boom in tourism, which created no environmental problems, partly because of the islanders' respect for their land. In 2003 separatist tension flared again after voters rejected a referendum to grant Corsica increased autonomy, but today Corsica and the mainland government are working together to build a peaceful future.

| | | | | | | |
|---|---|---|---|---|---|---|
| | **1966** FRC founded | | | **1981** University of Corte reopens | **2003** Referendum to increase regional autonomy is rejected | |
| **1942** Italian occupation | | | | | | |

*Logo of the University*

| 1925 | 1950 | 1975 | 2000 | 2025 |
|---|---|---|---|---|
| **1910–20** Great wave of emigration | **1943** Liberation of Corsica | **1976** FNLC founded | **1991** Regional autonomy law is passed | **2009** Expanded low-cost airline services and the launch of modern autorail rolling stock improve travel to and around the island |

# CORSICA
# AREA BY AREA

# Corsica at a Glance

Within a distance covered by a short drive, Corsica offers beaches that are not unlike those in tropical countries and wild mountains surrounded by woods. The island boasts extremely varied and fascinating landscapes, such as the coast carpeted with maquis vegetation, the hillside olive and chestnut groves, the valleys where rivers have created deep gorges, the mountains traversed by the GR20 long-distance path *(see pp22–7)*, and the beautiful surrounding waters and seabeds. In this natural setting, man-made splendour can also be found in prehistoric megaliths, Pisan Romanesque churches, Genoese citadels, and villages of old stone houses. The two cities that have played a major role in the history of the island, Ajaccio and Bastia, are joined by the "historical capital", Corte, along with Bonifacio, Calvi and Porto-Vecchio, famous for their beaches.

**Calvi's Citadel**
*The strongholds of Genoese power, the citadels still dominate the main cities in Corsica, surrounded by massive bastions. Calvi's citadel was built in the 15th century.*

**Pointe de la Parata**
*One of the most common sights along the coastline are the Genoese watchtowers, surrounded by the brilliant colours of the maquis. One such building features at Pointe de la Parata, the famous cape in the Golfe d'Ajaccio.*

**AJACCIO AND THE WEST COAST**
*see pp82–105*

**Megalithic Monuments**
*Relics of prehistoric Corsica can still be found in the interior of the island, which has many alignments of menhirs. The menhirs can be dolmens or the so-called* castelli *(castles).*

0 kilometres      20

0 miles      20

◁ **The citadel of Corte dominating the Gorges du Tavignano and the Vallée de la Restonica**

BASTIA AND
THE NORTH
*see pp54–81*

CORTE AND
THE INTERIOR
*see pp130–151*

BONIFACIO
AND THE SOUTH
*see pp106–129*

**Vieux Port, Bastia**
*Like so many other ports, the Vieux Port of Bastia, dominated by the citadel, exudes the spirit of the island's past. Hundreds of years ago, the foundations of the present-day cities rose up around natural harbours that were used for merchant vessels.*

**Rocks and Rivers**
*In the untamed Corsican interior, rugged mountains and deep valleys crossed by violent torrents offer an exciting and challenging landscape for hikers.*

**The Cliffs of Bonifacio**
*The white limestone cliffs in the Bonifacio area are perhaps one of the most famous sights in Corsica. The cliffs are also geologically interesting, since limestone is an unusual presence in this mostly granitic island.*

# BASTIA AND THE NORTH

*Bastia has a charm of its own, which can be found in the citadel and the historic centre, with its narrow alleys reminiscent of Italian villages. Indeed, the town owes its development and commercial success to Genoa. To get a true sense of Bastia, the best thing to do is join the locals in their rituals: a coffee in Place St-Nicolas, a pastis at the Vieux Port and shopping at the Sunday market.*

Geographically closer to Italy than to France, Bastia aims to become a regular stopover port for Mediterranean cruises and a base for ecological tourism thanks to its proximity to the mountains inland. Cap Corse is nearby, with villages squeezed between the sea and mountains and small harbours protected by old watchtowers. This region is a world unto itself and has always been more similar to Pisa, Marseille, Genoa and Livorno than to the rest of the island.

With their sailing prowess, the inhabitants of this peninsula made it a port for the shipment of wine, firewood, oil, cork and other local products. Thanks to their farming traditions, they transformed the steep mountainsides into cultivable terraces. This can be seen in the Rogliano and Patrimonio vineyards, among the best on the island. The proximity to and close relations with Italy have left their mark on the language, with its Tuscan influence, and on the architecture, which resembles that of Italy's Ligurian coast. In fact, the islands in the Tuscan archipelago are visible from the east coast of Corsica.

The other "microregion" in the north is sunny Balagne, famous for its beaches and hamlets nestled in productive olive orchards. The history of this region is linked with that of Pisa, which developed Balagne's agriculture. Beautiful Pisan churches can be found in Aregno, Lumio and Calenzana. When the Genoese arrived, they built the citadels of Calvi and Algajola, exploited the cork oak groves, and planted the olive trees that still surround the old stone villages.

**The small harbour at Meria, near Macinaggio, along the eastern coast of Cap Corse**

◁ **Maquis vegetation covering the cliffs of Cap Corse; in the background, the Tour de l'Osse**

# Exploring Bastia and the North

The main tourist localities in the northern region lie along the west coast, beyond the Col de Teghime. St-Florent boasts a lovely yacht harbour and boat service to the wild beaches in the Désert des Agriates. Calvi is renowned for its nightlife and its beach – a long stretch of white sand under the shade of a pine grove. The relatively short distances between interesting sights in this area make it possible to organize one-day excursions inland through Balagne or Nebbio. These villages have preserved their centuries-old architecture, including stunning Pisan Romanesque churches. The Cap Corse peninsula is for those who love cliffs or small pebble beaches. Visitors may also enjoy hikes along the coast or among the maquis to villages where time seems to have stood still.

**A slope in the Désert des Agriates covered with maquis undergrowth**

## KEY

| | |
|---|---|
| ▬ | Major road |
| ▬ | Minor road |
| – – | Hiking trail |
| ▬ | Scenic route |
| ▬ | Railway |
| △ | Summit |
| ✕ | Mountain pass |

**Two villagers soaking up the sunshine and taking it easy in the Balagne region**

L'ÎLE ROUSSE ⑰

ALGAJOLA ⑱

PIGNA ⑲   SANT' ANTONINO ㉑

AREGNO ⑳

CALVI ㉕

La Revellata

Lumio

STRADA DI L'ARTIGIANI ㉔

Muro

SPELONCATO ㉒

Feliceto

Pioggiola

CALENZANA ㉓

Argentella

Monte Corona 2144m

Monte Padro 2391m

Asco

Galéria

Corbara   Monticello   Lozari

Belgodère

Occhiatana

Castifac

Balagne

DÉSE

## SIGHTS AT A GLANCE

**BARCAGGIO AND CAP CORSE**

Tollare — Barcaggio **5**

**7 SENTIER DES DOUANIERS**

Ersa

Rogliano

**CENTURI 6**    **4 MACINAGGIO**

D253

D80    D80

**PINO 8**    • Tour de Sénèque

• Luri

Minervio    Marine de Porticciolo

**CANARI 9**    **3 PIETRACORBARA**

Marine de Pietracorbara

Albo    Sisco    Marine de Sisco

Monte Stello 1307m

**NONZA 10**    Castello

**Golfe de St Florent**    **2 ERBALUNGA**

Plage de Saleccia    San Martino di Lota

Plage de Loto    D80

Serra di Pigno 950m

**AGRIATES**    **PATRIMONIO**

**16**    **11**    **1 BASTIA**

**ST-FLORENT**    D81

**12**

Col de Teghime

D81    D82

**14**

D62    **15 OLETTA**

Col de San Stefano    N193

onte Asto 1530m    Rapale

Lama    Murato    **13 SAN MICHELE DE MURATO**

N1197    Borgo    Étang di Biguglia

Pietralba    D5

Lento    Casamozza    D107    La Canonica

N193    Golo

Ponte Leccia    • Aléria

Corte

## GETTING AROUND

The most convenient means of travelling is by car, which allows access to the most isolated villages. The main roads from Bastia to Bonifacio, Calvi and Corte are wide and well paved. The same cannot be said for the minor roads, however, such as those in Balagne or along Cap Corse. Those on the west coast have a seemingly endless number of curves and a surface that is not always in good condition. For this reason, it can be easier to get around by motorcycle. Always keep an eye on the petrol gauge – petrol stations are few and far between. Bicycles are popular and are available for hire, but they should only be used by experienced cyclists, and cycling is not advisable in the summer. The main road network is good. It runs from Bastia to Aléria, Porto-Vecchio, Bonifacio, Corte and Ajaccio. The CFC train links Bastia, Calvi and Ajaccio, via Ponte Leccia. There are also bus services connecting the main localities.

### SEE ALSO

• **Where to Stay** pp158–60

• **Where to Eat** pp172–5

0 kilometres        10

0 miles        10

Picturesque Macinaggio harbour, with its colourful boats and nets

# Bastia ●

With its colourful houses overlooking the sea, Bastia is the second-largest city in Corsica and is considered its economic capital. This is because of the port and the industrial zone that extends south of the old centre. Although the ancient Romans founded the city of Mantinon, mentioned by the Greek geographer Ptolemy, on the hills, Bastia was for centuries only the small port of the village of Cardo in the neighbouring hinterland. Wine was loaded on to ships here in the Middle Ages and taken to Pisa. It was not until the 15th century that the Genoese began to construct a tower and enlarge the fortress that protected the port (*bastiglia* in Italian, hence the name of the city). Genoa was responsible for the prosperity of Bastia and left its mark there – including a certain coldness towards foreigners. With a little time and patience, however, this city can provide many surprises.

The simple, elegant façade of the Chapelle St-Roch

### ⛲ Place du Marché

Dominated by the old Mairie (town hall) and a lovely fountain shaded by plane trees, this square is the heart of Terra Vecchia (the ancient port area), with streets winding around the Vieux Port, or old harbour. The name "marché" (market) derives from the stalls, which, especially on Sunday mornings, make for a colourful and noisy scene. As well as the stands with fruit, vegetables, cheese and charcuterie, there are those that make a sort of pancake with *brocciu*, the local sheep's-milk cheese, and an oyster and mussel vendor.

Detail of the fountain in Place du Marché

### 🏛 St-Jean-Baptiste

Place de l'Hôtel-de-Ville. **Tel** 04 95 55 24 60. ⬭ *Mon–Sat, Sun am.*
The largest church in Corsica is flanked by two bell towers and has an imposing, austere façade that rises majestically among the roofs of the Terra Vecchia area. It was built in the mid-1600s and redecorated in the following century in Baroque style. The façade stands on a narrow alleyway and is one of the most recognizable images of the island. The two-aisle nave displays marble decoration, gilded stucco work and trompe-l'oeil decorations. The high altar, pulpit and font are made of polychrome marble.

### 🏛 Oratoire de l'Immaculée Conception

Rue Napoléon. ⬭ *daily.*
Constructed in 1611, this chapel reveals a rich Baroque interior. Wooden panels and red Genoese velvet cover the walls, and there is a fresco on the central vault representing the Immaculate Conception. On the small square outside, black and white pebblestones are laid out in the shape of a sun.

### 🏛 Chapelle St-Roch

Rue Napoléon. **Tel** 04 95 32 91 66. ⬭ *Mon–Sat, Sun am.*
This chapel was dedicated to the saint who protected the population from the plague. It was built in 1604 for the St Roch Confraternity, founded in 1588 *(see p61)*. The work of Ligurian architects and artists, the chapel has 18th-century, Genoese-style wooden panelling and features a statue of St Roch, which is borne in local processions. The organ was made in 1750 and is housed in an interesting tribune made of sculpted, gilded wood.

### 🏛 St-Charles

Rue du Général Carbuccia. ⬭ *Mon–Sat, Sun am.*
Preceded by a stairway, this church with its impressive façade was constructed in 1635 for the Jesuits' college and dedicated to St Ignatius Loyola, the founder of the order. When the Jesuits were driven out of Corsica in 1769, the church became the seat of the St Charles Borromeo Confraternity *(see p61)*.

Inside are several restored paintings, an altarpiece of the miraculous *Virgin of Lavasina* and a statue of the *Virgin Mary and Child*.

The view across the rooftops of the Terra Vecchia quarter

The jetty known as Môle Génois, on the north of the Vieux Port

## Vieux Port

Nestled between Terra Nova, the citadel and the Terra Vecchia quarter, which frames it with its old buildings, the small cove of the medieval port has retained the atmosphere of an old maritime village. It was once the marina of Cardo, and fishermen still mend their nets here in the blue-and-white wooden boats that are flanked by luxury yachts. Lining the quays are cafés and restaurants that are frequented by the locals, who spend their evenings here. In the summer the road is closed to traffic and the old port is transformed into a large and lively pedestrian precinct, excellent for people-watching.

The tall façades lining the port have suffered erosion from the sea wind and salty air. Walks along the outer jetties are spectacular: the Môle Génois to the north, and the Jetée du Dragon to the south, ending at the 1861 lighthouse.

### VISITORS' CHECKLIST

**Road map** D2. 🚶 52,500.
✈ *Poretta, 25 km (16 miles)
(04 95 54 54 54).*
🚌 🚆 *Place Maréchal Leclerc
(04 95 32 80 61).*
⛴ *from Genoa, Savona, Livorno,
La Spezia, Nice, Marseille, Toulon.*
ℹ *Place St-Nicolas (04 95 54
20 40).* 🎬 *Italian Film Festival
(Jan–Feb); Black Christ (3 May); St
John's Feast Day (24 Jun); Relève
des Gouverneurs (mid-Jul).*
**www**.bastia-tourisme.com

## Jardin Romieu

At the right-hand jetty of the Vieux Port are steps that go up to the citadel along a winding – but not particularly steep – path. It crosses over the Jardin Romieu, an oasis of greenery and tranquillity in the middle of Bastia. With palm, pine and laurel trees and succulent plants, it offers a splendid view of the city.

### THE CENTRE OF BASTIA

Chapelle St-Roch ④
*Citadelle pp60–61* ⑩
Jardin Romieu ⑦
Oratoire de l'Immaculée
 Conception ③
Place du Marché ①
Place St-Nicolas ⑨
Quai des Martyrs de la
 Libération ⑧
St-Charles ⑤
St-Jean-Baptiste ②
Vieux Port ⑥

Gare SNCF 500 m (550 yards)
Gare Routière 250 m (300 yards)
PLACE ST-NICOLAS ⑨
Port de Toga 500 m (550 yards)
Cyrnarom

RUE MIOT
BOULEVARD PAOLI
RUE CÉSAR CAMPINCHI
RUE NAPOLÉON
COURS PIERRE-ANGELI
QUAI DES MARTYRS

Chapelle St-Roch ④
PLACE DU MARCHÉ
Oratoire de l'Immaculée Conception ③
St-Jean-Baptiste ②
St-Charles ⑤ St-Charles
①
TERRA VECCHIA
QUAI DU 1ER BATILON
Vieux Port ⑥
Môle Génois
QUAI DU SUD
Jardin Romieu ⑦
Jetée du Dragon

Cardo
BOULEVARD PAOLI
RUE FAVALELLI
R DES JARDINS
RUE DE LA MARINE
RUE GÉN CARBUCCIA
RUE DU COLLE
BOULEVARD AUGUSTE GAUDIN
RUE ST-ANGELO

Louis-XVI Gate
CHEMIN DES FILLIPINES
Pavillon des Nobles Douze
Palais des Gouverneurs
*Citadelle* ⑩
Oratoire Ste-Croix
PLACE D'ARMES
Ste-Marie
COURS DE DR FAVALE
VOIE RAPIDE

0 metres 180
0 yards 180

Étang de Biguglia
Poretta
25 km (16 miles)

**Key to Symbols** *see back flap*

# Bastia: the Citadelle

This impressive structure was built by the Genoese in the 15th–16th centuries. It is still surrounded by the original ramparts and lies in the Terra Nova quarter, which is quite different from Terra Vecchia. Unlike the ancient port area, which grew up almost at random, the Citadelle was laid out in keeping with rigorous town-planning principles, with houses of the same height and broad squares. After decades of neglect, a restoration campaign was initiated in the 1980s. The first houses to regain the original pastel colours typical of Ligurian tradition were those on Rue St-Michel, which has a splendid view of the Terra Vecchia quarter.

**Cherub in the Oratoire Ste-Croix**

The Citadelle seen from the sea, with the Jetée du Dragon in the foreground

**★ Ste-Marie**

*The cathedral in Bastia has a majestic yellow façade built in 1604–19. The bell tower is 71 m (233 ft) high. Ste-Marie was consecrated in 1570, when Bastia became a bishopric.*

**The rampart walls** of the Citadelle were built between 1480 and 1521 by the Genoese governor Tomasino da Campofregoso. This section of the walls extends furthest into the sea.

**★ Oratoire Ste-Croix**

*This gem of Rococo architecture boasts the Christ des Miracles, the protector of fishermen, which is borne in procession every third year on 3 May. Other sculptures include this angel.*

**STAR SIGHTS**

★ Ste-Marie

★ Oratoire Ste-Croix

**Louis XVI Gate**
*The monumental entrance to the citadel that directly connects Rue du Colle and Place du Donjon was built in the late 18th century.*

**The glacis** of the Citadelle offers the best panoramic view of Terra Vecchia and the old port.

## VISITORS' CHECKLIST

**Palais des Gouverneurs/ Museé de Bastia** Place du Donjon. **Tel** 04 95 31 09 12. for restoration until 2010; call for opening hours. **www**.musee-bastia.com **Ste-Marie** Rue Notre-Dame- de-la-Citadelle. daily.

**Palais des Gouverneurs**
*From the 15th to the 18th centuries, this palace was the residence of the Genoese governors. It is now home to a museum, currently closed for renovation, of the history and art of Bastia.*

**Pavillon des Nobles Douze**

**Place Guasco** is a square among the old houses, protected by trees.

## RELIGIOUS BROTHERHOODS

Religious brotherhoods, or confraternities, are groups that carry out charitable works and organize religious celebrations, such as processions on Christian holidays and feast days. They grew up in the 17th century and many are still quite active throughout the island. At Bastia there are also brotherhoods of people with a common profession (artisans, fishermen) that meet in oratories decorated with stucco work, sculptures, fabrics and paintings of high artistic value. The chapels of the local confraternities are in the side aisles of the Bastia cathedral.

**Singing during a religious procession**

**Luthiers in Bastia**
*In his workshop in Place Guasco, Christian Magdeleine makes stringed instruments, such as this cittern, decorated with wooden inlay.*

# Exploring Bastia

**Napoleon in Roman dress**

The centre of Bastia, facing the commercial port, can easily be explored on foot. Those travelling by car can park in the garage under Place St-Nicolas, the heart of the city and the junction between Terra Vecchia and the modern area. Bastia is relatively small, but for those who would rather not walk there is a small electric train that starts off from the square, a short distance from the tourist information office, and arrives at the citadel via the Quai des Martyrs and the tunnel under the Vieux Port. Guided tours of the Old Town are available, as is a tour of the outlying villages.

**Bric-à-brac for sale on Sundays in Place St-Nicolas**

**The Quai des Martyrs de la Libération**

### 🚇 Quai des Martyrs de la Libération

This quay, enlivened by cafés and restaurants, provides a pleasant walk along the seaside from Place St-Nicolas to the Vieux Port. One of the buildings on the quay is the Palais Monti Rossi, a residence of one of Corsica's old families and one of the finest 19th-century constructions in the city. The building miraculously remained intact after the American bombings that destroyed 90 per cent of the Terra Vecchia quarter in the late summer of 1943. Its façade boasts a pediment, arches and pilasters.

This street is known for its lively nightlife during the tourist season.

### 🚇 Place St-Nicolas

**Maison Mattei**

**Tel** 04 95 32 44 38 for tastings.

Facing the new port and shaded by the old palm and plane trees, this 300-m (980-ft) long square occupies the site of an old hospital for the poor that was destroyed in the early 19th century. In the middle of the square is a music pavilion where

concerts are held on summer evenings. On the south side of the square stands the white marble statue of Napoleon in the guise of a Roman emperor, while on the opposite side is a bronze sculpture group dedicated to widow Renno, a Corsican heroine who lost her sons in the wars of independence, and to all those Corsicans who lost their lives in war.

On the west side of the square are the bars and cafés where locals and visitors alike sit at alfresco tables. It is worth trying a glass of Cap Corse, the unique apéritif of the Maison Mattei, the historic establishment located on the square *(see opposite)*.

Every Sunday morning, Place St-Nicolas is enlivened by dozens of market stalls offering goods of every kind, and even some interesting antiques. Behind the charming cafés there are some elegant 19th-century buildings.

### 🏛 Cyrnarom

9 Avenue Monseigneur Rigo.
**Tel** 04 95 31 70 60. ⬜ daily (Nov, Jan–Mar: pm only).

Old perfume bottles, alembics and stills, as well as vials and period labels make a fine display on the shelves belonging to pharmacist and chemist Guy Cecchini. This local establishment is a laboratory and museum specializing in Corsican scents, including myrtle, pine, rockrose, lavender, rosemary and broom. The buds, flowers or leaves are distilled, becoming aromatic oils used to cure or prevent illnesses. There are also essences that smell like the sea breeze or have the intense and oily aroma of the maquis.

### ⚓ Port de Toga

When the Vieux Port proved unable to take the number of pleasure boats arriving there

**View of Port de Toga, also known as Port de Plaisance**

in the high season, an area was created between Bastia and Pietranera to cope with all this heavy traffic.

The Port de Toga is a long quay that has become a lively, trendy place frequented by young people, especially on summer evenings. The restaurant and disco bar tables almost touch the sea, their multicoloured lights reflected in the water. Some of the best nightspots that are open until late are Le Bounty, Le Café Cézanne and Le Maracana.

Façade of the church of St-Étienne in Cardo

## 🏛 Cardo

Today a chic suburb in the hills above Bastia, Cardo used to be a fishing village. Its marina, Porto Cardo, was the original nucleus of the city of Bastia in the Middle Ages. It became a municipality in its own right in 1844, by order of Louis Philippe. Cardo offers a spectacular view of the coastline, and there are many paths popular with hikers and cyclists.

The main monument here is the Neo-Classical church of **St-Étienne**, which has painted wooden statues from the 17th century and a Neo-Gothic organ tribune.

From Cardo, the D231 and then D31, the **Route de la Corniche Supérieure**, is a panoramic road running at around 300 m (980 ft) above sea level. It goes through the village of Pietrabugno and proceeds to San Martino di Lota and Miomo. In clear weather, the islands of the Tuscan archipelago can be seen on the horizon.

### THE MAISON MATTEI IN BASTIA

This renowned firm makes tobacconist's products, cork objects and, above all, liqueurs distilled from muscat grapes and flavoured with maquis herbs and quinine, including the famous Cap Corse *(see pp170 and 181)*. The Maison was established in Bastia in 1872 by Louis-Napoléon Mattei. Almost immediately the firm became a symbol of the spirit of enterprise, and its so-called "products of nostalgia" were exported throughout the world, especially where there

The stone sign on the façade of the Maison Mattei

were many Corsican emigrants. While the original cigarette factory at Toga closed in 1977, when the company was sold to a large group, the shop is still in Place St-Nicolas.

## 🦩 Étang de Biguglia
Lido de la Marana.
**Tel** 04 95 33 55 73.

On the southern outskirts of the city, between the airport, the industrial area and the strip of Marana coastline, is the Étang de Biguglia, a lagoon designated as a reserve to conserve the largest wet zone in Corsica. The lagoon consists of 18 sq km (7 sq miles) of pools and rivers that are part of the mouth of the Golo river and is connected to the sea in its northern part.

The scourge of malaria, which was an endemic disease in Corsica for centuries, was finally eliminated after World War II. The land was reclaimed and partly used for farming. Now the canebrakes and grassland

A flamingo in the wet Étang de Biguglia

are the ideal habitat for 100 species of birds, including the great cormorant, the purple heron and the flamingo. Other inhabitants of the lagoon are marsh tortoises. The reserve is also a habitual stop-over for birds migrating from Europe to Africa. The best seasons to observe the 60 or more species of migrators are spring and autumn.

The water, which used to be badly polluted, has been purified, resulting in the return of the mullet and eel populations. They are caught using traditional methods by a local fishermen's cooperative.

Since 1994, the Étang has been a regional reserve, with nature walks, a cycling path, and guided tours. The town of Biguglia, which overlooks the lagoon, was the capital of the island under the Pisans and the residence of the Genoese governors until 1372. The sandy belt that separates the sea from the lagoon is one of the loveliest beaches in Bastia.

Étang di Biguglia from the sea

White houses surrounding the small harbour of Erbalunga

## Erbalunga **②**

**Road map** D1. 🏠 *400.* 🚌 ℹ️ *Port de Plaisance, Macinaggio (04 95 35 40 34).* 🎭 *Procession de la Cerca (Maundy Thu & Good Fri); Music Festival (early Aug).*

A Genoese tower protects the small harbour lined with old stone houses and fish restaurants. Erbalunga, the marina of the district of Brando, was for centuries the port where Pisan ships landed to be loaded with local wine.

At the start of the village is the church of **St-Erasme**, home to the crosses of the Cerca procession: the men's crucifix weighs 60 kg (132 lb); the women's is 30 kg (66 lb). On the evening of Maundy Thursday, the procession winds through the streets to the Benedictine nuns' convent. On Good Friday it leaves early in the morning and proceeds for 7 km (4 miles), visiting the hamlets of Pozzo, Poretto and Silgaggia.

In Erbalunga, as in many other locations around Cap Corse, there are sumptuous country mansions known as *Maisons d'Américains*. These were built by Corsicans who had returned home wealthy after emigrating to Latin America. Rich families also had impressive mausoleums built, which can be seen from the D32 all over the cape *(see p29)*.

### Environs
In **Castello**, 3 km (2 miles) inland, there is a 13th-century fortress. A 15th-century Italian nobleman murdered his wife here, and she is said to haunt Castello. The chapel of **Santa Maria di e Nevi** lies a short walk south towards Silgaggia. It houses the oldest frescoes in Corsica, dating from 1386. **Pozzo** is the starting point for the path to **Monte Stello** (1,307 m/4,288 ft), which takes 6 hours to walk.

North of Erbalunga, along the D80, is the **Sisco Valley**. In Sisco is the Chapelle de St-Martin, housing a precious 13th-century silver mask of St John Chrysotom. From the main road a path leads to the Romanesque Chapelle de San Michele, built by the Pisans. Closer to the coast is the former Couvent de Santa Catalina, famous for once having housed relics of a fantastic nature, such as a lump of clay from which Adam was made and almonds from Paradise.

🔒 **Santa Maria di e Nevi**
Castello. **Tel** *04 95 33 20 84.*
📷 *Visits by guided tour only. Book one day in advance (06 86 78 02 38).*

## Pietracorbara **③**

**Road map** D1. 🏠 *350.* 🚌 ℹ️ *Port de Plaisance, Macinaggio (04 95 35 40 34).*

A broad, cultivated valley behind a long, sandy beach enclosed by a canebrake protects the village of Pietracorbara. A skeleton found here in 1990 and dating from 6000 BC is proof of the prehistoric origins of the site, which was later used by the Greeks and Romans as a base.

### Environs
Northwards, along the coast, is the 16th-century **Tour de l'Osse** (Bone Tower), one of best preserved in the area, and **Porticciolo**, a tiny marina with houses grouped around a pier.

Fishing boat in Macinaggio's busy harbour

## Macinaggio **④**

**Road map** D1. 🏠 *480.* 🚌 ℹ️ *Port de Plaisance (04 95 35 40 34).* 🎭 *Nautival, Sea Festival (end of May).*

Fishing boats are anchored next to the yachts that stop at Macinaggio after sailing across from Italy. The most popular tourist harbour in Cap Corse, it has always been a military and commercial port. Controlled by the Genoese for a long time, it was liberated by Pascal Paoli, after years of struggle, in 1761 *(see pp46–7)*. Plaques on the quay announce that Napoleon landed here, as did the empress Eugénie on her return trip from the Suez Canal inauguration in 1869, and that Paoli also stopped here. The port is divided into three basins that can take in over 500 boats and is surrounded by visitors' facilities.

The Genoese Tour de l'Osse near Pietracorbara

## Environs

Around the village are vine-yards, extending as far as **Rogliano**. Inhabited in Roman times, from the 12th to the 16th centuries it was ruled by the da Mare family, which had trade relations with Genoa.

At **Bettolacce**, the area's main village, a round tower bears witness to its former splendour. The church of Sant'Agnellu boasts a beautiful altar of white Carrara marble.

Île de la Giraglia opposite the tip of Cap Corse

## Barcaggio and Cap Corse ⑤

**Road map** D1. 🏘 480. 🚹 Port de Plaisance, Macinaggio (04 95 35 40 34).

On the northern tip of the peninsula are some villages that have retained the spirit of the past. One of these is Barcaggio, which has a beautiful beach where cows go to graze and a small harbour where time seems to have come to a halt.

The road leading here, the D80 followed by the D253, is simply spectacular. It descends among the maquis, holm oak groves and pastures covered in white asphodel, offering a fine view of the **Île de la Giraglia**. The northern-most part of Corsica, this green serpentine rock island is separated from the coast by 2 km (1 mile) of treacherous,

fast-flowing sea. This island has a square 16th-century Genoese tower and a lighthouse built in the 1940s that, until 1994, was inhabited by a keeper; now it is wholly automatic. Giraglia is famous because the sailing regatta that goes from Sanremo, in Liguria, to Le Lavandou, Provence, and back passes by here.

About 2 km (1 mile) west of Barcaggio is **Tollare**, another small harbour with a tuna fishery. From here, a small road winds back to the D80 and **Ersa**, whose church of **Ste-Marie** has a 17th-century wooden tabernacle. West of here, on Col de Serra is **Moulin Mattei**, an old, round mill offering a fabulous panoramic view. In a poor state of preservation, it was restored in the past by the Maison Mattei, the renowned apéritif makers (see p63).

## Centuri ⑥

**Road map** D1. 🏘 200. 🚹 Port de Plaisance, Macinaggio (04 95 35 40 34).

A narrow inlet lined by ochre, grey and white houses with green serpentine roofs is an apt description of the small port of Centuri, which for centuries was a loading point for wine,

A fisherman from Centuri making a lobster pot

wood, oil and citrus fruits that were then shipped to Italy and France. Today, Centuri, the ancient Roman Centurium mentioned by Ptolemy, is in fact the leading fishing centre in Cap Corse. The docks are covered with fishing nets and lobster pots that are still handmade. The port is full of the typical double-ended fishing boats that return laden with lobsters (3,000 kg/ 6,600 lb a year) that can be enjoyed in the local restaurants.

The sea floor here is a paradise for scuba divers, especially around the islet of Centuri, at the mouth of the bay, which was fortified in the 13th century.

From the port, an hour's walk up a path leads through luxuriant vegetation to the village of **Cannelle** (also accessible by car from the D80 road). Its simple stone houses hugging the mountainside are rich in bougainvillea, and its narrow streets and covered passageways offer views of the sea. On the D80 road, 3 km (2 miles) from Centuri, is the 16th-century **Couvent de l'Annonciation** dedicated to Our Lady of the Seven Sorrows. The church is considered the largest in Cap Corse. The monastery is not open to the public.

Fishing boats anchored in the Centuri harbour

# Tour of the Sentier des Douaniers ❼

Once used by customs officers to control smuggling activities (hence the name, "path of customs officers"), this coastal footpath runs along the tip of Cap Corse, in places offering stunning views. Similar paths run along the entire perimeter of Corsica, but the Sentier des Douaniers, going from Macinaggio to Centuri – among the junipers, mastics and asphodels, and over beaches and craggy cliffs – is simply breathtaking. This tour can be divided into three stages: Macinaggio–Barcaggio, Barcaggio–Tollare and Tollare–Centuri. It is not particularly difficult, but watch out for brush fires, especially in the summer. Drivers can reach the separate sights via inland paved roads.

**Barcaggio ③**
Past the Punta d'Agnello tower and promontory – one of the most panoramic spots in Cap Corse – is Barcaggio *(see p67)*. This is the first stage of the tour that is directly accessible by car, from the D253. The water in the bay is crystal clear.

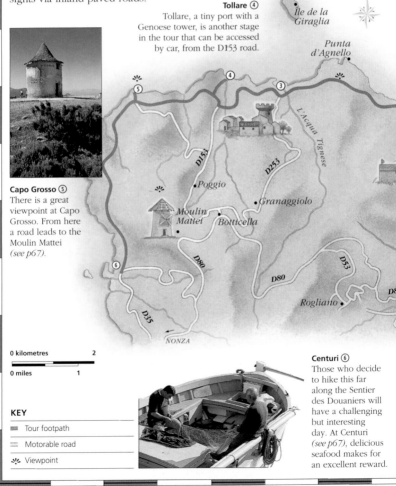

**Tollare ④**
Tollare, a tiny port with a Genoese tower, is another stage in the tour that can be accessed by car, from the D153 road.

*Île de la Giraglia*

*Punta d'Agnello*

*L'Acqua Tignese*

D153

D253

*Poggio*

*Granaggiolo*

*Moulin Mattei*

*Botticella*

D80

D53

D80

*Rogliano*

D35

*NONZA*

**Capo Grosso ⑤**
There is a great viewpoint at Capo Grosso. From here a road leads to the Moulin Mattei *(see p67)*.

0 kilometres    2

0 miles    1

**KEY**

▬ Tour footpath

═ Motorable road

⁜ Viewpoint

**Centuri ⑥**
Those who decide to hike this far along the Sentier des Douaniers will have a challenging but interesting day. At Centuri *(see p67)*, delicious seafood makes for an excellent reward.

## TIPS FOR HIKERS

ℹ️ *Port de Plaisance,
Macinaggio (04 95 35 40 34).*
**Length of tour**: *20 km (12
miles).* **Duration**: *Macinaggio–
Barcaggio 3 hours; Barcaggio–
Tollare 45 minutes; Tollare–
Centuri 4 hours.*
**Footpath**: *of average difficulty;
it can be taken all year long.*
**Stopping-off points**: *Macinaggio,
Barcaggio, Tollare and Centuri.*

**Chapelle de Santa Maria** ②
Further along the path is the
chapel of Santa Maria, built
in the 12th century over an
early Christian church. The
ruins of a Genoese tower
can be found on the coast
along Santa Maria bay.

**Macinaggio** ①
The tour begins at
Macinaggio *(see p66)*
and leads to the
beautiful beach
of Tamarone,
the entrance
to a reserve
opposite the Îles
Finocchiarola. These
craggy rocks with a
watchtower inhabited by
colonies of marine birds are
also a nature reserve. The
path then skirts the high
coastline, with continuous
fine views of the sea and
the coves below, where it is
possible to take a swim.

### CAP CORSE AND PATRIMONIO WINES

Appreciated since ancient times, the white wines of Cap
Corse come from terraces carved out of the mountainside.
The two AOC (*appellation d'origine contrôlée*) labels here
are Coteaux du Cap Corse and Muscat du Cap Corse (*see
p171*). They produce Malvasia, Muscat and Sciaccarellu
wines, and Rappu, a sweet white wine that can be purchased
only at the wineries. Among the most famous wineries is

the Clos Nicrosi, which
produces one of the best
Corsican whites. Another
AOC area is Patrimonio
(*see p70*); Domaine de
Pietri at Morsiglia has been
in business since 1786 and
at St-Florent there is the
Domaine Gentile. Both
make reds and whites, as
well as Rappu and Muscat.

**A wine label of Patrimonio,
a famous AOC region**

# Pino ❽

**Road map** D1. 🏘 *145.* ℹ️ *Port de
Plaisance, Macinaggio (04 95 35 40 34).*

This small village at the foot
of Col de Ste-Lucie lies in the
midst of luxuriant vegetation.
Umbrella pines protect the
Maisons d'Américains *(see
p66)*, including the Maison
Savelli and the family mausoleum with its tile roof. Other
monumental tombs surrounded
by cypress trees lie at the
junction of the D80 and D180
roads. The church of **Ste-Marie**
has a Baroque façade and,
inside, two fonts: one decorated with fish and salamanders,
the other with lions. The
**Couvent St-François**, built
in 1486 in Marina di Scalu, is
flanked by a Genoese tower.

### Environs
About 5 km (3 miles) from
Pino, on the D180 road going
up to Col de Ste-Lucie, is the
footpath for the **Tour de
Sénèque**. The tower is at the
top of **Monte Ventiggiola**,
564 m (1,850 ft) above sea
level, where the great Roman
playwright Seneca is said to
have been exiled. In reality,
the tower is medieval. It can
be reached after a steep climb
through the maquis that can
take over an hour. The view
is well worth the climb.

🏛 **Ste-Marie**
**Tel** *04 95 35 12 32.* ☐ *by appt.*

🏛 **Couvent St-François**
**Tel** *04 95 35 12 70.* ● *to the public.*

# Canari ❾

**Road map** D1. 🏘 *290.* ℹ️ *Port de
Plaisance, Macinaggio (04 95 35 40
34).* 🎉 *St Thomas's and St Erasmus's
feast days (Jul).*

Rather isolated from the D80
highway and divided into
various hamlets, the medieval
fiefdom of Canari boasts two
interesting churches. The 12th-
century Pisan Romanesque
**Santa Maria Assunta** has a
cornice decorated with animal
heads and human figures.
This church is open to the
public only on 15 August. **St-
François** was built in 1506 and
then rebuilt in Baroque style.
From 1932 to 1966, Canari
grew significantly due to a
local asbestos mine. Although
the mine was closed when this
mineral was found to be toxic,
it has left an ugly scar on
the landscape. The **Marine
d'Albo**, protected by a watchtower, is where, in 1588,
Hassan Pasha's fleet landed
and his men sacked the area.

🏛 **St-François**
**Tel** *04 95 37 80 17.*
☐ *ask for the keys at the Town Hall.*

**The old watchtower
at Marine d'Albo**

Panoramic view of Nonza, dominated by the cliff overlooking the sea

## Nonza ⑩

**Road map** D1. 🚶 85.
ℹ️ *Port de Plaisance, Macinaggio (04 95 35 40 34).* 🎭 *Culture in the Limelight (2nd week of Aug).*

One of the most fascinating villages in Corsica, Nonza clings to a black rock falling steeply down to the sea. Its old, pastel-coloured stone houses are surrounded by terraces and small gardens, and many are reached by steps rather than streets.

Steps also lead up to the church of **Ste-Julie**, built in the 16th century but enlarged in the 19th. Inside is a Baroque altar, a chapel dedicated to St Erasmus, patron saint of sailors, and a painting of St Julia, one of Corsica's patron saints. According to legend, this girl was crucified by a Roman prefect after refusing to take part in some pagan revelry. Nearby, 54 steps lead down to the **Fontaine de Ste-Julie**, which is said to have sprung up as she was martyred and to have miraculous water.

More steps lead down to the beach, 160 m (525 ft) below the village. Until the early 19th century, the inhabitants left from here in boats every morning to reach the then-fertile Désert des Agriates *(see p72)*. Today, the beach offers an awe-inspiring view up to the village and its 18th-century green schist tower built by Paoli. The dark colour of the sand is the result of pollution from an asbestos mine up the coast that was closed in 1966. It is safe to walk here, but bathing is not allowed. On

the D80 road to Albo there are many mortuary chapels and mausoleums *(see p29)*. These belonged to Corsican families that emigrated to find their fortunes and returned rich enough to have elaborate tombs built for themselves.

## Patrimonio ⑪

**Road map** D2. 🚶 650. 🚌 ℹ️ *Rte du Cap Corse, St-Florent (04 95 37 06 04).* 🎭 *Guitar Nights (3rd week Jul).*

At the foot of the Col de Teghime and the Serra di Pigno, this village in the heart of the Nebbio region is one of the main wine-producing centres on the island *(see p69)*. The vineyards, which all belong to small, family-owned wineries, dot the limestone hills that dominate Patrimonio.

While driving along the highway, it is worth stopping at one of the many wineries to taste and purchase the white Vermentino, or a fine red wine made from the Niellucciu grape. The latter is the ideal accompaniment for charcuterie and game.

Overlooking the village is the church of **St-Martin**, built in 1570 and reached by a stairway. At sunset, its façade takes on golden hues. Just down the lane, next to the church, is a megalithic menhir with a carved face.

🏛️ **St-Martin**
**Tel** *04 95 37 08 49.*
⏰ *daily; make enquiries at the Mairie (Town Hall).*

## St-Florent ⑫

**Road map** D2. 🚶 *1,350.* 🚌 ℹ️
*Route du Cap Corse (04 95 37 06 04).* 🎭 *Porto Latino: Latin-American music (mid-Aug).*

At the end of a long gulf, the village of St-Florent sits with its brightly coloured houses along the harbour and a lively promenade with boutiques, restaurants and cafés. In summer these are open till late at night.

Although it was inhabited in the Neolithic era and was an ancient Roman base, the village only really developed in the 15th century around the Genoese fort. The area was marshy and unhealthy, however, and was abandoned between the 17th and 19th centuries because of malaria.

The homes in the old town surround the parish church, which houses a statue of St Florent the Martyr.

At the edge of the village is **Santa Maria Assunta**, the old cathedral of the Nebbio region. This splendid Romanesque church dates back to 1140. Made of pale limestone, its façade has two superimposed tiers of blind arches and a niche with a *Virgin Mary and Child* statue. The basilica-style interior has pillars and pilasters whose capitals are decorated with shells and animal figures. In a glass case are the remains of St Flor, a Roman soldier mummified in the 3rd century AD.

🏛️ **Santa Maria Assunta**
⏰ *Jul–Nov: Mon–Fri & am Sat; Dec–Jun: call tourist office for opening times (04 95 37 06 04).*

The quay at the port of St-Florent

# San Michele de Murato ⑬

This 13th-century church is one of Corsica's best examples of Pisan Romanesque architecture. It lies just north of Murato village, 475 m (1,560 ft) above sea level, dominating the valley of the Bevincu river and the Nebbio region. San Michele de Murato has a simple structure, with a rectangular nave ending in a small semi-circular apse. The porticoed bell tower is set against the middle of the façade. The materials used were white limestone and green serpentine. All around the church are tiny blind arches. The consoles and cornices of the small windows have bas-reliefs with animal and plant motifs, as well as allegorical scenes, such as Eve taking the forbidden fruit or the Lamb attacked by other animals.

**VISITORS' CHECKLIST**

**Road map** D2. **Tel** 04 95 37 60 10. ☐ to view the frescoed interior ask for the keys at the Mairie (Town Hall) in Murato.

The central window of the apse with green serpentine decoration

**The square bell tower** in the middle of the façade was rebuilt and enlarged in the 19th century. It is the truly original element in this church, forming a colonnaded portico around the entry door.

**Consoles**
*The blind arches lie on consoles with various sculpted nature motifs.*

**Façade**
*Dominated by the bell tower, the façade has one entrance and three blind arches on the consoles of which are bas-relief sculptures of animals.*

**The sculpture decoration** in the church includes geometric patterns and scenes with birds and human figures.

**A feature of the Pisan Romanesque style** is the irregular checkerboard arrangement of different-coloured stone blocks.

**On the two columns** framing the portal, the limestone and serpentine alternate in irregular bands.

**Capitals**
*A garland surrounds the columns at the base of the capitals, which are carved in the shape of two simple volutes.*

**Symbols**
*The two figures flanking the three blind arches may be symbols of the political and religious power in Murato during that time.*

The village of Oletta, perched on the slopes of the Nebbio hills

# Nebbio ⑭

**Road map** D2. 🚌 ⓘ *Route du Cap Corse, St-Florent (04 95 37 06 04).*

Called the Golden Shell (Conca d'Oro) for its fertile land, the Alisu basin is an area with vineyards and olive and fruit orchards. Via the D38, D82 and D62 roads, there is a semicircular route that departs from and returns to St-Florent, passing through the Nebbio region's main towns, from Oletta up to Rapale. The roads lead to the passes of Col de Teghime (a small road goes up to Serra di Pigno, for an even better view) and Col de San Stefano. From here the stretch of D62 known as Défilé de Lancone descends to the coast in dangerously steep curves. A 30-minute walk from Rapale is the 13th-century **Chapelle de San Cesario**, with its green shale and white limestone façade. The parish church of **Murato** has a painting attributed to Titian, but the village is famous for the Romanesque church of San Michele *(see p71).*

**Detail of a monumental tomb in the Nebbio area**

hillside and is characterized by simple houses of white, ochre and pink. Oletta offers spectacular views of the Golfe de St-Florent and the Nebbio region, including the bell tower of the old **Couvent St-François**, the only remaining architectural element from the original complex. Dominating the view towards the hilltop is the **Mausoleum of Count Rivarola**, governor of Malta, one of the many monumental family tombs in this region. The 18th-century parish church of **St-André** has a bas-relief of the Creation on its façade and a wooden triptych inside dating from 1534.

The area around Oletta is renowned for its sheep's-milk cheese, which was once used to make Roquefort.

# Oletta ⑮

**Road map** D2. 🏔 880. 🚌 ⓘ *Rte du Cap Corse, St-Florent (04 95 37 06 04).*

Immersed in the greenery of the hills of Nebbio is the small village of Oletta. It seems to be clinging to the

# Désert des Agriates ⑯

**Road map** C–D2. ⓘ *Route du Cap Corse, St-Florent (04 95 37 06 04).*

Situated between St-Florent and the mouth of the Ostriconi river, this 160 sq km (60 sq miles) of green desert is virtually uninhabited. Only some shepherds and a few people in the hamlet of Casta live here. Until the mid-19th century, however, this area was the "bread basket" of Bastia and Cap Corse, and it produced wheat, olives and olive oil, wine and fruit. The farmers arrived by boat from Nonza, Canari and St-Florent to work the land. Today, the only remains of this area's fertile past are the barns and stone granaries. The fields are abandoned and the maquis has invaded the terrain.

The panoramic D81 highway crosses this sweet-smelling desert, which is extraordinary in spring. There are also two detours, negotiable only by four-wheel drives, that lead to the beaches of **Saleccia** *(see p21)* and **Guignu**. It is worth spending a few days on the 35-km (22-mile) coastal path, taking lodgings in the renovated barns. Boats also sail from the St-Florent port to the **Loto** beach, which is a 30-minute walk from Saleccia. The lovely, white-sand beach of **Ostriconi**, bounded by sand dunes and a pool, is more convenient and accessible.

Spring blossoms on the slopes of the Désert des Agriates

# Mediterranean Maquis

Known in the Corsican language as *macchia*, maquis is one of the most luxuriant types of vegetation in southern Europe. The low, thick undergrowth and bushes occupy vast areas along the coast and in the interior, covering a surface area of about 2,000 sq km (770 sq miles). The maquis is spectacular in spring, when it blossoms covering entire hills with white and pink rockrose flowers and yellow broom. The flowers are used to produce essences, as well as honey with a particular aroma. Despite the frequent fires, the maquis manages to grow back in a relatively short time compared to trees and tall shrubs. Besides rockrose, other herbaceous plants are asphodel thistle, cyclamen, lavender, heather and sarsaparilla. Typical shrubs include rosemary, juniper, myrtle, mastic shrub, phillyrea and strawberry trees. Among the trees are two kinds of oak – the cork oak and evergreen holm oak.

**White Montpellier cistus**

**Wild fennel** *has umbrella-shaped flowers that look like small white or yellowish clouds. It also has a strong, almost oleaginous scent that is quite characteristic of the maquis. It can be used for pot-pourri after being dried.*

**Cistus, or rockrose,** *is a typical maquis plant that can also grow in the mountains, up to an altitude of 1,200 m (3,950 ft). This is a low-growing shrub with slightly fleshy leaves. Its five-petalled flowers frame a centre of golden-yellow stamens.*

**Wild rosemary** *exudes an intense scent that infuses the entire maquis. Its aromatic leaves are used to flavour food and as a perfume and a medicine.*

**Myrtle** *is considered a sacred plant, the symbol of fertility. It has aromatic leaves, white flowers and dark berries from which a liqueur is distilled.*

**Broom** *inflames the sides of hills and mountains from April to late summer with its dazzling yellow flowers, which cover the green, arched and spiny stems.*

The red granite rocks around the bay of L'Île Rousse

## L'Île Rousse **⓱**

**Road map** C2. 🏘 2,800. 🚌
🚉 Route du Port. 🚢 from Genoa, Savona, Marseille, Nice, Toulon.
🛈 Ave Calizi (04 95 60 04 35).
🎭 Festimare (early May).

A busy beach with fine sand, a pleasant, Riviera-style promenade, shops and a lively port sum up L'Île Rousse. It was founded in 1758 by Pascal Paoli, who had the port built to counter the presence of the Genoese at Calvi and Algajola. L'Île Rousse revolves around Place Paoli, with its mix of cafés, shops and *pétanque* players in the shade of palm and plane trees. In the middle of the square is a fountain with the statue of Paoli.

The square is the starting point for the little train that skirts the bay and goes to Isola di La Pietra. This islet is linked to the mainland by a pier with a tower and a lighthouse built by Paoli in 1857.

At one end of Place Paoli is the covered market, a 19th-century structure similar to a Greek temple, which sells charcuterie, vegetables, cheese, maquis-flower honey, fish and home-made bread. For shops and restaurants, try the old quarter north of the square, with its well-kept houses and paved streets that descend to the seaside.

Outside the town is the popular but less urban Rindara beach, which can be reached by a dirt track.

L'Île Rousse is also the starting point for excursions in the Balagne region (*see*

*pp76–7*). This area of Corsica boasts the island's best artisans, whose products are exported all over the world.

The area is also renowned for its idyllic villages surrounded by olive groves, such as **Monticello**, overlooked by the 13th-century Castel d'Ortica. Further inland, the road climbs up to **Santa Reparata di Balagna**. Here the church of Santa Reparata, with its origins in the 11th century, offers a great view from its terrace.

## Algajola **⓲**

**Road map** C2. 🏘 200. 🚉
🛈 Place Gare (04 95 62 78 32).

Fringed by a beach of golden sand some 2 km (1 mile) long, Algajola makes an excellent base for water sports, especially windsurfing. Founded by the Phoenicians, Algajola was used by the Romans as a base for their legions, and then chosen by the Genoese because of its central position in the region. Sacked repeatedly

**Music box by Scat'a Musica in Pigna**

by the Saracens, the village enjoyed a period of splendour in the 1600s, when the bastions were built.

The church of **St-Georges** was also fortified after a Barbary pirate raid. Its interior houses a 17th-century painting of the Deposition attributed to the Italian artist Guercino.

**🔒 St-Georges**
**Tel** 04 95 62 78 32. ⬜ for religious services only.

## Pigna **⓳**

**Road map** C2. 🏘 90. 🛈 Ave Calizi, L'Île Rousse (04 95 60 04 35).
🎭 Estivoce (Jul).

This thriving hamlet in the Balagne is perched on a slope alongside olive orchards. It has retained its medieval character, with stepped paths, narrow alleys and vaulted passageways. By the tree-lined central square stands the local church with two bell towers.

Pigna has become famous as a centre for traditional Corsican music and for its many handicraft workshops. The **Casa Musicale** (Music House), which also has hotel facilities (*see p160*) and a restaurant, is the centre for the safeguarding of Corsican music and the island's major traditions. In the workshops, ancient instruments are built in traditional style, including various types of cittern. Another workshop, **Scat'a Musica**, sells musical boxes. In summer, the Estivoce festival celebrates traditional songs.

The Corsican-produce boutique A Merendella is also worth a visit.

**🎵 Casa Musicale**
**Tel** 04 95 61 77 34.
**www**.casa-musicale.org

### Environs

The Franciscan **Couvent de Corbara**, 2 km (1 mile) from Pigna, was founded in 1456, destroyed during the French Revolution and rebuilt by the Dominicans in the 1800s. Pascal Paoli was a guest here. To arrange a visit call 04 95 60 06 73.

The sea wall at Algajola protecting the port at the foot of the citadel

# Aregno ❷⓿

**Road map** C2. 🏘 600. 🚍 *Ave
Calizi, L'Île Rousse (04 95 60 04 35).*
🎪 *Almond Festival (early Aug).*

The village of Aregno,
surrounded by olive and
citrus-fruit trees, should be
visited for its two churches:
the Baroque parish church
of **St-Antoine** and the Pisan
Romanesque church of the
**Trinité et San Giovanni**. Built
in 1177 of green, white and
pink granite, the latter
has a façade with four blind
arches over the portal. It also
has a pediment decorated
with small arches, in the
centre of which is a statue
of a man holding his foot while
pulling a thorn from it. The
chapel interior has two 15th-
century frescoes: *St Michael
and the Dragon* and *The
Four Doctors of the Church*.

🏛 **Trinité et San Giovanni**
**Tel** *04 95 61 70 34.*
⏰ *Jul–Aug; during other
months, ask for the keys at
the Mairie (Town Hall).*

# Sant'Antonino ❷❶

**Road map** C2. 🏘 60. 🚍 *Ave
Calizi, L'Île Rousse (04 95 60 04 35).*

An eagle's nest 447 m
(1,467 ft) above sea level,
this hamlet overlooks the
Regino and Tighiella river
valleys. Its unique position
affords a magnificent view,
from the snow-capped
mountains to the sea.
Sant'Antonino is laid out in
a circle and was one of the

**Steps going up to the village of
Sant'Antonino**

**The Baroque church and campanile at Feliceto, near Sant'Antonino**

fiefdoms of the Savelli family.
It was an impregnable fortress
that took in the entire valley
population when Saracen
pirate ships appeared on the
horizon. Along the alleys of
this hamlet, which are for
pedestrians only, there are
steps and passageways. The
dark-granite houses have
been restored and shops
featuring local handicrafts
have been opened.

**Environs**
About 10 km (6 miles) along
the D663 road is **Feliceto**,
which has a Baroque church
and a mill producing olive oil.
In the opposite direction
is the Giussani region, with
the villages of **Pioggiola** and
**Olmi-Cappella**, linked by a
number of footpaths. The
latter is known for its olive oil.

# Speloncato ❷❷

**Road map** C2. 🏘 194. 🚍 *Ave
Calizi, L'Île Rousse (04 95 60 04 35).*

Perched on a spur of Monte
Tolo, this village offers a fine
view of the surrounding
Balagne region. It is named
after the *spelunche*, the
caves in the vicinity, which
include the 8-m (25-ft) long
**Pietra Tafonata**. Supposedly,
twice a year, on 8 April and
8 September, the setting
sun is visible through the
tunnel, briefly illuminating
the village square with
the Baroque church of
**San Michele**.

# Calenzana ❷❸

**Road map** C2. 🏘 1,535. 🚍 *Place
Paoli, L'Île Rousse (04 95 60 04 35).*
🎪 *Ste-Restitude's Feast Day (end
of May).*

Olive oil, wine and honey
are still the mainstays of the
economy of this town, one
of the liveliest in the Balagne
region. It is also the starting
point of the GR20 long-
distance path *(see p22).*
The Baroque collegiate
church of **St-Blaise**, designed
by the Milanese architect
Domenico Baina, was built
in the late 17th century. The
ceiling over the nave has an
18th-century fresco, *St Biagio
Healing a Child*. At the foot
of the campanile, a plaque
commemorates the battle
of Calenzana, fought on
14 January 1732 between
Corsican nationalists and
the Genoese Republic,
in which 700 German
mercenaries lost their lives.
About 1 km (half a mile)
away is **Ste-Restitude**, a 12th-
century church built over
a Roman necropolis. It is
dedicated to a martyr killed in
Calvi in the 3rd century and
venerated in the entire region.
Her story is told in two 14th-
century frescoes, and her
sarcophagus is in the crypt.

**Environs**
A short way along the D151 is
**Montemaggiore**. This village,
built on a promontory, has a
lovely Baroque church and
views of the Golfe de Calvi.

# Tour of the Strada di l'Artigiani ㉔

**A typical music box made in Pigna**

The "Artisans' Road" is a route that covers the most characteristic craftsmen's workshops in Balagne, the fertile region behind Calvi and L'Île Rousse. These shops are located in villages perched on hilltops and are a popular tourist attraction thanks to their handicraft production. The main centre is Pigna *(see p74)*, with its Casa Musicale, an organization committed to safeguarding the island's rich cultural heritage. The road signs indicate different ways to reach Calenzana, Corbara, Santa Reparata, Feliceto, Pigna, Lumio, Monticello, Occiglioni, Lozari, Palasca, Olmi-Capella, Cateri and Occhiatana, all of which are fascinating villages thanks to their architecture and panoramic views.

**Pigna ④**
Musical instruments, music boxes and pottery, along with many natural products such as wine, honey, olive oil and cheese, can be found in Pigna. This village is the leading handicraft centre in the region, with all kinds of workshops – as if the best artisans in Corsica had decided to settle here.

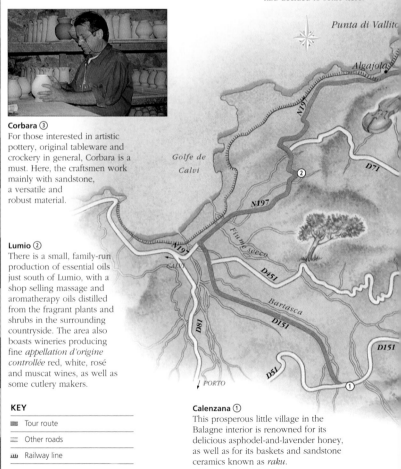

**Corbara ③**
For those interested in artistic pottery, original tableware and crockery in general, Corbara is a must. Here, the craftsmen work mainly with sandstone, a versatile and robust material.

**Lumio ②**
There is a small, family-run production of essential oils just south of Lumio, with a shop selling massage and aromatherapy oils distilled from the fragrant plants and shrubs in the surrounding countryside. The area also boasts wineries producing fine *appellation d'origine controllée* red, white, rosé and muscat wines, as well as some cutlery makers.

**KEY**

| | |
|---|---|
| ▬ | Tour route |
| ═ | Other roads |
| ᴖᴖᴖ | Railway line |

**Calenzana ①**
This prosperous little village in the Balagne interior is renowned for its delicious asphodel-and-lavender honey, as well as for its baskets and sandstone ceramics known as *raku*.

## OLIVE OIL IN BALAGNE

Among the many local gastronomic specialities in the Balagne region, the extra-virgin olive oil is outstanding.

Olive trees and their products are an integral part of Corsican tradition. It has been proven that the trees are endemic to the island, as are myrtle and the Corsican pine, and many of them are over 500 years old. The olives are gathered by setting large nets under the trees and shaking the branches. The olives are then pressed in hydraulic presses. Olive oil is a true "fruit juice", wholly natural, with many nutritious qualities.

**Olive harvesting**

### TIPS FOR DRIVERS

ℹ️ *Calvi tourist information, 97 Port de Plaisance (04 95 65 16 67), or any other in the Balagne region have leaflets about the tour.*
**Length of tour**: *50 km (30 miles).*
**Duration**: *one day for the route suggested here, while more time will be needed for an extended tour to take in other localities in the area or to make an additional gastronomic tour.*
**Stopping-off points**: *there are many in all the localities.*

**Feliceto ⑤**
This village features precious blown-glass objects that are handmade by two local craftsmen. Feliceto also has two wineries, one in the heart of the village, the other a little way out. Both offer wine-tasting tours.

**Occhiatana ⑥**
Sandstone wares are available in Occhiatana as well as in Corbara. Here, craftsmen make vases, lamps, candlesticks, and an entire range of objects and souvenirs of Corsican culture to decorate the home.

0 kilometres    2

0 miles    2

# Calvi ㉕

CIVITAS · CALVI
SEMPER · FIDELIS

**Plaque over the citadel entrance**

Situated on a rocky promontory, the 15th-century Genoese citadel dominates the yacht harbour and the promenade of Calvi. Massive bastions protect it on all four sides, three of which overlook the sea. In 1794, the citadel was bombarded by 30,000 cannon shots fired by the British fleet. Inside, there is a quiet atmosphere, which contrasts with the liveliness of the rest of the town. A series of alleys leads to the Palais des Gouverneurs Génois and the cathedral of St-Jean-Baptiste. The latter was almost destroyed in 1567, when an arsenal of gunpowder exploded. A walk along the ramparts, including the Tour de St-Antoine and the Teghiale and Malfetano bastions, offers magnificent views.

**Sentries' lookout walkway along the ramparts of the citadel**

**Citadel Entrance**
*A sign made of glass with the symbols of the Genoese maritime republic greets visitors before they enter the citadel.*

## Palais des Gouverneurs Génois
*Built in 1492, this building was the residence of the Genoese governors from 1545–47 and after 1652. It now houses Caserne Sampiero, the barracks of a division of the Foreign Legion.*

### STAR SIGHT

★ St-Jean-Baptiste

## Oratoire St-Antoine
*Built in 1510, this structure was used for meetings of the St Anthony and Annunciation confraternities (see p61). Inside are some 15th-and 16th-century frescoes and an ivory statue of Christ attributed to the Italian artist Sansovino.*

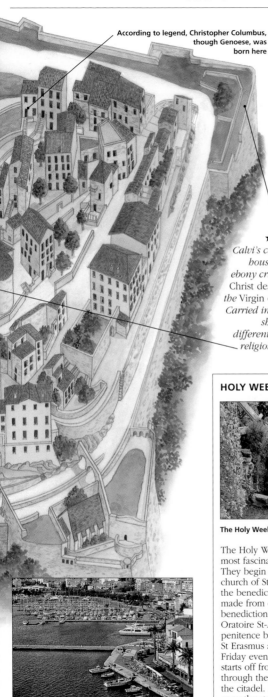

According to legend, Christopher Columbus, though Genoese, was born here

Teghiale Bastion

## VISITORS' CHECKLIST

**Road map** B2. 👥 *5,600.*
✈ *Ste-Catherine, 4 km (2 miles)
(04 95 65 88 88).* ▭ 🚉 *Avenue
de la République (04 95 65 00 61).*
⛴ *from Marseille, Nice, Toulon
and Savona.* 🛈 *97 Port de Plaisance (04 95 65 16 67).* 🎭 *La
Granitula (Holy Week); Jazz Festival
(late Jun); Polyphonic Music (mid-
Sep); Festiventu (mid-to late Oct).*
**www**.balagne-corsica.com

★ **St-Jean-Baptiste**
*Calvi's cathedral* (see p80)
*houses a 15th-century
ebony crucifix known as*
Christ des Miracles, *and
the* Virgin of the Rosary.
*Carried in processions,
she is dressed
differently for each
religious festival.*

## HOLY WEEK

**The Holy Week Procession**

The Holy Week celebrations are among the
most fascinating and beautiful in Corsica.
They begin on Maundy Thursday in the
church of Ste-Marie-Majeure *(see p80)*, with
the benediction of the *canistrelli* (biscuits
made from chestnut flour). Another
benediction of *canistrelli* takes place in the
Oratoire St-Antoine after a procession of
penitence by Calvi's two confraternities,
St Erasmus and St Anthony. On Good
Friday evening, the Granitula procession
starts off from St-Jean-Baptiste and winds
through the streets of the lower city and
the citadel. Members of the confraternities
carry the statues of the *Christ des Miracles*
and the *Virgin of the Rosary*, who is
dressed in black. Some penitents follow
the procession barefoot, wearing a white
habit and carrying wooden crosses.

**View from the Bastions**
*The impressive citadel walls and
Tour de St-Antoine overlook the
yacht harbour and the lower city.*

# Exploring Calvi

Frieze, Notre-
Dame-de-la-Serra

The capital of Balagne is one of the most beautiful seaside resorts in Corsica, partly because of its long beach. Calvi was founded by the Romans in the 1st century AD. From 1278 onwards it was the main Genoese stronghold – the wealthy capital of the island governed by this maritime republic. It comprises the upper sector, the citadel with its centuries-old Genoese ramparts, and the lower town, with houses overlooking the harbour and the animated atmosphere typical of seaside resorts. Calvi claims to be the real birthplace of Christopher Columbus.

Sunbathers enjoying the white-sand beach paradise at Calvi

## 🔒 St-Jean-Baptiste
Perched in the centre of Calvi's towering citadel is the St-Jean-Baptiste cathedral, whose foundations date from the mid-13th century. Boasting a dramatic history, the original church burned down in 1481, was heavily damaged in a Turkish siege in 1553, and, just 14 years later, was virtually destroyed when a nearby gunpowder store exploded. In 1576, the cathedral was rebuilt in its present Greek cross form.

Stop in for a peek at the *Christ des Miracles*, the consecrated crucifix that sits to the right of the marble altar. During the 1553 siege, locals paraded through the streets carrying the ebony sculpture, which according to legend, caused the Turks to hastily abandon the city.

The Calvi War Memorial

## 🏛 Place Christophe Colomb
At the foot of the citadel is a square linking the old and new towns, the ideal starting point for a walking tour of the city (partly thanks to the large car park). In the middle of the square is a bronze statue commemorating those who died in World War I, while a stone pays homage to the first battalion of the French Liberation Army, which liberated Corsica in 1943. A stairway descends to the Rue Clemenceau, a pedestrian precinct with restaurants and shops selling beach accessories.

## 🔒 Ste-Marie-Majeure
Rue Clemenceau. ⬜ *daily.*
This rose-coloured church can be found on a small square next to Rue Clemenceau, in the heart of the lower city. Begun in 1765, with the bell tower added in 1838, it is Baroque in style, with a softly rounded dome.

It houses some statues, including one of St Erasmus, the fishermen's patron saint who is popular here, and an *Assumption* that is carried through the city in a procession. The chapel in the choir has a 15th-century oil painting on leather from Cordoba.

## 🖼 Marina
The marina in Calvi is one of the loveliest in all Corsica, with luxury yachts berthed next to simple fishing craft and other small boats. The marina is the starting point for day-long boat tours of the west coast that go to the Scandola Nature Reserve

*(see pp104–5)*, the Calanques de Piana *(see pp100–101)*, continuing even as far as Ajaccio. Much of this coast, with its fascinating red granite rock formations, can be seen up close only from the sea.

The harbour also hosts the boats that belong to the diving centres. These take scuba divers to the best spots, such as those around the nearby Pointe Revellata promontory *(see p191)*, where short courses for beginners are available.

## 🏛 Quai Landry
This promenade, with its hotels, cafés and restaurants shaded by palm trees and colourful awnings, is the liveliest spot in Calvi. Many relaxing hours can be spent at one of the tables, enjoying a refreshing drink, watching the boats anchoring or setting off or observing the passers-by along the quay.

Under the citadel at the end of the quay is the **Tour**

The lively Quai Landry, with Ste-Marie-Majeure in the background

*For hotels and restaurants in this region see pp158–60 and pp172–5*

**du Sel**, a medieval lookout post once used as a salt storehouse. Further along is the lighthouse, which dominates the entrance to the harbour.

### 📷 The Beach

Calvi's beach is 4.5 km (3 miles) long, from the marina to the mouth of the Figarella river. It is bordered by a pine grove that was laid out in the 19th century, when the marshland was reclaimed. It has fine white sand and low dunes protected by fencing. The sea is shallow and free from rocks.

The Chapelle de Notre-Dame-de-la-Serra, with views of the bay

**View of the Pointe Revellata promontory, a popular site for divers**

Camp sites and establishments offering deckchairs and other beach items can be found among the pines. It is also possible to swim and sunbathe off the rocks at the foot of the Citadelle.

### Environs

About 4 km (2 miles) along the Ajaccio road leading south out of Calvi there is a steep road on the left that climbs into the maquis among rocks sculpted by wind erosion. From here there is a fine view of the **Pointe Revellata** promontory, a scuba divers' paradise *(see p191)*. The road ends at **Notre-Dame-de-la-Serra**, a 19th-century chapel built over the ruins of a 15th-century complex destroyed during the 1794 siege, when British and Corsican troops surrounded Calvi. This is a popular picnic spot. The terrace with the statue of Notre-Dame-de-la-Serra affords a fabulous view of the bay and the city below.

**CALVI**

Beach ⑦
*Citadelle (see pp78–9)* ①
Marina ⑤
Place Christophe
　Colomb ③
Quai Landry ⑥
St-Jean-Baptiste ②
Ste-Marie-Majeure ④

Anse de Fontanaccia

La Maison Colomb
Citadelle ①
② St-Jean-Baptiste
Oratoire St-Antoine
Palais des Gouverneurs Génois
*Pointe Revellata, Notre-Dame-de-la-Serra*
③ Place Christophe Colomb
QUAI LANDRY
Tour du Sel
Port de Commerce
④ Ste-Marie-Majeure
AVENUE NAPOLÉON
RUE DE L'URUGUAY
VILLAS ST-ANTOINE
BVLD WILSON
RUE CLÉMENCEAU
PL ST-CHARLES
AVENUE SANTA MARIA
⑥ QUAI LANDRY
LA PORTEUSE D'EAU
Gare SNCF
⑤ Marina
RUE JOFFRE
AVENUE DE LA RÉPUBLIQUE

Beach ⑦

**Key to Symbols** *see back flap*

| 0 metres | 200 |
|---|---|
| 0 yards | 200 |

# AJACCIO AND THE WEST COAST

*A rugged, craggy coastline beaten by the wind, white sandy beaches and red granite cliffs: Corsica's west coast offers no end of grand, natural scenery. This stretch of land has three gulfs – Porto, Sagone and Ajaccio – that highlight the jagged nature of the western coastline, which is so different from the rather straight profile of eastern Corsica.*

The Golfe de Porto has retained its wild beauty thanks to the regional nature reserve that protects the Scandola peninsula and the smaller Golfe de Girolata, which can be reached only on foot or by sea.

The sandy beaches of the gulfs of Ajaccio and Sagone have led to the creation of tourist facilities, which fortunately have not altered the beauty of the area. Most of this coastline can also be explored on foot by following the shrub-lined mule tracks that go to Girolata or traverse the rock formations of the Calanques, between Piana and Porto.

Just outside Ajaccio there are other panoramic footpaths, ending opposite the Îles Sanguinaires and the beaches of Capo di Feno. The capital of Corse-du-Sud *(see p49)*, Ajaccio owes its foundation and prosperity to the Genoa Maritime Republic *(see pp41–5)*, but it is linked mostly to Napoleon Bonaparte, who was born here. Ajaccio jealously preserves Napoleon's memory: his name and effigy are everywhere to be seen in the city, on plaques, statues and souvenirs.

As well as a stunning coastline and some of the most interesting sea beds in the Mediterranean, Corsica offers valleys full of olive, pine and chestnut trees. Some mountain villages have maintained their old pastoral traditions, linked to wild-pig breeding and the exploitation of the woods. The rivers have created deep and spectacular canyons, such as the Gorges de Spelunca at Evisa and the Gorges du Prunelli near Bastelica. On the old stone bridges the sounds of sheep and mules have been replaced by those of hikers on the panoramic *Mare a Mare* (Sea to Sea) and *Mare e Monti* (Sea and Mountains) paths.

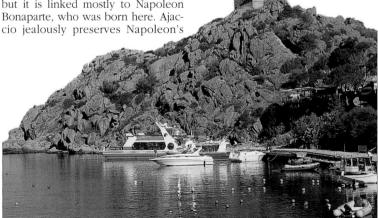

The Genoese tower, dominating the Golfe de Porto, still seeming to be defending the city

◁ Dramatic granite cliffs along the Château Fort path, a classic route in the Calanques de Piana

# Exploring Ajaccio and the West Coast

The west coast of Corsica, with the gulfs of Porto, Sagone and Ajaccio, offers spectacular marine landscapes, from the porphyry cliffs in the Scandola Nature Reserve *(see pp104–5)* to the white beaches of Porticcio. Apart from Ajaccio, with its museums and stylish streets, the most interesting sights in western Corsica are nature-based. Some of them are part of the Parc Naturel Régional de la Corse *(see p99)*: Evisa and the Forêt d'Aïtone, the Vallée du Fango, the Gorges de Spelunca, the Calanques de Piana, the Gorges du Prunelli and the Golfe de Girolata. This area is ideal for hiking, especially the region around Porto, which offers numerous waymarked routes of varying degrees of difficulty.

Calvi

Argentella

*Punta Ciuttone*

D81b

GALÉRIA **18**

RÉSERVE
NATURELLE DE
SCANDOLA
**19**  **17** GIROLATA

*Forê
du Fa*

*Col de
la Croix*          Partine

*Golfe de
Porto*

D81

PORTO **14**

CALANQUES
DE PIANA **13**        Ot

**12** PIANA

*Capo
Rosso*

*Plage d'
Arone*          D81

*Plage de
Chiunt*

CARGÈSE **11**

SAGONE **10**

TIUCCIA

*Golfe de
Sagone*          *Tour
d'Ancone*

Plage de Verghia, a cove with a sandy beach and transparent sea
in the Golfe d'Ajaccio

A natural arch of typical red rock in the
Scandola Nature Reserve

### KEY

— Major road

═══ Minor road

– – Hiking trail

— Scenic route

— Railway

✕ Mountain pass

*Capo di
Feno*

AJACCIO

POINTE **3**
DE LA PARATA
ROUTE DES
SANGUINAIRES
**2**

**4** ÎLES
SANGUINAIRES

*Golfe
d'Ajaccio*

0 kilometres          10

0 miles          5

### SEE ALSO

• *Where to Stay* pp161–3

• *Where to Eat* pp175–6

*Punta di
a Castagna*

## SIGHTS AT A GLANCE

Young Laricio pines in the intriguing Forêt d'Aïtone

View of a village in one of the interior valleys on the west coast

### GETTING AROUND

Around Ajaccio, the roads to Corte and Sartène are wide and quite fast. However, minor mountain roads and those on the stretch of coast between Galéria and Porto are very narrow and overhang the sea, so careful driving is required. A car is the best way to get around Corsica, but you can also use the Ajaccio–Bastia railway line, which stops at Bocognano, the starting point for many paths going through the Vallée de la Gravona. Boat excursions along the west coast are quite interesting: those from Ajaccio and Sagone go to the Îles Sanguinaires and the Golfe de Porto. Porto is the starting point for trips to Girolata and the Scandola Nature Reserve.

# Ajaccio **❶**

**Sculpture on Ajaccio Cathedral**

The largest city in Corsica, as well as the island's political centre, Ajaccio has a typically Mediterranean look. It is divided into three sectors: the old Genoese town, with its narrow streets and houses with pastel-coloured façades; the modern city, with tree-lined avenues and outdoor cafés; and the outskirts, which extend up to the hills and offer a marvellous view of the gulf, dominated by the Citadelle.

A Roman settlement during the Imperial Age, Ajaccio began to develop in 1492 thanks to the Genoese. In 1553 the city was conquered by Sampiero Corso *(see p45)* for the French, but in 1559 it was returned to the Genoese as part of the treaty of Cateau-Cambresis. Under Genoa Ajaccio prospered, thanks to commerce, agriculture and coral fishing, but not until 1592 were the locals granted the right to live here. In 1723 the city became the capital of West Corsica. Ajaccio is famous because Napoleon Bonaparte was born here on 15 August 1769.

**The Tino Rossi harbour, bordered by the Jetée de la Citadelle**

## 🏛 Citadelle
🚫 *to the public.*
The construction of the Citadelle, on a rocky spur jutting over the sea, began in 1554, by order of the French Marshal de Thermes, and was completed by the Genoese in 1559. The building faces the innermost part of the gulf and overlooks the Jetée de la Citadelle, a jetty that encloses the Tino Rossi harbour. With its sentry walkways, walls and ramparts, the Citadelle towers over the old Genoese quarter.

As a military zone, the Citadelle is not open to the public, but its majestic profile can be admired from the beach, from the breakwater or from Boulevard Danielle Casanova, named after the Ajaccio-born French-Resistance heroine who died in Auschwitz in 1943.

## 🏛 Ajaccio Cathedral
Rue Forcioli-Conti.
**Tel** 04 95 21 07 67. ⬚ *daily.*
Dedicated to the Virgin Mary, the cathedral of Ajaccio was built in 1582–93 by Giacomo della Porta in Venetian Renaissance style, but has Baroque elements. The simple façade contrasts with the lavish interior, which features polychrome marble and gilded decoration. In July 1771, when he was almost two, Napoleon was baptized at the font.

The first chapel on the left has a painting by Eugène Delacroix, the *Madonna of the Sacred Heart*. The next chapel, dedicated to Our Lady of Mercy, the patron saint of Ajaccio (celebrated on 18 March with a procession, *see p32*), contains an impressive 18th-century marble statue of the Virgin Mary. The high altar, made of white marble with black tortile columns, was donated to the cathedral in 1811 by Elisa Bacciochi, Napoleon's sister and princess of Lucca and Piombino.

## 🏛 St-Erasme
Rue Forcioli-Conti.
Founded in 1617 as the chapel of the Jesuit College, St-Erasme later became the chapel of the Royal College. During the French Revolution the church was closed to the public and turned into a city office. In 1815 it was reconsecrated and dedicated to the sailors' patron saint, Erasmus. Inside are model ships, three processional crosses and a statue of St Erasmus with angels. On 2 June the statue is carried in a procession down to the seaside.

## 🏛 Rue Bonaparte
This street was the old *carrugio dritto* (straight alley) of the Genoese city, inhabited by merchants and leading citizens. During Genoese rule Rue Bonaparte divided Ajaccio into two quarters: to the north was the Macello, where the poor lived, and to the south was the area of the upper middle classes. Today this is a pleasant, lively street with

**The simple façade of Ajaccio Cathedral**

**The study of Napoleon's father, furnished in the style of a bedroom of the late 1700s**

antique shops and boutiques catering to all tastes.

### 🏛 Maison Bonaparte

Rue St-Charles.
**Tel** 04 95 21 43 89.
◯ Tue–Sun. 🖼 🕭 ♿ 🔈
**www**.musee-maisonbonaparte.fr

The house that belonged to the Bonaparte family from 1682, and where Napoleon was born, features an austere façade overlooking the small, tree-lined Place Letizia, where there is a bust of the emperor's son.

In 1793 Napoleon and his family were forced to flee the house (through a trap door) by supporters of eventual liberator Pascal Paoli (see pp46–7). The Paolist mob was seeking revenge because Napoleon (then an officer in the French army) had ordered his troops to fire at a local rally. The house was then impounded by the British (1794–6) and partly used as an arsenal. In 1797 Letizia Bonaparte, Napoleon's mother, returned to Ajaccio and obtained compensation to refurbish the house. Since 1923 Maison Bonaparte has been a state-managed, three-storey museum illustrating the fascinating and turbulent history of the Bonaparte family.

**VISITORS' CHECKLIST**

**Road map** B4. 🏛 58,500.
✈ Campo dell'Oro, 7 km
(4 miles) E (04 95 23 56 56).
🚌 🚆 Place de la Gare (04 95
23 11 03). ⛴ from Porto Torres,
Marseille, Nice, Toulon (04 95 51
21 80). 🛈 3 Boulevard du Roi
Jérôme (04 95 51 53 03). 🎭 Our
Lady of Mercy Feast (18 Mar);
Blues Festival (Jul); Celebrations in
Honour of Napoleon (mid-Aug).
**www**.ajaccio-tourisme.com

### ⛲ Place Foch

The true heart of Ajaccio, this square is lined with cafés with tables outside in the shade of the palm and plane trees. Formerly called Piazza Porta, it used to be the only gate to the Citadelle. Place Foch is dominated by the white marble statue of Napoleon as First Consul, in the middle of the Four Lions Fountain, which was sculpted by Jérôme Maglioli.

**Marble bust of Napoleon**

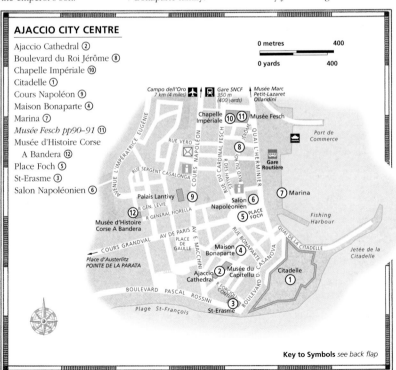

**AJACCIO CITY CENTRE**

0 metres    400
0 yards    400

Campo dell'Oro
7 km (4 miles)

Gare SNCF
350 m
(400 yards)

Musée Marc
Petit-Lazaret
Ollandini

Chapelle Impériale ⑩ ⑪ Musée Fesch

RUE VERO

Port de Commerce

⑧

Gare Routière

AVENUE L'IMPÉRATRICE EUGÉNIE

RUE SERGENT CASALONGA

COURS NAPOLÉON

RUE DU CARDINAL FESCH

RUE DES HALLES

QUAI L'HERMINIER

Palais Lantivy

⑨

R GÉN. LEVIE

Salon ⑥
Napoléonien

⑦ Marina

⑫

R GENERAL FIORELLA

⑤ PLACE
FOCH

Fishing
Harbour

Musée d'Histoire
Corse A Bandera

COURS GRANDVAL

AV. DE PARIS

PLACE
DE
GAULLE

AV. MACCHINI

RUE BONAPARTE

QUAI DE LA CITADELLE

Jetée de la
Citadelle

Place d'Austerlitz
POINTE DE LA PARATA

Maison ④
Bonaparte

QUAI DU CASANOVA

Ajaccio ②
Cathedral

Musée du
Capitellu

Citadelle
①

BOULEVARD PASCAL ROSSINI

R FORCIOLI
CONTI

BOULEVARD D. CASANOVA

Plage St-François

③ St-Erasme

**Key to Symbols** see back flap

# Exploring Ajaccio

**The Petit Train logo**

Ajaccio is a relatively small town and can easily be explored on foot. One of its main thoroughfares, Rue Cardinal Fesch, is a pedestrianized area with craft shops and boutiques. In Cours Napoléon and along the seafront, on the Quai Napoléon and Quai l'Herminier, it is quite enjoyable to sit at one of the outdoor cafés and watch the world pass by. Ajaccio can also be discovered by *Petit Train (see p184)*. It leaves from Place Foch for a tour of the city (45 mins) or goes to the Pointe de la Parata (90 mins).

The *Petit Train* leaving Place Foch for a tour of the city

## 🏛 Salon Napoléonien
Avenue Antoine Serafini.
**Tel** 04 95 51 52 62. ⬜ Mon–Fri.
⬤ public hols. 📷
Housed on the first floor of the town hall (Hôtel de Ville), the rooms of the Napoleonic Museum are accessed via a grand staircase. The museum displays documents and paintings relating to the life of Napoleon and his family. In the Grand Salon, under the large Bohemian crystal chandelier donated for the 200th anniversary of the birth of Napoleon, there are large portraits of the family and several busts, including one of Napoleon's mother, Letizia. A painting by Domenico Frassati celebrates the *Glory of the Emperor* (1840). Other interesting items are Napoleon's baptism certificate and a replica of his bronze death mask. The Hall of Medals features a fine collection of coins and gold, silver and bronze medals.

*First Consul Bonaparte, detail*

## 🚢 Marina
At the foot of the Citadelle, a long breakwater protects this harbour from the west wind. Next to the passenger terminal of the port, where the large ferries land, are the yacht harbour and the fishermen's port, with many brightly coloured boats filled with fishing nets. Every morning from 7am, in the open space in front of Place Foch, there is an animated market offering fresh fish. This quay is also the departure point for the boats taking visitors on excursions to the Îles Sanguinaires, the Golfe de Porto and Porticcio.

## 🚽 Boulevard du Roi Jérôme
Lined with hotels and restaurants, this boulevard is a favourite with locals, who gather here to have a *pastis* or play a game of *pétanque*. Every morning, the area behind the town hall facing the sea becomes a colourful open market offering typical Corsican products: *brocciu* cheese, *lonzu* (smoked fillet of pork), *coppa* (pork neck), *prizuttu* (cured ham), pâtés, honey, fig jam and myrtle liqueur. Vegetables and flowers also fill the market with their scents and colours.

The hubbub and gaiety invade the adjacent streets, as well as the pedestrianized Rue Cardinal Fesch, once the main thoroughfare in the Genoese quarter, which from the 16th century onwards grew outside the city walls. Halfway down this street is the Palais Fesch, built by Cardinal Fesch, one of Napoleon's uncles, in 1827–37 and now a museum containing part of his huge fine art collection (see *pp90–91*).

## 🚽 Cours Napoléon
The main street in Ajaccio crosses the city from northeast to southwest. It is intersected by smaller streets that go down to the sea or up to the hills. Cours Napoléon is lined with cinemas, shops, banks and cafés, including the famous Café Napoléon, built in 1821 by the architect Carrayol. Towards the railway station the street becomes wider, forming Place Abbatucci, which was once the border between the old town and the countryside.

Typical Corsican products for sale on Boulevard du Roi Jérôme

*For hotels and restaurants in this region see pp161–3 and pp175–6*

**Detail of the statue of Napoleon on horseback in Roman dress**

About halfway down Cours Napoléon is the Chapelle de St-Roch, built in the late 1800s, while towards the southern end of the street is the **Palais Lantivy**, now home to the prefecture and the General Council. The street ends at Place de Gaulle, a large square dominated by a statue of Napoleon in the guise of a Roman emperor on horseback, surrounded by his four brothers.

### 🔒 Chapelle Impériale
50 Rue du Cardinal Fesch.
*Tel 04 95 21 48 17.*
⭕ *call for opening hours.*
When Emperor Napoleon III had Cardinal Fesch's palace restored in 1857 by the architects Corona, Casanova and Paccard, he decided to use the right-hand wing as a chapel to house the remains of the nine members of the Bonaparte family, including Napoleon I's parents – Carlo Bonaparte and Letizia Ramolino (Napoleon's tomb is in Les Invalides, Paris), and Cardinal Fesch himself. The sober Renaissance exterior is made of light St-Florent limestone.

Inside, the trompe-l'oeil dome was painted by the Ajaccio-born architect Jérôme Maglioli, and is decorated with the cardinal's insignias, which are also on the stained-glass windows. On the high altar is a gold crucifix that Napoleon gave to his mother when he returned from his campaign in Egypt. The remains of the nine family members are all in the round crypt under the dome.

### 🏛 Musée Fesch
*See pp90–91.*

### 🏛 Musée d'Histoire Corse A Bandera
1 Rue du Général Levie.
*Tel 04 95 51 07 34.* ⭕ *daily.*
🌑 *Sun (winter).*
Just behind the prefecture is a picturesque building, the façade of which is decorated with portraits of the leading figures in Corsican history. This is the home of a museum that illustrates the history of the island through its main political and military events, from prehistory to World War II. This is done over five halls with documents, objects, photographs and large maps.

The museum is a good starting point for an understanding of Corsican culture. Of particular interest are the maps showing the location of the megaliths on the island, the models of Genoese ships, the paintings of the battles for independence, and the accounts of the Resistance against the Italian and German occupation and the liberation of Corsica in September 1943.

### 🏛 Place d'Austerlitz
At the western end of Place Foch begins Cours Gandval, a street running parallel to the sea in the direction of the Pointe de la Parata *(see p92)*. Cours Gandval ultimately leads to Place d'Austerlitz, a square dominated by an imposing structure, known as U Casone, which features a statue of Napoleon. Preceded by two eagles and a stone that commemorates his victories and exploits, this monument represents the emperor in a riding coat and wearing his famous two-cornered hat as he looks towards Ajaccio, his native town.

To the left of U Casone is the cave where, according to legend, Napoleon pretended he was an emperor when he was a child. Every year, around 15 August, his birthday, Ajaccio commemorates Napoleon's imperial period with impressive parades in period costumes *(see pp33–4)* during the lively *Journées Napoléoniennes*.

### 🏛 Musée Marc Petit–Lazaret Ollandini
Route d'Aspretto 20090.
*Tel 04 95 10 85 15.*
⭕ *Mon–Thu.*
www.lazaretollandini.com
Built in the mid-1800s, the Lazaret originally served as the quarantine for the port of Ajaccio. It was classified as a national historic monument in 1977, and opened to the public as a museum in 2008. The museum houses 32 large-scale sculptures by Marc Petit in its permanent collection, as well as other drawings and sculptural works. The building is also open for cultural events throughout the year.

**Mural in the Musée A Bandera**

**The monument to Napoleon in Place d'Austerlitz**

# Ajaccio: Musée Fesch

**Cardinal Joseph Fesch's insignia**

Cardinal Fesch, Napoleon's uncle, had this palace built in 1827. He dedicated three wings to housing works of art, which were donated to the city when he died, in 1839. The main building has the most important collection of Italian paintings in France after the Louvre, as well as works by Spanish, Flemish and Dutch artists. The first floor contains 13th– 17th-century Italian art, including many canvases of the Virgin Mary and Child. On the second floor are works dating from the 17th and 18th centuries, with a fine collection of still lifes. The basement is given over to Napoleon, with statues and paintings of the emperor, as well as various objects bearing his image. The left wing houses the City Library, founded by Lucien Bonaparte, Napoleon's brother. The renovated museum re-opened to the public in 2010 with a new exhibit of modern Corsican paintings added to the main collection.

**Jesus and the Samaritan**
*This work is by Étienne Parrocel, an 18th-century Corsican artist. Above is a detail of the Samaritan.*

**Holy Family**
*This detail of a painting by 17th-century Italian artist Benedetto Gennari shows the attention he paid to minutiae.*

**The Grande Galerie**
contains large-scale Italian paintings.

**The collection**
of early Italian Renaissance paintings is the core of the museum.

**Auditorium**

## CARDINAL FESCH

**Cardinal Fesch**

Joseph Fesch (1763– 1839) was Napoleon's uncle, but he was only six years older than the emperor. He was the archdeacon of Ajaccio and arch-bishop of Lyon. In 1803 he became a cardinal and moved to Rome, where he collected 16,000 works of art, some of which are on display in the museum, while others were donated to many churches in Corsica. It was thanks to his diplomatic intervention that Pope Pius VII agreed to go to Paris in 1804 to crown Napoleon emperor. In 1811 Fesch fell into disgrace for siding with the Church in the conflict between the Pope and Napoleon.

★ **Virgin Mary and Child with Angel**
*This early master-piece by the Italian artist Sandro Botticelli (1445–1510) is one of the loveliest works in the museum. It is innovative from an iconographic point of view because the Virgin is standing, and also because of her open display of affection.*

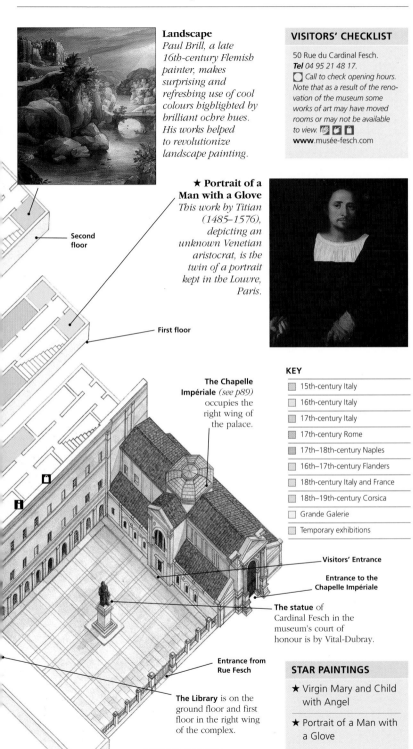

**Landscape**
*Paul Brill, a late 16th-century Flemish painter, makes surprising and refreshing use of cool colours highlighted by brilliant ochre hues. His works helped to revolutionize landscape painting.*

**★ Portrait of a Man with a Glove**
*This work by Titian (1485–1576), depicting an unknown Venetian aristocrat, is the twin of a portrait kept in the Louvre, Paris.*

**Second floor**

**First floor**

**The Chapelle Impériale** *(see p89)* occupies the right wing of the palace.

**KEY**

| | |
|---|---|
| ▨ | 15th-century Italy |
| ▨ | 16th-century Italy |
| ▨ | 17th-century Italy |
| ▨ | 17th-century Rome |
| ▨ | 17th–18th-century Naples |
| ▨ | 16th–17th-century Flanders |
| ▨ | 18th-century Italy and France |
| ▨ | 18th–19th-century Corsica |
| ☐ | Grande Galerie |
| ☐ | Temporary exhibitions |

**Visitors' Entrance**

**Entrance to the Chapelle Impériale**

**The statue** of Cardinal Fesch in the museum's court of honour is by Vital-Dubray.

**Entrance from Rue Fesch**

**STAR PAINTINGS**

★ Virgin Mary and Child with Angel

★ Portrait of a Man with a Glove

**The Library** is on the ground floor and first floor in the right wing of the complex.

**Entrance to the Library**

One of the many beaches on the Route des Sanguinaires

# Route des Sanguinaires ❷

**Road map** B4. 🛈 *3 Boulevard du Roi Jérôme, Ajaccio (04 95 51 53 03).*

This panoramic road, the D111, runs along the northern shore of the Golfe d'Ajaccio, passing by the locals' favourite sandy beaches. There are also many cafés and restaurants with terraces from where it is possible to admire the cormorants in flight and, with a bit of luck, see dolphins playing.

As well as by car or bicycle, this coastline can be explored by bus or by the *Petit Train* (departure from Place Foch in Ajaccio, *see p88*).

The coastal route begins at Boulevard Lantivy and continues along Plage St-François, the most central beach in Ajaccio, at the foot of the walls of the Citadelle. It then proceeds along Boulevard Pascal Rossini, where every Sunday from 8am to noon there is a colourful flea market in front of the Fesch Lyceum, with second-hand objects and antiques.

The road continues through residential quarters, which offer a view of the gulf and are surrounded by lush Mediterranean gardens.

At the edge of the city, at Place Emmanuel-Arène, is the **Chapelle des Grecs**, a small Greek Orthodox church built in 1632 and used by the Greek community that had fled from the Peloponnese seeking political asylum. Not far from the main road is the cemetery, with Baroque and Neo-Classical chapels.

Some 5 km (3 miles) from the heart of town, the road skirts the beaches of Scudo, with bathing facilities and restaurants, the beautiful Marinella cove, and Vignola beach. The latter also marks the end of the **Chemin des Crêtes**, a popular, easy-to-follow ridge path with a superb view of the gulf. Waymarked with spots of paint, it starts in the centre of Ajaccio, at Bois des Anglais, behind Place d'Austerlitz (*see p89*), and takes about three hours. The number 5 bus travels back into town.

# Pointe de la Parata ❸

**Road map** B4. 🚌 *from Place de Gaulle, Ajaccio.* 🛈 *3 Boulevard du Roi Jérôme, Ajaccio (04 95 51 53 03).*

A black granite headland, the Pointe de la Parata makes for a dramatic end to the D111 road. The cape is dominated by the **Tour de la Parata**, a tower built by the Genoese in 1608 to defend the island from pirate raids. A path leads to the end of the cape (about 30 minutes there and back). From here the view of the red Îles Sanguinaires is grandiose, especially at sunset.

Another, longer route starts about 500 m (1,600 ft) before the restaurant at the Pointe de la Parata. Once on the far side of the headland, a path winds through tall maquis to a lovely beach at Anse de Minaccia (90 mins), also accessible via the D111-B road from Ajaccio. From here it is possible to continue to windswept Capo di Feno, with its Genoese watchtower (60 mins).

# Îles Sanguinaires ❹

**Road map** B4. 🚢 *from Ajaccio.* 🛈 *3 Boulevard du Roi Jérôme, Ajaccio (04 95 51 53 03).*

The red rock seems to have been the reason behind the name ("sanguinary") of the maquis-covered cliffs that emerge from the sea a short distance from the Pointe de la Parata. However, because the islands mark the southern border of the Golfe de Sagone, some people claim that the name derives from the Latin *Sagonares Insulae*, or Islands of the Gulf of Sagone.

The largest of the islands is the Grande Sanguinaire, also called Mezzumare. There is a lighthouse, built in 1840, as well as the ruins of the Genoese tower and a leprosy hospital. In spring this island is clad in white thanks to Montpellier rockrose in bloom. The Grande Sanguinaire is home to cormorants, herring gulls and other birds.

In 1863 the French author Alphonse Daudet lived in the lighthouse. He described the Sanguinaires as wild islands populated by wild goats, Corsican ponies and an osprey.

The other three islands are very small, little more than cliffs emerging from the sea.

View of the Îles Sanguinaires with their reddish rocks

The long beach at Porticcio, with its fine white sand

## Porticcio **5**

**Road map** B4. 👥 *320.* 🚌 *from Ajaccio.* 🚌 ℹ️ *Porticcio (04 95 25 10 09).* **www**.porticcio-corsica.com

Just opposite Ajaccio, on the southern coastline of the gulf, is Porticcio. This seaside resort is filled with hotels, residential complexes and lovely beaches with fine sand and facilities for watersports, from sailing to diving.

The beach with the best facilities is **La Viva**, while the most spectacular are **Agosta** and **Ruppione**, separated by the Isolella peninsula, which has coves with turquoise water.

On the headland is an old Genoese tower called Tour de l'Isolella. Another tower, Tour de Castagna, is further south, at Punta di a Castagna. Built in 1584, it is now off limits, since it stands in a military zone. The headland can be reached by taking the D55 road, past the Port de Chiavari and the little Portigliolo cove. From here are fine views of the Golfe d'Ajaccio and of Île Piana, a maquis-covered island.

## Forêt de Chiavari **6**

**Road map** B5. ℹ️ *Parc Naturel Régional de la Corse, 2 Rue Major Lambroschini, Ajaccio (04 95 51 79 10).*

The large Forêt de Chiavari extends for 18 sq km (7 sq miles), from the coast to an altitude of about 600 m (1,970 ft) on top of the hills separating the Golfe d'Ajaccio from the Golfe de Valinco.

The forest consists mainly of holm oaks, eucalyptus (imported from Australia in the 19th century to reclaim the land and help eliminate malaria), maritime pine and shrubs such as strawberry trees, mastic trees, ruscus and thyme. It also has many footpaths and mountain-bike paths of all levels of difficulty and for all tastes. One of the most pleasant is the Sentier de Myrte ("Myrtle Path"), which starts and ends at Plage de Verghia, a beach with a café.

At 485 m (1,600 ft), perched on a hill at the edge of the forest, is the hamlet of **Côti-Chiavari**, with a tree-lined terrace offering a splendid panoramic view of the gulf. Destroyed in the 16th century by Barbary pirates, this village was repopulated in 1713, when the Genoese government decided to transfer here the inhabitants of Chiavari, a locality in the Gulf of Tigullio, in Liguria, hence the name.

Not far from Côti-Chiavari there are interesting viewpoints that take in both sides of the surrounding hills and the two large gulfs on the west coast, Golfe d'Ajaccio and Golfe de Valinco.

On the narrow D55 road that leads up to Côti-Chiavari from Verghia is the old agricultural penal colony that was constructed in 1855. The mortality rate of the prisoners who worked the land here was very high because of malaria and the unhealthy climate. The prison was therefore abandoned in 1906 and the inmates were transferred to Cayenne.

**A village at the edge of the Forêt de Chiavari**

### THE COASTLINE TOWERS

As well as the fortified cities that defended their ports, the Genoese rulers left another symbol in Corsica: the series of 67 coastline towers that were constructed in the early 16th century along the entire perimeter of the island. Built to spot pirates and, in some cases, to afford refuge for the populations of the small seaside villages, these towers are either square or round and their size differs to quite an extent. Some, such as the towers of Girolata (*see p103*) or Campomoro (*see p128*), were the centres of true fortresses, while in other cases the towers were merely outposts built on sites that could easily be seen from the villages or from the neighbouring towers. Normally, a tower contained storehouses and a cistern to collect rainwater, since sources of drinkable water were very scarce so close to the sea.

**Round watchtower**

A characteristic sight on the west coast: craggy granite rocks and a Genoese watchtower at Porto ▷

# Gorges du Prunelli **❼**

**Road map** C4. 🛈 *Parc Naturel Régional de la Corse, Rue Major Lambroschini, Ajaccio (04 95 51 79 10).* **www**.parc-corse.org

The Prunelli torrent flows from Monte Renoso, which stands 2,352 m (7,716 ft) high, to the Golfe d'Ajaccio. The torrent has carved a deep canyon, or gorge, partly irrigated by the water from an artificial lake created by a dam.

From Ajaccio, the D3 twists along the north bank of the torrent. At the village of **Eccica-Suarella** a stone commemorates the site where Sampiero Corso, the enemy of Genoa in the 16th century *(see p45)*, was killed.

A little further along the D3, at the pass of **Col de Mercuju**, 716 m (2,349 ft) above sea level, a path begins. It leads to a belvedere with great views.

Overlooking the lake is **Tolla**, a small village surrounded by orchards. From here the road joins the D27 leading up to **Bastelica**. This hamlet on the slopes of Monte Renoso is known for its wild-pig charcuterie and for being the birthplace of Sampiero Corso. The national hero is portrayed in a bronze statue in front of the parish church. The house he was born in is in Dominacci, a nearby hamlet.

If driving back towards Ajaccio, it is possible to follow the D27 along the south side of the gorge. Here, between Col de Cricheto and Col de Marcuggio, is the **Forêt de Pineta**, with pine, beech and chestnut trees. A footpath descends from the road towards the Èse torrent and the Genoese bridge of Zipitoli.

### Environs

Continuing north from Bastelica, the D27 first ascends to Col de Scalella, then descends to Tavera, a village in the Vallée de la Gravona. Another panoramic road from Bastelica is the D27-A, leading southeast to the Val d'Èse ski resort, 1,700 m (5,577 ft) above sea level.

Convolvolus berries

# Vallée de la Gravona **❽**

**Road map** C4. 🛈 *Parc Naturel Régional de la Corse, Rue Major Lambroschini, Ajaccio (04 95 51 79 10).* **www**.parc-corse.org

This wide valley is traversed by the N193 highway, one of Corsica's main roads, which leads to Corte and Bastia. Parallel to the N193, but further up on the slopes, are the winding and panoramic roads leading to the villages of **Peri**, **Carbuccia**, **Ucciani** and **Tavera**, on the south side of the Vallée de la Gravona.

At the hamlet of Carbuccia is **A Cupulatta**, a reserve for 166 species of tortoise and the largest of its kind in Europe. **Bocogna-no**, the main village in the valley, lies at the foot of Monte d'Oro and is surrounded by chestnut trees. The village marks the start of many paths. The most popular begins 4 km (2 miles) southwest of the village, down the D27, and leads to the Cascade du Voile de la Mariée ("Bride's Veil Falls").

**View of coves and beaches on the road to Tiuccia**

# Tiuccia **❾**

**Road map** B4. 🏛 *150.* 🚌 🛈 *Sagone (04 95 28 05 36).*

On the Golfe de Liscia, between the Genoese towers of Ancone and Capigliolo, is Tiuccia. This small seaside resort is dominated by the ruins of the Capraja Castle, which once belonged to the Counts de la Cinarca. In the 13th–16th centuries, this family resisted Genoese rule and established its hold over the south of the island.

The mouths of the Liscia river and, further north along the coast, of the Liamone river have created long, sandy beaches surrounded by hills covered in maquis. These secluded beaches and coves can be reached via the Ancone footpath along the coast.

Tiuccia is also the starting point for boat excursions towards Girolata *(see p103)*, the Calanques de Piana *(see pp100–101)* and Capo Rosso.

### Environs

The valley of the river Liscia forms **La Cinarca**, a fertile area covered with woods, olive and orange trees and vineyards. Livestock raising is the main activity here. At an altitude of 400–600 m (1,300–2,000 ft) are villages with splendid views of the coast, such as Sari d'Orcino and Calcatoggio.

This area was once the home of some famous bandits, including Spada, also known as "the Tiger of Cinarca".

**The dam at Gorges du Prunelli**

# Corsican Charcuterie and Cheeses

The gastronomic products *prisuttu* (cured ham), *lonzu* (smoked pork fillet), *coppa* (smoked pork shoulder) and *figatellu* (smoked liver sausage) are typical of Corsica. They are prepared by hand and smoked on the *fucone*, an open fireplace that burns chestnut wood and grapevine stumps. The wild pigs used for these products are allowed to roam freely, a factor reflected in the meats' unique flavour. Other typical products are cheeses made of goat and sheep's milk. They are named after their areas of production, such as Niolo, Balaninu, Orezzincu, Bastelicaccia and Venaco. Niolo is one of the best-known strong, aged cheeses. Usually, cheese is eaten with fig preserves and nuts. *See also pp168–9.*

Nuts to be eaten with cheese

**Sheep can be found** *almost anywhere, especially in upper Corsica. Their milk is used to make a variety of cheeses, including* brocciu *and* toma. *Goats are common above all in the Balagne and Castagniccia regions.*

**There are about** *45,000 wild pigs in Corsica. They live in woods along the roads, feeding on chestnuts, acorns and aromatic herbs that give their meats a special flavour.*

*Partly aged cheeses*

*Salsiccia*

*Goat's milk cheese*

*Lonzu*

**Lonzu** *is raw pork fillet rolled with salt and pepper, tied into thick sausages and smoked.*

*Cheese with herbs*

*Fresh herbs*

## CORSICAN FLAVOURS
In tourist resorts there is no shortage of delicatessens selling gift baskets filled with tempting food items. But produce can also be purchased directly from the farmers.

**Prisuttu** *is a very savoury cured ham. It is best when it is cut by hand in thick, compact slices, so that its taste can be enjoyed to the full.*

FROMAGE DE LACTOSERUM DE CHÈVRE ET DE LAIT FRAIS DE BREBIS
**BROCCIU**
Appellation d'Origine Contrôlée
PASSU

**Brocciu** *is a ewe's- or goat's-milk cheese similar to ricotta, prepared with whey and heated milk. It can be fresh or salted to last longer. Since 1983 its trademark has been registered.*

Boats moored in the Golfe de Sagone

## Sagone 🔟

**Road map** B4. 🏠 250. 🚌 🛈 *Residence Sagone Plage (04 95 28 03 46).*

The wide Golfe de Sagone, between Punta di Cargèse to the north and Capo di Feno to the south, has long, sandy beaches formed by the silt carried by the Liamone, Sagone and Liscia rivers.

The small village of Sagone was once a major Roman city and owed its prosperity to timber from the Forêt d'Aïtone. In the 6th century AD it became a bishopric, and in the 11th century the cathedral of **Sant'Appiano** was built near the port. Its ruins can still be seen there. In the Middle Ages, however, the town declined because of malaria from the stagnant river water.

Thanks to land reclamation, Sagone is now a pleasant seaside resort. Among the activities on offer are sailing, scuba diving and boat trips to Scandola and Girolata.

#### Environs

A beautiful 15-km (9-mile) road goes up the Liamone river valley to **Vico**, a large, hilly village with narrow houses packed around two squares. Until the 18th century, Vico was the residence of the bishops of Sagone.

The church of the Couvent St-François has a lovely

wooden crucifix that was sculpted in the 15th century and that is considered one of the oldest in Corsica.

The road continues through lush vegetation to **Guagno Les Bains**, a tiny spa with two springs: the Occhiu (37° C/98.6° F), which is used to cure eye and throat ailments, and the Venturini spring (52° C/125.6° F), used by those afflicted by sciatica, rheumatism and obesity. Among the illustrious guests at this spa were Pascal Paoli and Napoleon's mother, Letizia.

Further along the road is the village of Soccia, the starting point for a footpath to the **Lac de Creno**, a lake surrounded by Laricio pines (2 hours return trip).

**Sign for the spa of Guagno Les Bains**

## Cargèse 🔟

**Road map** B3. 🏠 1,000. 🛈 *Rue Dr Dragacci (04 95 26 41 31).* Greek-Orthodox procession (Easter Monday).

In the mid-17th century a group of Greek families that had fled from the Peloponnese following the Turkish invasion asked the Genoese for political asylum. First they settled at Paomia, 50 km (31 miles) from Ajaccio, and then at Cargèse, where they were allowed to retain their traditions and religion. To this day this village, which is about 100 m (330 ft) above sea level, reflects its

Greek history. Two churches, both from the 19th century, stand opposite each other: a Greek-Orthodox church, with Byzantine-style icons and a 13th-century double-sided panel of the *Deposition of Christ*; and a Latin church, with a Neo-Classical interior. The terraces of both offer fine views of the Golfe de Sagone.

## Piana 🔟

**Road map** B3. 🏠 500. 🚌 🛈 *Place de la Mairie (04 95 27 84 42).* Brocciu Day (date depends on cheese production). **www**.otpiana.com

With its white houses, large Baroque church and the granite formations of the Calanques in the background, Piana occupies a panoramic position overlooking the Golfe de Porto. The village is the ideal base for excursions along this stretch of coastline, which has many beautiful beaches and is one of the most fascinating in Corsica.

Among the beaches is the **Anse de Ficajola**, situated among red rocks at the end of a winding road descending to the sea. The panoramic D824 road leads to **Plage d'Arone**, a pretty, undeveloped beach surrounded by maquis.

A difficult hike (4 hours return trip) from the roadside 2 km (1 mile) above the beach leads to **Capo Rosso** and the Tour de Turghiu, which, from its position 300 m (1,000 ft) above sea level, offers a spectacular view of the area.

**Panoramic view of Piana, surrounded by forest**

# Parc Naturel Régional de la Corse

With a surface area of 3,300 sq km (1,274 sq miles) and 143 towns, this park occupies nearly two thirds of Corsica, including the peaks of Monte Cinto, Rotondo, d'Oro, Renoso and Incudine, up to the Aiguilles de Bavella and the Massif de l'Ospédale. The park was founded in 1972 to support the mountain

The park logo

economy and protect the island's natural wonders: its forests (Aïtone, Valdu-Niellu, Vizzavona, Bavella and Ospédale), its rugged gorges (Spelunca, Restonica, l'Asco), the Calanques, and lakes such as Creno and Nino. The park is traversed by all the main hiking paths, including the GR20 long-distance path *(see pp22–7).*

Cork oak *is one of the most widespread species of trees in Corsica and is protected in the park.*

Elderly Corsican women are often dressed in black clothes.

Wheel to untangle the wool

The wheel is fastened to a chair

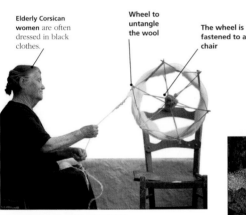

**LOCATOR MAP**

The park area

**The Gorges de l'Asco** *are a stunning example of the many deep canyons created by the rivers that flow from inland Corsica to the sea.*

## TRADITIONS AND NATURE

The Parc Naturel Régional was established not only to protect the Corsican flora and fauna, but also to safeguard the traditional activities of the hill and mountain environments. Most of the inhabitants in the park area are people whose families have lived and worked here for centuries and have forged the region's history and traditions.

**The donkey** *is one of the many domesticated or semi-domesticated animals linked to the economic activities of mountain life.*

**This bergerie** *at Cagna exemplifies mountain architecture. Bergeries are used in the summer for transhumance (the movement of livestock). In 1973–8 Father Doazan wrote about 20 notebooks describing this activity and the life of Corsican shepherds.*

# Tour of the Calanques de Piana ⑬

Typical rock in the Calanques

The granitic rock formations known as the Calanques de Piana feature sensational colour changes from gold to pink to bright red depending on the time of day. The wind and water have sculpted the granitic rock, creating awesome cavities, known as *tafoni*, and intriguing formations. Although it is possible to cover this whole route in half a day, or a full day with a lunch break, it might be more relaxing to explore the Calanques in the course of two separate walks, especially during the hottest period of the year. For those who are driving, this stretch of the D81 road is at its most beautiful and impressive at sunset.

**Tête du Chien** ①
The "dog's head" rock, eroded by the sea and wind, is one of the many intriguing shapes in the Calanques. It is near the parking area on the D81 road and is the starting point for many excursions.

**Château Fort** ②
This massive block of granite that looks like a fortress forms a panoramic terrace overlooking the gulfs of Porto and Girolata and Capo Rosso. It can be reached on foot in 30 minutes from the Tête du Chien through a maze of sculpted rocks, cavities and pinnacles that in spring are covered by flowering shrubs.

*Dardo*

**Café les Roches Bleues** ④
In one of the most spectacular spots along the D81 highway is the Roches Bleues café. Drinks are served on the terrace overhanging fantastically shaped rocks: to the left is the Tortue ("turtle", seen here), and to the right the Aigle ("eagle").

*Mezzanu*

*D81*

*PIANA* ← *D81*

⑥

**The D81 Road** ⑥
Once back on the D81, walk about 500 m (500 yards) towards Piana. Along this stretch of road the Calanques can be appreciated at their most beautiful. Turn back and follow the D81 all the way back to the parking area.

**KEY**

▬▬ Tour route

═ Other roads

☀ Viewpoint

🅿 Parking

## THE TAFONI

In Corsican *tafone* means a large hole, and this term is used to indicate a natural cavity in the rock of areas where the dry season is very long and the terrain is steep. Erosion begins when even just one crystal of granite is corroded

by the humidity and swings in temperature that occur in this area. The shapes the rock then takes on are truly astonishing. The *tafoni* became part of the Corsican way of life in ancient times, when these holes were used as burial sites or as primitive dwellings.

**A *tafone* formation in the Calanques de Piana**

### TIPS FOR HIKERS

**i** *Place de la Mairie, Piana (04 95 27 84 42).*
**Length of tour**: *3 km (2 miles).*
**Duration**: *about four hours, without stops, to do the paths, plus 45–60 minutes to get back to the parking area.*
**Difficulty**: *average. Wear comfortable shoes and carry a hat and sunglasses, a supply of water and a detailed map of the area (free from local tourist offices).*
**Stopping-off point**: *Café les Roches Bleues.*
**www**.otpiana.com

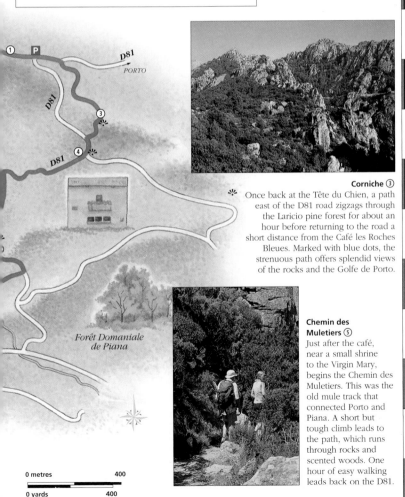

**Corniche ③**
Once back at the Tête du Chien, a path east of the D81 road zigzags through the Laricio pine forest for about an hour before returning to the road a short distance from the Café les Roches Bleues. Marked with blue dots, the strenuous path offers splendid views of the rocks and the Golfe de Porto.

Forêt Domaniale de Piana

**Chemin des Muletiers ⑤**
Just after the café, near a small shrine to the Virgin Mary, begins the Chemin des Muletiers. This was the old mule track that connected Porto and Piana. A short but tough climb leads to the path, which runs through rocks and scented woods. One hour of easy walking leads back on the D81.

PORTO

0 metres      400

0 yards       400

**The Genoese watchtower at Porto**

# Porto ⓮

**Road map** B3. 460.
i La Marine (04 95 26 10 55).
**www**.porto-tourisme.com

A modern seaside resort with facilities for watersports of every kind, Porto is also an ideal base for visitors who want to make inland excursions. Its favourable geographic position was providential for Porto, which, during the Genoese period, was the only outlet to the sea in the agricultural zone of Ota.

On either side of the village are tall cliffs that conceal enchanting beaches. Over-looking the village's harbour is the impressive Genoese tower that defended the small port, the river and the valley. This quadrangular construction was built in 1549 on levelled red-granite cliffs and offers magnificent views of the gulf, where the red rock contrasts with the blue sea.

Next to the village, with its many hotels, cafés and boutiques, is the **Marina**, which has a wide beach of grey pebbles backed by a large grove of centuries-old eucalyptus trees. The Marina can be reached via a charming wooden footbridge leading over the estuary of the little river where fishing boats and yachts are anchored. This tiny port is the departure point for many excursions by boat along the entire coastline. The Golfe de Porto, part of the Parc Naturel Régional (see p99), can be seen in all its splendour from the sea – the tourist boats go as far as the Scandola Nature Reserve (see pp104–5) and the Calanques de Piana (see pp100–1).

**A strawberry tree laden with fruit**

### Environs
South of Porto loom the magnificent Calanques, which reach an altitude of 1,294 m (4,245 ft) at Capo d'Orto. North of Porto, among the coast's granite cliffs, are some beautiful beaches that can be reached either by car (by taking turn-offs from the D81 road) or by boat. Among the most scenic are the pebble beaches of **Bussaglia** and **Gradelle**, the latter on the way to Osani; and the **Caspio** beach, with its dark rocks. Caspio can be reached by taking the detour after the hamlet of Partinello.

The stretch of the D81 road to Galéria is arguably the most difficult and spectacular in all Corsica. This high, narrow road with numerous bends offers wide-ranging views of the Golfe de Porto and coast. Small lay-bys along the road make for good viewpoints, as does the **Col de la Croix**, from which a path leads to the beaches of Tuara (75 minutes return) and Girolata (3 hours return; also accessible by boat).

# Gorges de Spelunca ⓯

**Road map** B3. i La Marine, Porto (04 95 26 10 55).

Behind Porto is a splendid valley from where it is possible to admire this gorge, formed by the Aïtone and Tavulella torrents. Fine views of the Gorges de Spelunca can be had from the D84 road that goes up to Evisa on the south side of the valley.

On the north side of the valley, at an altitude of 310 m (1,017 ft), is **Ota**, a mountain village with simple stone houses that was once famous for its citrons, which were exported to Europe. Today the orchards are partly overrun by scrub. Ota is one of the stops on the *Mare e Monti* path (see p27) in the Parc Naturel Régional (see p99).

Interesting sights in this area are the Genoese bridges, about 2 km (1 mile) along the road to Evisa. The first of these, at **Pianella**, is a perfect arch. The nearby bridge of **Ota** lies where the Aïtone and Tavulella torrents meet and passes over both of them. This point also marks the start of the old mule track that once linked Ota and Evisa through the spectacular gorges, passing over the **Vecchju** and **Zaglia** bridges (90 minutes return). The latter, built in 1745, is one of the gems of Genoese architecture.

The entire area is reminiscent of American canyons, and there is a ravine that can be followed along the path hewn out of the rock.

**The Genoese bridge of Ota, with its characteristic arch**

**Laricio pines in the Forêt d'Aïtone**

## Forêt d'Aïtone ⑯

Road map C3. ℹ Jun–Sep: Paesolu d'Aïtone (04 95 26 23 62). Other times: Parc Naturel Régional de la Corse, Ajaccio (04 95 51 79 10). www.parc-corse.org

With the atmosphere of an enchanted forest, the Forêt d'Aïtone can be explored through its easy, enjoyable and well-marked footpaths.

An ancient forest, its name seems to have derived from the Latin word *abies*, meaning fir tree. The forest covers an area of 24 sq km (9 sq miles) at an altitude of 800–2,000 m (2,600–6,500 ft). The Genoese used the wood to make their ships and, in the 16th century, built a road to transport the trunks to Sagone (see p98). The forest is made up mostly of Laricio pines, a sweet-scented variety of *Pinus nigrus* that can grow to more than 45 m (150 ft) high and live for 200 years. There are also maritime pines, firs, beeches and larches that protect the rich undergrowth and its wild fruit and mushrooms. The forest is inhabited by foxes, wild boars and mouflons.

Just west of the forest, at 830 m (2,723 ft) above sea level, is **Evisa**. Surrounded by chestnut groves that yield high-quality fruit, this village plays host to a famous chestnut festival in November. Evisa is situated at the junction of the *Mare a Mare* and *Mare e Monti* footpaths (see p27) and is therefore a great starting point for excursions.

About 4 km (2 miles) from Evisa, on the road to Col de Verghio (see p151), is the starting point of the path that leads to the **Cascades d'Aïtone** (30 minutes return), a series of waterfalls formed by the Aïtone torrent, at the foot of which are limpid pools perfect for a swim.

The **Sentier de la Sittelle** (the French word for the nuthatch, a local bird) is a path beginning by the park information centre of **Paesolu d'Aïtone** and going through the forest along the **Sentier des Condamnés** (2 hours 30 minutes), a circular path named after convicts who, in the 19th century, felled the trees for firewood.

**The ramparts and keep of the Genoese fort at Girolata**

## Girolata ⑰

Road map B3. 🏠 100. ℹ La Marine, Porto (04 95 26 10 55).

A fishermen's hamlet facing a splendid cove sheltered from the wind, Girolata can be reached only on foot (90 minutes from Col de la Croix, see p102) or by one of the boats that offer excursions from Porto in the summer. On the headland is the majestic square Genoese fort, which is protected by a defensive wall.

It was in the sea in front of Girolata, that, in 1540, the Genoese led by Andrea Doria captured the infamous Turkish pirate Dragut Rais.

In the summer the bay area becomes crowded with yachts and loses much of its charm, even though the sea beds and red cliffs are still beautiful.

## Galéria ⑱

Road map B3. 🏠 300. 🚌 ℹ Carrefour des Cinq Arcades (04 95 62 02 27).

The only residential area of any importance between Calvi (see pp78–80) and Porto, this isolated village is a great base for visits to the Scandola Nature Reserve (see pp104–5), dives and watersports in general. Galéria is also the departure point for excursions along the coast, where a panoramic path that also penetrates the maquis skirts the Golfe de Galéria from Punta Ciuttone to the north to Punta Stollu to the south.

Just behind Galéria is the **Vallée du Fango**, created by the river Fango, the mouth of which forms a vast pebbled beach. The valley was a transhumance route along which flocks of sheep from the mountains above the Vallée de Niolo were moved to the sea for winter. They stayed there until spring, when they made the return trip.

The D351 road penetrates the valley for about 10 km (6 miles), traversing the Forêt du Fango. Here the Fango river flows between low rock faces, creating transparent water-holes ideal for a swim. Shortly before the village of Barghiana is the spectacular meeting point of the Fango and the Taita torrent.

**The Taita torrent in the Vallée du Fango**

# Réserve Naturelle de Scandola ⓙ

Red granite cliffs plunge into the transparent sea at the Scandola Nature Reserve, while cormorants and shearwaters perch on the rocks and ospreys circle in the sky. Under the water's surface is a blaze of colours created by sponges, yellow anemones and corals. The reserve, which is on the UNESCO World Heritage list, protects 9.2 sq km (3½ sq miles) of land and 10 sq km (4 sq miles) of sea between Punta Mucchilina to the south and Punta Palazzo to the north. The park boasts an unparalleled wealth of flora, rare bird species and an abundance of underwater fauna: 450 species of algae and 125 species of fish are protected by bans on fishing, on mooring for more than 24 hours, and on gathering marine fauna and flora.

**Cliffs of beautiful red volcanic rock**

**Volcanic Rock**
*The entire Scandola peninsula is part of a volcanic complex, the rocks of which date back to the Upper Permian era (248 million years ago). Among these are porphyry flows at Cala Ficaccia, the lava and rhyolite domes at Punta Palazzo, and the prismatic organ-pipe shapes at Elbo, shown above.*

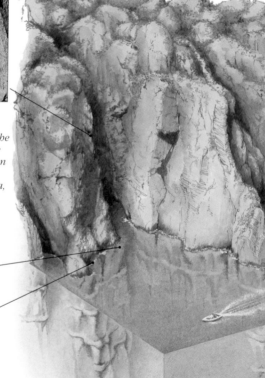

Algae platform ⎯⎯⎯

**Clinging to the volcanic rocks,** at the water's surface, are sea urchins and anemones, as well as numerous crustaceans.

**Algae platform above the water**

## THE ALGAE PLATFORM

*Lythophyllum* is a calcareous algae forming encrustations that hang over the surface of the water and are often as thick as 30 cm (12 in). At Punta Palazzo is the largest algae platform in the Mediterranean, about 100 m (330 ft) long and 2 m (6½ ft) wide. Though they seem robust, algae platforms are extremely fragile.

**Underwater layers**

### Euphorbia Dendroides

*Growing as much as 1 m (3 ft) high, this shrub is one of the most common in the reserve. It blossoms in May, when it tinges the cliffs yellow; at the end of spring, as it becomes dry, it takes on a bright-brown hue. Only in late summer, with the first autumn rain, does it become green again.*

### VISITORS' CHECKLIST

**Road map** B3. *La Marine, Porto (04 95 26 10 55).* excursions (by boat) from Ajaccio, Calvi, Cargèse, Galéria, Porto, Propriano, Sagone. (Snorkelling excursions are also available.) Jul–Aug: six excursions a day; Apr–Jun & Sep–Oct: four excursions a day.

### FAUNA IN THE RESERVE

The Scandola Nature Reserve is above all the domain of marine birds and fish. Here the birds find shelter and abundant food in the crevices of the rocks, where they nest. Cormorants, peregrine falcons and ospreys can all be observed here, as can a species of bat. The pure water also favours underwater life: flora lives as deep as 45 m (150 ft) down and the range of sea creatures is truly exceptional.

**The nest** of the osprey, a large white bird of prey with brown wings, is one of the features of these cliffs. After being close to extinction, there are now about 20 pairs of ospreys in the Scandola Nature Reserve.

**The cormorant,** *one of the largest sea birds, makes acrobatic manoeuvres on the water.*

**The osprey** *builds its nest on the steep cliffs of the Scandola Nature Reserve.*

**The grouper** *is a large fish that can be as much as 1.5 m (5 ft) long. It is recognizable by the light spots on its brownish dorsal portion.*

**The sea bream** *is highly prized and much in demand for its tasty meat, but in this park it is protected by the ban on fishing.*

**Over 450 species** of algae live here as a result of the exceptional clarity of the water.

### Panorama

*The coast along the Scandola Nature Reserve is one of the most evocative in Corsica. Here steep red rock formations plunge into the crystalline sea.*

# BONIFACIO AND THE SOUTH

*T*he fortified city of Bonifacio, with its narrow streets from which Sardinia can be seen on the horizon, is one of the most ancient on the island. But long before the Pisans, Genoese and Spanish fought for control here, southern Corsica was the centre of a prehistoric indigenous population that left amazing traces of its presence in the alignments of menhirs and casteddi.

The inlet of Bonifacio, on the cliffs of which are the defensive walls of the old Genoese city, is an ideal starting point for boat excursions along the precipitous white coastline. The menhirs at Filitosa are among the best-known aspects of Corsican history, but this is only one of the many sites where it is possible to admire Neolithic architecture. North of the Golfe de Porto-Vecchio are the impressive walls of the *casteddu* (castle) of Araggio, while south of Sartène the alignments of menhirs at Palaggiu, Stantari and Renaggiu are eloquent reminders of Corsica's early history.

The natural scenery in this area is quite varied and splendid: from the forests around the Aiguilles de Bavella to the white rocks on the islands of Lavezzi and Cavallo – protected by an international marine park that extends over the Straits of Bonifacio – the landscape offers incomparable views. There are many walking tours, and indeed the interior of southern Corsica should be explored, at least to some degree, on foot. A series of small villages occupies the most protected part of the mountain valleys, where olives and chestnuts grow and where traces of Corsica's medieval past can be found.

Amid small churches and old houses there is still an atmosphere of peace and quiet – the region is far removed from the world most of the year, becoming animated with tourists only in the summer. A low-season visit is highly recommended.

Three of the best-known anthropomorphic megaliths at the prehistoric site of Filitosa

◁ The famous cliffs of Bonifacio, resembling the hull of a huge ship

# Exploring Bonifacio and the South

Southern Corsica is divided into two adjacent areas that are quite different to one another. Starting off from Bonifacio, two main routes are worth exploring. Along the south coast there are many small coves, peaceful beaches and sheer rocks overlooking the sea. This is the area with the most popular tourist resorts, such as Bonifacio, Propriano, Solenzara and Porto-Vecchio, which in summer all become crowded. The inland route, after crossing the Alta Rocca region, leads to the Col de Bavella zone, which offers wonderful spots for nature hikes and many small secluded villages. The best-preserved prehistoric sites in Corsica – Filitosa, Palaggiu, Renaggiu, Fontanaccia and Stantari – are only a short driving distance from the town of Sartène, while near Levie, the sites of Cucuruzzu and Capula are also worth a visit.

View of the citadel of Bonifacio

Menhirs at Palaggiu, one of the prehistoric sites on the Cauria plateau

## GETTING AROUND

The main communication routes on the south coast of Corsica are the N196 and N198 roads, connecting Bonifacio to Propriano and Sartène, and Porto-Vecchio respectively. The N198 then proceeds northwards towards Bastia. The D368 road, with its many hairpin bends, goes from Porto-Vecchio into the mountains; in the village of Zonza it merges with the D268 road and leads to Col de Bavella. To explore the prehistoric sites it is necessary either to take minor roads, some of which are unpaved, or to go on foot. The main coastal towns are connected to Ajaccio and Bastia by bus service, while Bonifacio is a stopover for the ferries from Sardinia.

### SEE ALSO

• **Where to Stay** pp163–5

• **Where to Eat** pp177–9

## SIGHTS AT A GLANCE

0 kilometres 10

0 miles 5

Characteristic granitic rocks on Îles Lavezzi, shaped by the wind and sea

### KEY

— Major road

= Minor road

- - Hiking trail

— Scenic route

△ Summit

Transparent water and wild beauty on the exclusive Île Cavallo

# Bonifacio ●

**Rose window, Ste-Marie-Majeure**

This stunning medieval town on a striking limestone promontory was developed by Bonifacio, Marquis of Tuscany, who passed by upon his return from an expedition in Africa in 828. For three centuries the fortified harbour lived on fishing and piracy and was partly under the rule of Pisa. In 1195, Bonifacio became a Genoese colony and took in a number of immigrants from Liguria. At about the same time, it became a republic, was granted the right to mint its own money and began construction of the massive walls. Bonifacio was conquered in 1553 by the French before being recaptured by the Genoese, and in the 17th century it was fortified with modern military structures. Although the town fell definitively under French rule in the 18th century, it has kept an Italian flavour and a certain sense of isolation from the rest of Corsica.

**Outdoor cafés along the Marina**

### Marina

The quays of the old port of Bonifacio are now a popular promenade filled with cafés and restaurants. This is the departure point for cruises to the Grotte du Sdragonatu *(see p114)* and the Îles Lavezzi *(see p117)*. In the summer, this area remains quite lively until late at night.

Further along, towards the mouth of the inlet, is the commercial port with the Gare Maritime (passenger terminal). In the Middle Ages the port was entrusted to the benevolence of St Erasmus, the patron saint of sailors and fishermen who is celebrated on 2 June *(see p33)* and honoured by a church named after him in the Marina.

### To the Haute Ville

The old town can be reached by walking up the stairs known as Montée Rastello, next to St-Érasme, and then up Montée St-Roch, which leads to the old Porte de Gênes. It is also possible to drive along the road that goes past the Porte de France. This road skirts the foot of the Bastion de l'Étendard and a war memorial that consists of an ancient Roman column found on a nearby islet, and leads to the car park in the upper town *(haute ville)*, next to the monument to the Foreign Legion soldiers.

### Bastion de l'Étendard
◐ *Jul–Aug: daily; Apr–Jun & Sep–Oct: Mon–Sat.*

The silhouette of this massive bastion towering over the quays of the Marina and the port is one of the most famous features of the city. The bastion was built in the 16th century by modifying the existing fortifications, and its function was to house the powerful heavy artillery that at that time was bringing about a drastic change in military architecture. Along with the Porte de Gênes, it was the strong point of the walls of Bonifacio, which proved impregnable on several occasions.

The upper platforms of the bastion afford a magnificent panoramic view of the narrow inlet of Bonifacio and the Marina below.

Four halls in the interior are now a small museum featuring reconstructions of significant moments in Bonifacio's history.

### Porte de Gênes

During Genoese rule, the Porte de Gênes was the only entrance to Bonifacio's upper town. Surrounded by tall ramparts, the gate gave access to the Place d'Armes, beyond the walls. These walls were so thick that, to get to the square, one had to pass through eight successive barriers made of wood reinforced with iron.

In 1588, a drawbridge was added at the end of these barriers. The drawbridge was raised and lowered by a complex system of counterweights that can still be seen inside the structure.

**The massive Bastion de l'Étendard towering over the Marina**

*For hotels and restaurants in this region see pp163–5 and pp177–9*

**Open and blind double lancet windows, Ste-Marie-Majeure**

### 🔒 Ste-Marie-Majeure

Rue de la Loggia. ⬜ *daily.*
Bonifacio's cathedral was the heart of the city's religious and cultural life for centuries. At the front of the building is a vast loggia with porticoes, which, in the past, was the meeting point for the town notables and the seat for administering justice. The structure was built over a large cistern that is now used as a conference room.

Construction of Ste-Marie-Majeure was begun in the 12th century, before the Genoese conquered the city, by Pisan artisans, and was completed a century later. This extremely long delay has led to a mixture of styles that does not, however, diminish the beauty of the whole. The first floor of the bell tower, for example, is Romanesque, while the upper three are Gothic with some Aragonese relief decoration. The three-aisle interior is partly Baroque.

Inside, to the left of the entrance, is a 3rd- or 4th-century Roman sarcophagus surmounted by a magnificently wrought tabernacle executed by Genoese masters in the mid-1400s. The high altar dates from 1624 and is clearly Baroque in style. In the sacristy is a relic of the True Cross.

### VISITORS' CHECKLIST

**Road map** C6. 🏘 *3,400.*
✈ *Figari-Sud-Corse, 21 km (13 miles) NW (04 95 71 10 10).*
🚢 🚌 *from Sardinia.* 🛈 *2 Rue Fred Scamaroni (04 95 73 11 88).*
🎉 *St Erasmus's Feast Day (2 Jun); St Bartholomew Procession (24 Aug).* **www**.*bonifacio.fr*

In the past, during particularly dangerous times and when there were heavy storms, the curate and mayor carried the Cross in a procession through the streets of Bonifacio.

**The loggia of Ste-Marie-Majeure**

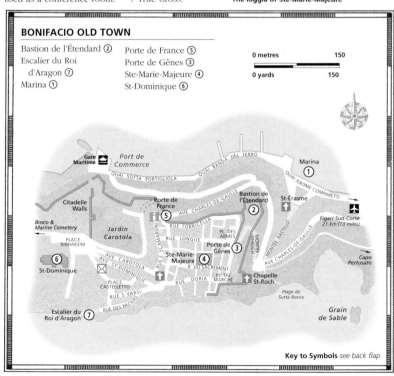

### BONIFACIO OLD TOWN

Bastion de l'Étendard ②
Escalier du Roi d'Aragon ⑦
Marina ①
Porte de France ⑤
Porte de Gênes ③
Ste-Marie-Majeure ④
St-Dominique ⑥

0 metres 150
0 yards 150

Gare Maritime
Port de Commerce
QUAI SOTTA PORTIGLIOLA
QUAI BANDA DEL FERRO
Marina ①
QUAI JEROME COMPARETTI

Citadelle Walls
Porte de France ⑤
AVE CHARLES-DE-GAULLE
Bastion de l'Étendard ②
St-Érasme

Bosco & Marine Cemetery
PLACE BIRHAKEIM
Jardin Carotola
RUE F SCAMARONI
RUE TORRICELLA
RUE LONGUE
PL. DES ARMES
Porte de Gênes ③
MONTEE ST-ROCH
MONTEE RASTELLO
AVE CHARLES-DE-GAULLE
Figari-Sud-Corse 21 km (13 miles)
Capo Pertusato

⑥ St-Dominique
AVE CAROTOLA
AVE ST-DOMINIQUE
Ste-Marie-Majeure ④
R DU SACREMENT
RUE DORIA
PLACE CASTELLETTO
RUE 5 VARSI
PL DU MARCHE
Chapelle St-Roch
Plage de Sutta Rocca

Escalier du Roi d'Aragon ⑦
RUE DES PACHAS
Grain de Sable

**Key to Symbols** *see back flap*

# Exploring Bonifacio

The heart of Bonifacio is the *haute ville* (upper town), which perches on the promontory high above the fjord-like inlet that forms Bonifacio's harbour. Bordered by Avenue Charles-de-Gaulle and the massive ramparts, this is the oldest section of the city. Around the cathedral, tall, narrow houses line the streets, the outer rows balancing dangerously on the cliff's edge. Further out on the promontory, west of the city walls, the wind-battered Bosco area stretches out towards the sea, offering panoramic views from the Esplanade St-François.

## 🏰 Porte de France

In addition to the Porte de Gênes, a second entrance to the *haute ville* was created in 1854, when the French Army Engineers' Corps built a road to the St-Nicolas fort. This new gate also featured a drawbridge. Within the city walls around the Porte de France, traces of the oldest quarters of Genoese Bonifacio can still be seen. These include the Fondaco, or staple (commercial ware-house), that once stood in the Place Montepagano area.

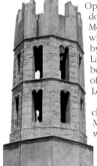

**The bell tower of St-Dominique**

## ⛪ St-Dominique

Haute Ville, near Place Birhakeim.
🕐 *Jul–Aug.*
Outside the city walls, but inside the fortifications that once protected the Pisan quarter, is this church dating from 1343. It stands on the site of an earlier Romanesque church, which was begun by the Pisans and finished by the Knights Templars. The present church was built by the Dominicans and, until the French Revolution, was part of a monastery complex.

The Gothic bell tower is unusual: its square base is surmounted by an octagonal section topped with battlements, and the white limestone façade is decorated with an ogival portal. Inside are groups of statues depicting Mary and the other holy women at the foot of the Cross and an image of St Bartholomew.

Opposite the church doorway are the Montlaur barracks, which were built by the Genoese. Later this building became the home of the Foreign Legion troops.

Next to the church is the Mairie (Town Hall), which is linked to St-Dominique by an arch that was once part of the old Dominican monastery.

## 🌿 Bosco

At the tip of Bonifacio's promontory is the Bosco area. Here there is a cemetery, with many small, light-coloured mortuary chapels. Near the edge, the structure of the St-Antoine battery was constructed in the period between the two World Wars. The position of the battery allowed complete control of the maritime traffic in the Straits of Bonifacio.

## 🏰 Escalier du Roi d'Aragon

Rue des Pachas. 🕐 *Apr–Oct.* 📷
On the west side of the headland, where the craggy cliff is at its most precipitous, this steep rock-cut stairway descends to sea level. According to legend, its 187 steps were hewn in only one night, during the Aragonese siege of 1420. It is, in fact, more likely that the stairway was built in a much earlier period and served as access to a well with good drinking water.

The Escalier could be clearly monitored from above, and was never used by any of the foreign troops that tried to storm Bonifacio.

**The impressive Escalier du Roi d'Aragon**

### THE TRINITE PROCESSIONS

When heading out of Bonifacio on the D196 road towards Sartène, after about 3 km (2 miles) there is a junction, the left branch of which leads to the Ermitage de la Trinité. A narrow road winds between two walls of maquis to the open space in front of this little church, which affords a magnificent view towards Bonifacio and the Anse de Paragnano. On 13 May (feast day of Our Lady of Fatima) and on 8 September *(see p34)*, the inhabitants of Bonifacio come here in procession, creating such a traffic jam that it is advisable to go to the Ermitage on foot. The small church dedicated to the Trinity contains offerings and vows left by people who survived dangerous trips in the Straits of Bonifacio during heavy storms.

**View from the hermitage**

# Parc Marin de Bonifacio

To preserve the coastal habitats of southern Corsica, the first marine reserves were established in the early 1980s. They now include the islands of Lavezzi, Bruzzi, Monaci and. Cerbicale. Underwater fishing was prohibited and rigorous regulations were applied even to professional fishermen. In 1986, the idea for an international marine park in the Straits of Bonifacio – the stretch of sea between Corsica and Sardinia – started to take shape. In 1992 the Italian and French ministers of ecology decided to work

**A yacht in the straits**

together for the park. Although they could not block shipping of loads that could cause damage in case of an accident, the authorities did restrict the limits of the navigable channel and set up an emergency plan that goes into effect whenever the wind, which is quite strong in this part of the sea, blows at more than 4 or 5 knots. Because the wind is never lacking here, the straits are a paradise for yachtsmen, whose boats can always be seen slicing through the frothy waves, often during a regatta.

### THE CORSICAN COAST
The French side of the Straits of Bonifacio has one of the best-known coasts in the Mediterranean, characterized by tall white cliffs in which layers of limestone are clearly visible. The profile is extremely jagged and the tiny coves squeezed between the craggy rocks can often be reached only by boat. One of the problems of the marine park is how to limit the damage to the environment caused by mass tourism.

**Red coral**, *according to popular legend, originated from the blood of Medusa after Perseus cut off her head and tossed it into the sea.*

**The sea anemone** *is an inhabitant of the coast of the straits. Although it seems to be an immobile plant, the sea anemone is an exceptional predator.*

**Lobsters**, *crustaceans with highly prized meat, find refuge in this area, where fishing is strictly regulated.*

### THE SARDINIAN COAST
On the other side of the Straits of Bonifacio, the Sardinian coastline is as jagged as Corsica's, but generally much lower, with beautiful sandy coves and colourful sea beds. Not far away to the east is the Maddalena archipelago, made up of seven main islands, including La Maddalena and Caprera, and several smaller islets, such as Isola Budelli, famous for its pink-sand beach.

# Bonifacio: the Coast and the Cliffs

Perched on its promontory, keeping guard over the
deep inlet below, the fortified city of Bonifacio owes
its charm and importance to the sea, fishing and
commerce. Only an exploration from beneath the
cliffs, at sea level, reveals all of Bonifacio's particular
beauty and the reason why it has been likened to a
ship carved out of rock. On the jetties of the Marina
many companies offer boat tours of the coastline as
far as the sea caves, the Grain de Sable and to the
open sea, skirting the headlands and coves that
lead to the Îles Lavezzi.

**The houses of Bonifacio on the
steep cliffs overlooking the sea**

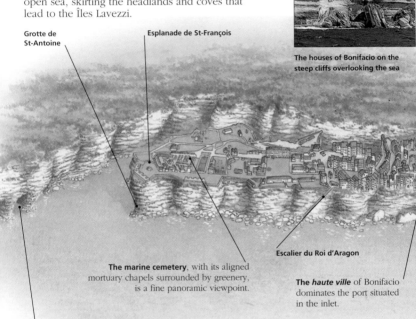

**Grotte de
St-Antoine**

**Esplanade de St-François**

**The marine cemetery**, with its aligned
mortuary chapels surrounded by greenery,
is a fine panoramic viewpoint.

**Escalier du Roi d'Aragon**

**The *haute ville*** of Bonifacio
dominates the port situated
in the inlet.

### Grotte du Sdragonatu
*Created by water erosion, this
sea cave is illuminated by the
sun, which penetrates through
a crack in the vault. The local
tourist guides claim that this
long, narrow opening resembles
the shape of Corsica.*

## A GEOLOGICAL ANOMALY

The coast around Bonifacio is made up of
a chalk outcrop that created the famous
cliffs. Extending as far as south as Capo
Pertusato and towards Pointe de Sperone,
these cliffs are friable sedimentary rocks
that over time have been sculpted by the
wind and sea to create this much-admired
craggy coastline. The presence of limestone here is
a geological
anomaly on an
island mostly
made up of
magmatic rocks,
in particular
granite (Col
de Bavella and
the Calanques
de Piana) and
volcanic rhyolite
(Scandola Nature
Reserve).

**Typical layers of
limestone in the cliffs**

### Grain de Sable
*This solitary stack, which now has the curious nickname of "grain of sand", broke off from the cliff 800 years ago. It is one of the most recognizable cliffs around Bonifacio.*

**VISITORS' CHECKLIST**

**Road map** C6. 2 Rue Fred Scamaroni, Bonifacio (04 95 73 11 88). Apr–Oct: excursions leave from the Marina of Bonifacio every 15 minutes for the sea caves and the Grain de Sable (duration: 1 hour). **www**.bonifacio.fr

### Capo Pertusato Lighthouse
*Clearly visible at night from the coast of Sardinia, this lighthouse was built on the southernmost point of Corsica.*

### Craggy Cliffs
*The cliffs near Bonifacio have many fine belvederes from which the beauty of this splendid coastline can be fully enjoyed. Among the birds that nest in this wild stretch are shags, herring gulls and the rare Andouin's gull.*

### Capo Pertusato
*Viewed from the sea, the southernmost point of Corsica appears quite rugged and shaped by the waves. A view from the land highlights a colossal cave carved out of the limestone. Capo Pertusato was named after this natural opening – in Genoese dialect, the language of the former rulers of Bonifacio, the word pertusato means "perforated".*

# Bonifacio: the Îles Lavezzi

Continuing along the coast after Capo Pertusato, the cliffs remain quite high, and the few beaches here can only be reached via steep paths. Past the Pointe de Sperone, the view opens on to the group of the Îles Lavezzi and Île Cavallo. This fascinating archipelago is made up of granitic-rock islands fringed by small sandy beaches. Inland, although the scenery appears to be extremely barren, there are plenty of endemic plant species. The Îles Lavezzi lie in the middle of a large marine reserve and mooring is strictly regulated. Today, there are about 20 people working here, including park wardens and marine biologists.

Aerial view of Île Cavallo, with its runway in the middle

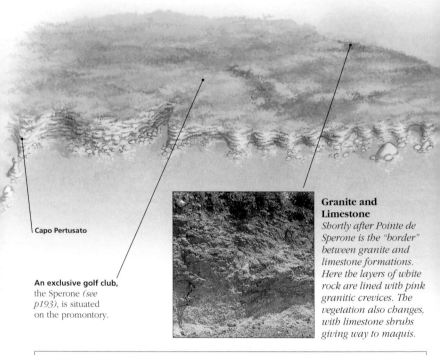

**Capo Pertusato**

**An exclusive golf club,** the Sperone *(see p193),* is situated on the promontory.

### Granite and Limestone
*Shortly after Pointe de Sperone is the "border" between granite and limestone formations. Here the layers of white rock are lined with pink granitic crevices. The vegetation also changes, with limestone shrubs giving way to maquis.*

---

## THE *SÉMILLANTE* SHIPWRECK

The Straits of Bonifacio have been the dramatic scene of many shipwrecks. One of the most famous was that of the *Sémillante,* a French frigate that set sail from Toulon in February 1855 with a crew of 301 to take 392 French soldiers to Crimea. On the night of 15 February a terrifying storm caused the ship, which was full of gunpowder, to explode on the rocks of Île Lavezzi. The *Sémillante* sank quickly and there were no survivors. The bodies found were buried in the two small cemeteries of Lavezzi. A year after the tragedy, a monument commemorating the victims of this shipwreck was built on one of the island's promontories.

The monument to the victims of the *Sémillante* shipwreck, on a promontory of Lavezzi

### Pointe de Sperone

*This wind-beaten, maquis-covered promontory is a perfect example of the untamed nature of this stretch of coast. Many sea birds nest and live here.*

### Île Cavallo

*This beautiful island is private property. Hidden among the rocks and low vegetation are luxury villas, and there is even a small airport. Mooring is forbidden along the entire coastline.*

**The islet of San Bainsu** was used by the ancient Romans as a granite quarry.

**Cormorants** and Corsican gulls find ideal nesting places among the rocks of Lavezzi.

**The flora on Lavezzi** includes endemic species, the presence of which is somewhat of a mystery. Some of these exist only here, in Australia and in South Africa.

### Île Lavezzi

*Like the rest of the archipelago, this island is a nature reserve. Little more than a rock, it is full of fascinating stone formations but also has a range of flora and fauna that is interesting from a scientific point of view.*

**The marina of Bonifacio, dominated by the massive Bastion de l'Étendard** ▷

# Tappa ❷

**Road map** C6. 🛈 *Rue Camille de Rocca Serra, Porto-Vecchio (04 95 70 09 58).* ⭕ *daily.*

The impressive *casteddu (see p39)* of Tappa stands about 7 km (4 miles) from Porto-Vecchio on the D859, in the village of Ceccia. This Neo-lithic settlement, which consists of fortified dwellings built around two gigantic structures, went through some difficult times in recent years, when it was treated as an open-air quarry. Tappa was saved from a worse fate by a private citizen who bought the land to protect it.

From above, the plan of the site reveals stretches of walls that were added to fortify the natural defence of the small settlement. On the basis of their finds, archaeologists have established that Tappa was already inhabited by the Torréens *(see p37)*, so called because of their tower structures, in the second millennium BC, which makes this one of the most ancient settlements in Corsica.

On the southwestern side of the settlement is a round, non-fortified monument dating from 1350 BC. Access was gained via a steep rock-cut stairway. A round cell in the interior was used to preserve foodstuffs and other valuable materials. Besides serving as a store-house, this monument was probably also used as a place of worship and as a watchtower.

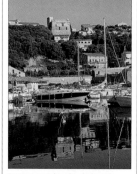

**Boats moored in the sheltered port of Porto-Vecchio**

# Porto-Vecchio ❸

**Road map** C6. 👥 *8,400.* 🚢 *from Genoa, Livorno, Marseille, 04 95 70 06 03.* 🛈 *Rue Camille de Rocca Serra (04 95 70 09 58).* **www**.ot-portovecchio.com

It was the Genoese governors of the Bank of St George *(see pp44–5)* who decided, in the early 16th century, to found Porto-Vecchio. Its function was to fill a long gap in the series of strongholds on the coastline between Bastia and Bonifacio. Porto-Vecchio was also known as the "City of Salt" after its most precious natural resource. However, due to its proximity to the marshes created by the Stabiacciu and Osu rivers, Porto-Vecchio was plagued by malaria for centuries.

Around 1553, the period of the revolt headed by Sampiero Corso *(see p45)*, Porto-Vecchio became a refuge for pirates;

then, until the mid-1900s, the town lived off the cork industry and the local salt works.

At the end of World War II, land reclamation stemmed the danger of malaria, paving the way for future development, such as tourism, commerce and small industries. Porto-Vecchio is now an important town, famous above all for the lovely beaches in its vicinity. In the upper part of town there are still traces of the Genoese fortifications and in the historic centre, in the summer, tourists flock to the many outdoor cafés and restaurants.

## Environs
Along the southern coast of the Golfe de Porto-Vecchio there is a series of very popular tourist resorts. Past the watershed that ends at **Punta di a Chiappa** are the famous white sand beaches of **Palombaggia** and **Santa Giulia** *(see p21)*, which face the Îles Cerbicale reserve.

**The beach at Palombaggia, south of Porto-Vecchio**

# Massif de l'Ospédale ❹

**Road map** C5.
🛈 *Rue Camille de Rocca Serra, Porto-Vecchio (04 95 70 09 58).*

Behind the town of Porto-Vecchio is a large wooded and rocky region that offers panoramic views of the sea and many fine footpaths.

The village of **Ospédale** lies 800 m (2,600 ft) above sea level, halfway up the mountain of the same name. It may owe its name (hospital) to the fact that, in the past, affluent Porto-Vecchio families used to come here to spend the hot season away from the unhealthy marshes.

The panorama from here includes a broad section of the coastline below.

**The ruins of the *casteddu* at Tappa, a prehistoric settlement**

**The artificial lake below the peaks of the Massif de l'Ospédale**

One of the recommended hikes starts from the hamlet of **Cartalavonu**, 4 km (2 miles) further up the hill, and leads to the 1,315-m (4,300-ft) high **A Vacca Morta** peak, which offers marvellous views.

Beyond Ospédale, a maritime pine forest spreads out, covering the entire massif and surrounding the artificial lake of Ospédale. The whole area is part of the Parc Naturel Régional *(see p99).*

## Araggio (Araghju) ❺

**Road map** C5. 🚹 *Rue Camille de Rocca Serra, Porto-Vecchio (04 95 70 09 58).* **www.**araggio.com

North of Porto-Vecchio, towards the interior and the hills, the small hamlet of Araggio is the departure point for a steep walkway leading to the nearby *casteddu (see p39).* This mule track is quite narrow and hard to climb, ascending without a break along a stony ridge. Then, suddenly, the loose stones and sheepfolds are interrupted by the light-coloured walls of a massive fortress standing on a rocky spur. The walls of the *casteddu* of Araggio are about 4 m (13 ft) high and 2 m (6 ft) thick. The megalithic complex inside the fortifications consists of a series of rooms that in prehistoric times (16th–12th centuries BC) served as living quarters, kitchen and storehouse for foodstuffs. Close-up these structures are reminiscent of the great prehistoric nuraghi complexes in Sardinia. From here there is a splendid view of the gulf and the countryside around Porto-Vecchio.

## Punta Fautea ❻

**Road map** D5. 🚌 *from Porto-Vecchio (in summer).* 🚹 *Solenzara (04 95 57 43 75).*

North of the low coastline of the gulf of Porto-Vecchio is the Cala Rossa promontory, which marks the beginning of a rocky stretch interspersed by a few beaches, including the beautiful **Plage de Pinarellu**.

About 20 km (12 miles) from Porto-Vecchio, towards Solenzara, is the turn-off for Punta Fautea. Here, not far from the main road, is a restored **Genoese watchtower** built in the late 16th century and partly destroyed by fire in 1650.

From here to Solenzara is the **Côte des Nacres**, a rocky coast with many coves, crystal-clear waters and fascinating sea floors. The name of this coast derives from the large triangular shells that can be found locally. They are as much as 50 cm (20 in) long and the inside is covered by a thin layer similar to mother-of-pearl (*nacre* in French).

**Mermaid mural at the port of Solenzara**

## Solenzara ❼

**Road map** D5. 🏘 *1,200.* 🚌 *from Porto-Vecchio.* 🚹 *04 95 57 43 75.*

What was once only a tiny hamlet at the mouth of the Solenzara torrent has become one the most lively and well-appointed tourist resorts in southeast Corsica. Solenzara has a port that can take in about 450 boats and a sandy beach bounded by eucalyptus trees. **Sari**, a tiny hamlet above Solenzara, overlooks the plain and is worth visiting for the splendid views of the Bavella.

**The restored ruins of the 16th-century Genoese watchtower at Punta Fautea**

# Col de Bavella **8**

A mouflon

The jagged pinnacles of the Aiguilles de Bavella make for one of the most thrilling landscapes in Corsica. This group of needle-shaped peaks lies at the foot of the Monte Incudine massif, which, at 2,134 m (7,001 ft), is the highest mountain range in south Corsica. The road going over the Col de Bavella passes through rocks that glow red at sunset, pine groves and meadows covered with thyme flowers in spring, and offers one of the most breathtaking views in Corsica. The area boasts many footpaths, including the southernmost stretch of the GR20 *(see pp22–7)* and the more demanding alpine route through the Aiguilles themselves.

One of the marvellous views from the Trou de la Bombe

**Laricio pines** are very tall. They often live for a considerable time; many are three or four centuries old and some have even reached the venerable age of 800 years. In the past the pine trunks were used to build ships.

**Calamint in Bloom**
*When spring arrives, the meadows lining the road and the footpaths take on the pink colour of calamint flowers, which bumblebees love for their abundant nectar.*

## THE TROU DE LA BOMBE

There are several holes *(tafoni, see p101)* created by wind erosion in the hard rocks of Corsica. Expertise in hiking or climbing is not necessary to get to the Trou de la Bombe, a hole about 9 m (30 ft) high at the Punta Tafonata di Paliri. The walk, which takes a couple of hours there and back, starts off from the U Canone fountain, a short distance beyond the Col de Bavella in the direction of Solenzara. From here a forest road, then a footpath with red markings lead to a rocky amphitheatre and then to the base of the huge *tafone*. From here the view of Monte Incudine and of the pines among the rock crevices is remarkable.

Approaching the Trou de la Bombe

### Aiguilles de Bavella

*The rugged needles of these peaks are a real favourite with hikers and rock climbers. Those with no head for heights can enjoy the spectacular beauty of the Aiguilles while travelling along the D268 road.*

**The Aiguilles massif is** the habitat of many species of birds of prey. Mouflons (called *muvrini* in the Corsican language) can also be spotted.

### Paths and Signs

*The many hiking itineraries in this area are all well marked. Easy-to-read wooden signs show the altitudes and distances of the hikes, while other markings painted on rocks or trees indicate the direction to take.*

**The shrubs** are a sign that the wooded area is ending to give way to alpine meadowlands.

### Inspiring Landscape

*The Bavella area has always been popular, even at the time when tourism was only for the privileged few. Edward Lear, the English artist and traveller, depicted the region in this 1870 watercolour called* Forest of Bavella, Corsica.

The village of Zonza; in the background, the famous profile of the Aiguilles de Bavella

## Zonza ❾

**Road map** C5. 🏛 *1,800.* 🚌 ℹ
*Office du Tourisme de l'Alta Rocca,*
*Place de la Mairie (04 95 78 56 33).*

In the middle of the Alta
Rocca region, among pine
and oak forests and high along
the course of the Asinao river,
is Zonza. During the summer
this small town, with the bulk
of the Aiguilles de Bavella in
the background, is a magnet
for those who love outdoor
activities. Along the main
street are shops selling guides
with descriptions of climbing,
rafting, trout fishing and hiking
itineraries. There are also many
associations of tourist guides.
   In 1953, the sultan
Mohammed V of Morocco
lived in Zonza in exile, but
the climate proved too harsh
for him, and he asked to be
transferred to L'Île Rousse
*(see p74),* on the north coast.

## Cascade Piscia di Gallo ❿

**Road map** C5. ℹ *Office du Tourisme*
*de l'Alta Rocca, Zonza (04 95 78 56 33).*

Although the Cascade Piscia
di Gallo can only be reached
on foot, it is possible to park
in the vicinity, near the top
of the D368 road leading
to the pass of the Massif
de l'Ospédale.
   After some streams is a
larger watercourse, where,
over time, the current has
sculpted large round pools,
commonly known as

**Marmitte dei Giganti**. Further
along the path, the river
suddenly rushes through a
narrow rock crevice, creating a
waterfall that is about 46 m
(150 ft) high. The best viewpoint for the Cascade Piscia
di Gallo can be reached by
following the path that goes
around the rocks and then
descends to the right. The
whole walk will take about 90
minutes to the viewpoint and
back and for a long stretch
consists of rocky terrain,
so suitable hiking boots or
robust shoes should be worn.

## Quenza ⓫

**Road map** C5. 🏛 *750.* 🚌
ℹ *Office du Tourisme de l'Alta*
*Rocca, Zonza (04 95 78 56 33).*

This village at the foot of the
ascent leading to the Col de
Bavella is surrounded by a
thick oak and chestnut forest.

The façade of the Chapelle de
Ste-Marie, just outside Quenza

Quenza has two churches,
**St-Georges**, in the village,
has a pulpit carved in the
form of a Moor's Head
supported by sea monsters.
The second church, the
Romanesque **Chapelle de
Ste-Marie**, was founded
around the year 1000 and
stands on the road to Aullène.

## Levie ⓬

**Road map** C5. 🏛 *2,200.* 🚌
ℹ *Office du Tourisme de l'Alta
Rocca, Zonza (04 95 78 56 33).*

The area around Levie, a
short distance from the
Aiguilles de Bavella, is one
of the most interesting
prehistoric zones in Corsica,
with many important sites
unearthed by digs.
   Levie also houses one of the
main archaeological museums
in Corsica. Recently moved to
a new and more modern
home, the **Musée Départemental de Levie** boasts the
famous *Dame de Bonifacio,*
the skeleton of an old woman
who was buried in 6570 BC.
It is the most ancient relic of
the island's past. The museum
also features a fascinating
display of cardial ware
(named after the decorative
patterns carved with the use
of the sharp edges of the
*Cardium* cockle shell; *see
p38*), skeletons of small
mammals and an ancestor
of the cow. The explanations
and descriptions given by
the museum staff are very
enlightening and offer a

**The ancestor of the cow at the Musée Départemental de Levie**

better understanding of the evolution of prehistoric civilization on the island.

**🏛 Musée Départemental de Levie**

Quartier Pracu. **Tel** 04 95 78 00 78. ⬜ call ahead of your visit for opening times. ⬤ public hols. 🖼

### Environs

About 8 km (5 miles) from Levie, across the deep Fiumicicoli river valley, is **Carbini**. It was in this small village that, around the end of the Middle Ages, the religious sect of the Giovannali was founded (1352) and thrived. Inspired by St John the Baptist and founded by Giovanni Martini, a Franciscan monk from Marseille, this cult found fertile ground in Carbini and then spread throughout the island. The meeting place of the followers was the Pisan Romanesque church of St-Jean-Baptiste, which was built in the 14th century. The church is flanked by a structure – still visible – thought to correspond to the foundations of an earlier church dedicated to San Quilico and destroyed during the tragic repression of the Giovannali. As a result of the 1362 crusade ordered by Pope Urban V against the "satanic heretics", the members of this sect were burned at the stake at the foot of the Monte Kyrie Eleison, the name of which (Greek for "Lord, have mercy") has a particularly poignant ring in this context.

# Cucuruzzu and Capula ❾

**Road map** C5. 🛈 *Maison d'Accueil des Sites Archéologiques, Office du Tourisme de l'Alta Rocca, Zonza (04 95 78 48 21).* ⬜ *Apr–Oct: daily. By request during the other months.* 🖼 🏠 🔓

The visit to the archaeological site of Cucuruzzu and the medieval castle of Capula is organized as a pleasant walk in the oak and chestnut forest on the plateau.

Right by the ticket office, where audio-guides are handed out, is the start of a mule track. The ruins of Cucuruzzu appear after a 15-minute walk. This *casteddu (see p39)*, with its wall, fireplaces, and inner stairway leading to the upper levels, dates from the second millennium BC. Digs carried out in the 1960s brought to light an entire citadel covering a surface area of 1,200 sq m (12,900 sq ft). Some of the enormous blocks that make up the citadel's walls weigh more than one tonne.

Once back on the trail, a short walk leads to the Chapelle San Lorenzo, which was built using stone blocks from an earlier church, the ruins of which can also be seen here.

A short distance above these are the ruins of the medieval castle of Capula, a Roman fortification that was destroyed in 1259 by Giudice della Rocca, who had been

**The bell tower at Carbini**

made count of Corsica by the Pisans. This site of Capula had already been inhabited in pre-historic times, as confirmed by the nearby menhir-statue of an armed prehistoric warrior (Capula I), which was unearthed during the course of archaeological digs.

# Ste-Lucie de Tallano ❿

**Road map** C5. 🚣 520. 🛈 *Office du Tourisme de l'Alta Rocca, Zonza (04 95 78 56 33).*

On the road descending west from the Alta Rocca plateau towards the Golfe de Valinco is the village of Ste-Lucie de Tallano, famous for its **Couvent St-François**, a monastery founded in 1492 by the local lord, Rinuccio della Rocca. St-François is being restored, call the tourist office for more information.

On the village square is the church of **Ste-Lucie**, which contains a beautiful Catalan-style altarpiece with Christ, St Peter and St Paul in the middle, and three small figures of saints below them. The altarpiece is attributed to the Master of Castelsardo, an artist from the late 15th to the early 16th centuries who probably came from the large Franciscan monastery of Castelsardo, in Sardinia. The church of Ste-Lucie also boasts a *Crucifixion*, which some art historians have attributed to the same artist.

**🏠 Ste-Lucie**
⬜ daily (call the tourist office for opening hours).

**View of the hamlet of Ste-Lucie de Tallano**

The austere grey houses of Sartène perched on the rocks

## Sartène ⑮

**Road map** C5. 🏘 3,600. 🚌
ℹ️ Cours Soeur Amélie (04 95 77 15 40). 🎭 Catenacciu Procession (Good Friday).

Prosper Merimée, who in the mid-1800s was the Inspector of Antiquities in Corsica, described Sartène as "the most Corsican of Corsican towns". Located in the middle of an area rich in prehistoric ruins, this town with a history of vendettas lies halfway up the hill in the valley of the Rizzanese river.

The old town has a maze of narrow streets lined with dark-coloured houses as well as many aristocratic mansions. The alleyways are often surmounted by arches and vaults.

On Good Friday evening, the Baroque church of **Ste-Marie**, in Place de la Libération, is the starting point for the Catenacciu Procession (see p32). One of the most ancient religious ceremonies in Corsica, it re-enacts the crucifixion walk to the Golgotha. The Catenacciu ("chained one") represents the Great Penitent. After spending two fasting days in isolation, he dons the traditional long red tunic and a hood covering his face while bearing the Cross and heavy chains through the streets. The White Penitent, who represents Simon of Cyrene, helps him carry the large oak cross, while behind them eight black-clad figures bear

the statue of the Dead Christ. A traditional chant, "Perdonu miu Diu" (Forgive me, Lord), accompanies the slowly moving procession, which comes to a halt back in front of the church where it started. After the blessing, the ceremony ends.

Sartène is also worth a visit for the **Musée de Préhistoire Corse et d'Archéologie**, which is similar to the one in Levie (see pp124–5) and features the long, ancient history of the island. The museum was renovated in 2009, and is now based in a larger, more modern building. Among the items on display, the cardial ware (see p38) is worth a look,

as are the obsidian arrowheads from Sardinia and the collection of funerary vases dating from the second and first millennia BC.

🏛 **Musée de Préhistoire Corse et d'Archéologie**
1 Rue Croce. **Tel** 04 95 77 01 09.
◯ Mon–Sat. 🖼 ♿

## Roccapina ⑯

**Road map** B6.

About 25 km (16 miles) south of Sartène, on the N196 road towards Bonifacio, a terrace on a hilltop affords a fine panoramic view of the Golfe de Roccapina and the Pointe de Roccapina promontory, with its characteristic pink granite rocks, which were inhabited in prehistoric times. One of these rocks, which is flanked by a massive Genoese tower, looks very much like a colossal crouching lion, hence the name **Le Lion de Roccapina**, or Lion's Rock.

**View of the Golfe de Roccapina**

### HANDMADE KNIVES

With their curved blades and handles that fit perfectly in the hand, knives have always been one of the shepherds' most indispensable work tools. Traditionally, the top of the blade also had a sawtoothed section and the handle was made of wood or goat's horn. Called *cursina* in the local language, this type of knife is now protected by a registered trademark and is still handmade by a dozen craftsmen. Their size and the ratio between the blade and handle have always been the same, but the artisans' creativity has led to the use of new materials. Thus, the blades are now made of damask steel and the handles range from white cedar to manta-ray skin. Corsican tradition has also produced the *runchetta*, a jackknife, and the *temperinu*, a small, pointed knife. Most famous of all is the *stiletto*, which, along with pistols, was part of the bandits' arsenal in the 19th century and is now sold as a souvenir, with the word "Vendetta" carved on it.

**Two cursine, typical knives**

# Tour of the Megaliths of Cauria ⑰

In the region of Sartène alone, after almost two centuries of archaeological research, no fewer than 500 prehistoric sites have been explored. According to the experts, the southern part of Corsica was much more densely populated than the north in prehistoric times. A tour of the barren plateau of Cauria, south of Sartène, allows the chance to visit some of the island's most important sites with megalithic monuments *(see p39)*, which here are in the form of alignments. Although it is not easy to reach Palaggiu, it is worth the effort, because this is one of the most important menhir alignments in the world.

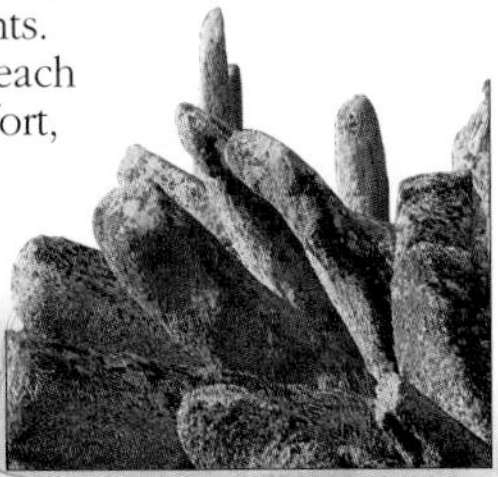

**TIPS FOR DRIVERS**

ℹ️ *Cours Soeur Amélie, Sartène (04 95 77 15 40).*
**Length of tour**: *from Sartène to Palaggiu, ca 15 km (9 miles); from D48-A turn-off to Stantari, ca 5 km (3 miles).* **Duration**: *1 day.* **Stopping-off points**: *Sartène and Tizzano.*

**Palaggiu** ①
With its 258 menhirs, discovered in the late 1800s, Palaggiu is an amazing sight. About 5 km (3 miles) after the Cauria turn-off on the D48 road, on the right is a mule track marked by a metal gate. A 20-minute walk leads to the "stone forest".

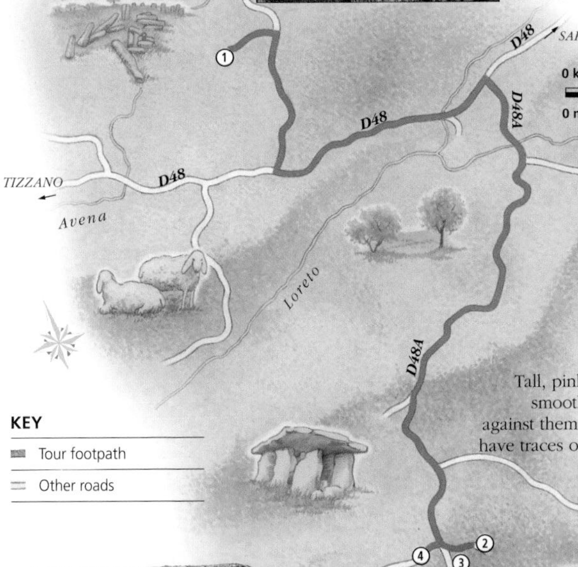

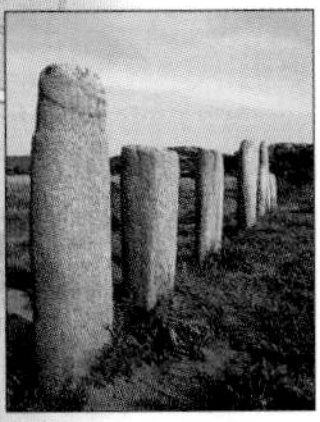

0 kilometres 1
0 miles 0.5

**Stantari** ②
Tall, pink at sunset and made smooth by animals rubbing against them, the Stantari menhirs have traces of faces and weapons.

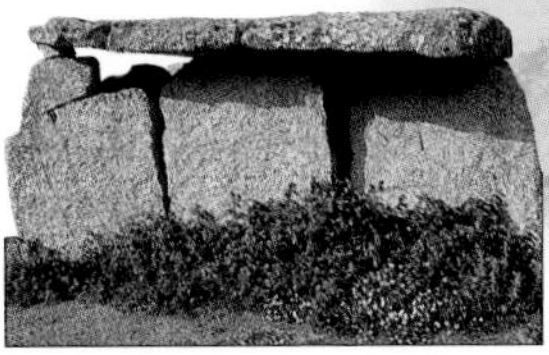

*Chiusu di a casa*

**KEY**

▨ Tour footpath

═ Other roads

**Fontanaccia** ④
Discovered in 1840 by Prosper Merimée, then Inspector of Antiquities in Corsica, this is the island's best-preserved dolmen. It stands about 100 m (320 ft) from the parking area.

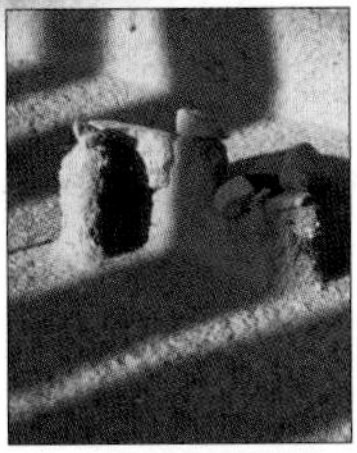

**Renaghju** ③
Here is the most ancient Neolithic settlement in Corsica, with two alignments of menhirs. The most ancient ones date from 4000 BC; around their bases are remains of round fireplaces.

The tranquil bay of Campomoro, with its crystal-clear sea

## Campomoro ⑱

**Road map** B5. 🏛 *260.* 🛈 *Quai St-Erasme, Propriano (04 95 76 01 49).* **Tour de Campomoro** ◯ *Apr–Nov: daily.* 🖼

Situated on the south coast of the Golfe de Valinco, the small village of Campomoro is a peaceful place to relax, even during the tourist season.

A ten-minute walk along a well-marked path dotted with informative signs leads to the door of the **Tour de Campomoro**, built in the 16th century by the Genoese. This fortress, the largest in Corsica, allows visitors to explore the interior of a typical defensive tower and offers magnificent views of the gulf.

Experienced hikers can also explore another splendid coastal path that runs south from Campomoro to Tizzano.

The round Genoese tower at Campomoro

## Propriano ⑲

**Road map** B5. 🏛 *3,500.* 🛲 🛈 *Quai St-Erasme (04 95 76 01 49).* **www**.propriano.net

The town of Propriano lies at the innermost point of the Golfe de Valinco, tucked in between the green hills behind it and the transparent blue sea. It is an attractive and popular yacht harbour and seaside resort thanks to the beautiful beaches and coves dotting the gulf.

Because of its strategic position, Propriano was much sought after throughout its history. In ancient times it developed as a famous port, and as a landing place and trade centre for Etruscans, Greeks, Carthaginians and Romans, especially in the 2nd century BC. In the 1980s, while restructuring work was being carried out on the port, numerous remains from this period were found.

During the Middle Ages Propriano was governed first by the Pisans and, then, from 1230 onwards, by the Genoese. In 1563 Sampiero Corso (*see p45*) landed here and initiated a period of anti-Genoa revolts. His actions, however, proved to be disastrous for Propriano, because the village was then left at the mercy of pirate raids and virtually destroyed. The same period also saw the demise of the beautiful Santa Giulia di Tavaria abbey, mentioned in chronicles but now in ruins.

In the 19th century Propriano came to life again, becoming a commercial port for the entire region, a role consolidated in the early 20th century.

Now the village is a lively tourist locality.

The beautiful beaches and well-developed facilities make it one of the leading resorts on the island.

### Environs

About 9 km (6 miles) from Propriano, going northwest on the N196 road, is **Olmeto**, a large hamlet 870 m (2,850 ft) above sea level that dominates the gulf. Just above the village are the ruins of the **Castello della Rocca**, the fortress that Arrigo della Rocca used as a base when he began his rebellion against the Genoese rulers. In 1376–90, he governed the entire island, leaving only Bonifacio and Calvi to the foreign invaders.

The white lighthouse at Propriano looming over the sea

## Porto-Pollo ⑳

**Road map** B5. 🏛 *340.* 🛲 🛈 *Office du Tourisme de Sollacaro (04 95 74 07 64).*

At the mouth of the Taravo river, Porto-Pollo is a small seaside resort. During the summer it is popular with people who are attracted by the tranquillity of the place and its delightful beach along the Golfe de Valinco.

Not far from the village, on top of the Pointe de Porto-Pollo, is the Genoese **Tour de Capriona**.

The sea and sea bed along the promontory are very popular with scuba divers, who love to dive down to the so-called *cathédrales*, rocky pinnacles at a depth of about 10 m (32 ft).

# Filitosa ㉑

**Road map** B5. **i** *Office du Tourisme de Sollacaro (04 95 74 07 64).* ◯ *Apr–Oct: daily; Nov–Mar: by appointment (04 95 74 00 91).* 🏛 📷 www.filitosa.fr

The most famous prehistoric site in Corsica is managed with great care by the heirs of Charles-Antoine Cesari, who made the first discoveries here in 1946.

Filitosa offers almost 5,000 years of history. Populated in very ancient times because it was both fertile and easy to defend, the area was filled with large constructions and menhirs from 1800 BC to 1100 BC. The fortified town dominated the valley of the small Taravo river. It was here, among the stones of one of the structure's walls, that one of the most significant alignments of

**The front of Filitosa V**

anthropomorphic menhirs *(see below)* was found. Details of the faces, weapons and helmets of ancient warriors are still clearly visible on the surface of these rocks.

Most of the ruins of Filitosa date from between the late second millennium BC and 700 BC. With the rise of Christianity, the menhirs were considered pagan and therefore destroyed. Their remains were heaped together in piles, like mere stones, and had to wait many centuries to be rediscovered.

The tour of Filitosa begins with a splendid statue (Filitosa V) standing on the track that leads to the fortified settlement, also known as *oppidum*. Here are the ruins of a village and three monuments, the middle one

**Detail of the central monument**

of which is well preserved. Below, in a small valley, is the quarry where the stone for the sculpture was extracted. Some statues found in the surroundings have been placed around the quarry.

Next to the entrance to the site is a small museum that illustrates the history of the site. It displays fragments of three menhir statues, the most famous of which is the Scalsa Murta menhir (1400 BC). Armour and weapons can be seen on these menhirs, as well as holes on the upper part of the head, probably where ornamental ox horns were placed.

---

## THE EVOLUTION OF THE ANTHROPOMORPHIC MENHIRS

Megalithic monuments, used to worship the dead in the Neolithic era (6000–2000 BC), were found on five Mediterranean islands: Corsica, Sardinia, Malta, Majorca and Minorca.

The Corsican megalithic culture (3500–1000 BC) is divided into three periods – Megalithic I, II and III – which show an evolution in burial practices. The early subterranean tombs on mounds of earth sealed with long stone slabs were replaced by outdoor monuments known as dolmens, consisting of horizontal monoliths representing the souls of the deceased.

In the Megalithic III period, which, in turn, is divided into six stages, the horizontal

monolith becomes a vertical anthropomorphic statue, that is, one resembling a human.

These statues have different features, depending on the populations that sculpted them. In the period of invasions, for example, they were armed, but later they became plain again. Near the end of Megalithic III the so-called Torréens *(see p37)* settled in Corsica, introducing tower-like structures. Over time these towers replaced the anthropomorphic statues.

**The front of Filitosa IV**

---

**Statues of Stages 5 and 6 of the Megalithic III period.** *The statues seen below are among the most famous in Corsica. They were named after the localities in which they were discovered; their numbers indicate that more than one statue was found on the same site.*

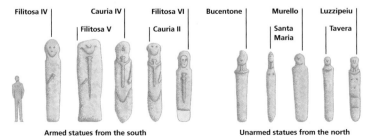

| Filitosa IV | Cauria IV | Filitosa VI | Bucentone | Murello | Luzzipeiu |
|---|---|---|---|---|---|
| | Filitosa V | Cauria II | | Santa Maria | Tavera |

**Armed statues from the south**      **Unarmed statues from the north**

# CORTE AND THE INTERIOR

T*he ancient Romans who conquered Corsica in 259 BC were aware of the strategic importance of Corte as the geographical heart of the island. Originally a fortress, the city soon became the symbol of all Corsica and its struggle for independence, the home of the island's parliament, university and national heroes. Corte is also the starting point for excursions into the valleys in the interior.*

The colours of the sea, the jagged coastline and the iridescent sea beds are perhaps the best-known features of Corsica. But also deserving of a visit are the mountains inland, which, with Monte Cinto, reach a height of 2,706 m (8,877 ft). Traversed by valleys and paths leading to refuges, in the summer the mountains are ideal for a wide range of hiking excursions.

In the middle of this natural setting made up of rocks, spring waters and forests, lies Corte. The town's fortunate geographic location meant that on several occasions potential conquerors, including the Romans, had to stop short of this region. In the 18th century, Corsica's first National Constitution was drafted here and ever since then Corte has been the symbol of the island, of its culture and yearning for independence. From its Citadelle, which is the home of the Musée de la Corse, there are commanding views of the surrounding territory. To the west are the wildest valleys and tallest peaks; to the east are hills covered with woods, small villages and remains of the past. These hills descend towards the sea of Aléria, the first Roman colony in Corsica. The regions of Bozio, Fiumorbo and Castagniccia (named after its rich chestnut groves) have a series of chapels and churches that bear witness to various artistic styles and that reach in the Romanesque church of La Canonica and the Baroque church of La Porta the apogee of Corsican religious tradition.

Fresco decoration in the small church of San Pantaleo, Castagniccia

◁ Punta Larghia, one of the peaks in the Haut-Asco area

# Exploring Corte and the Interior

Corte is the geographic heart of Corsica, as well as
its cultural centre. The city is skirted by a region of
tall, rugged mountains forming the very backbone of
the island: Monte Rotondo, Monte d'Oro and Monte
Renoso stand southwest of Corte, while Monte Cinto
and Capo Tafonato are northwest of the city. To the
northeast, descending towards the coast, are the hilly
regions of Bozio and Castagniccia, where, from the
period of Genoese domination (late 12th century)
onwards, the less harsh terrain favoured the birth of
many small villages. The area surrounding Corte is
also known for its gastronomy, which includes
game, wild boar and traditional cheeses.

**KEY**

━━ Major road

═══ Minor road

− − Hiking trail

━━ Scenic route

━━ Railway

△ Summit

✕ Mountain pass

Soveria, a village in the vicinity of Corte, with a
view of the magnificent mountains in the background

## GETTING AROUND

Corte lies on the N193 road, which, coming from Ajaccio,
crosses the Col de Vizzavona in the inland valleys. North
of Corte, at Ponte Leccia, the N193 divides, going either
northeast in the direction of Bastia (N193) or north to
L'Île Rousse and Calvi (N1197 and N197). Other roads
branch off from this main artery, traversing the splendid
side valleys both west, towards the mountains, and east,
towards Bozio and Castagniccia. An enjoyable way to
travel to Corte from Bastia or Ajaccio is to take the small
train – jokingly called the TGV, or Train of Great Vibrations –
which stops at almost all the stations along the way.

### SEE ALSO

- **Where to Stay** p165
- **Where to Eat** p179

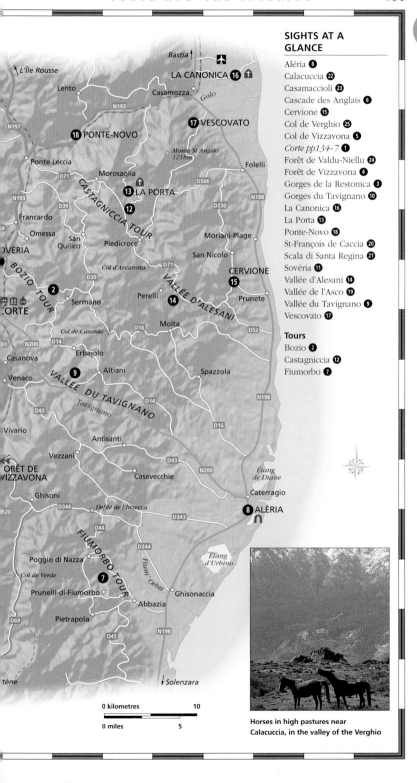

**Horses in high pastures near Calacuccia, in the valley of the Verghio**

# Corte ❶

Located in the heart of Corsica, Corte was fortified in 1419 by the viceroy of Aragón, Vincentello d'Istria. Later, it was ruled intermittently by the Genoese and the French. In 1735 it became the cradle of Corsican patriotism when the constitution for an independent state was drafted here. In 1755, when Corsica was liberated by Pascal Paoli, Corte became its capital. Ten years later Paoli founded the island's first university here.

Corte still maintains a proud spirit of nationalism. It is part of the city's charm and can be discovered through a walk in the old town and a tour of the Citadelle. The latter, the symbol of the military power of past ages, is now home to the Musée de la Corse, one of the leading centres of Corsican culture. A hike to the Belvedere overlooking the Gorges du Tavignano and the Gorges de la Restonica reveals the natural beauty of the area.

**The nave in the Église de l'Annonciation**

**Place Gaffori and the monument to the hero of the taking of Corte**

## 🏛 Place Paoli

At the foot of the upper city (*haute ville*) is a large and lively square named after Pascal Paoli *(see p47)*. Laid out in the early 20th century by Huguenin, the centre of the square features a large monument to the patriot and hero of Corsican independence.

## 🏛 Place Gaffori

West of Place Paoli are the ramps of Rue Scoliscia, which lead to the heart of the city and Place Gaffori. In the middle of this square is the statue commemorating General Jean-Pierre Gaffori. On the pedestal are two bas-reliefs depicting his feats and those of his brave wife Faustina *(see p46)*. Also on the square is the Église de l'Annonciation and the house where Gaffori was born.

## 🔒 Église de l'Annonciation

Place Gaffori. ☐ *Mon–Sat.*
Founded around the mid-15th century, this church is one of the oldest buildings in Corte. However, the façade as it stands today dates from the 18th century. Commissioned by Alexandre Sauli, who later became bishop of Aléria, it has five pilasters with Corinthian capitals. The tall, slender bell tower that dominates the entire quarter is Baroque. Inside the church is a series of Baroque statues and an altar made of the local grey marble.

A short, steep descent along Rue Feracci leads to a pretty Baroque mansion known as Maison Palazzi.

## 🔒 Chapelle Ste-Croix

Rampe Ste-Croix. ☐ *Mon–Sat.*
Past the Maison Palazzi is the austere façade of the 17th-century church of Ste-Croix. The pillarless nave has a barrel vault and an aisle paved in grey marble. By the altar is a colourful Baroque retable and a large medallion with a relief of the *Madonna of the Apocalypse*.

This church is also the home of the Ste-Croix Confraternity, which has always played a leading role in the religious life of the city.

### JEAN-PIERRE GAFFORI

The hero of the Corsican independence movement along with Pascal Paoli, Jean-Pierre Gaffori was born in 1704 in Corte and studied medicine. In 1745, during the armed revolt against the Genoese occupation, he was elected as one of the triumvirate of the "Protectors of the Nation". One of his exploits was the taking of Corte in 1746.

According to local lore, during the battle against the Genoese troops, Gaffori realized that his enemies were using one of his sons as a shield. He was uncertain about what to do, but his courageous wife Faustina urged the Corsican patriots to continue attacking, allegedly shouting: "Don't think about my son, think about your country!" Made a general, Gaffori managed to conquer most of the island but was assassinated in an ambush organized by his brother, who was in the service of the Genoese. In the square named after him is his statue, and on the façade of his house, opposite the Église de l'Annonciation, there are still marks of the shots fired by the Genoese during the 1746 siege of Corte.

**Statue of Jean-Pierre Gaffori**

**Fontaine des Quatre-Canons**

A short descent along a ramp in front of the church leads to the square and the Fontaine des Quatre-Canons.

#### Fontaine des Quatre-Canons
Place des Quatre-Canons.
Commissioned by Louis XVI, this fountain ("of the four cannons") was completed in 1778. Its purpose was to channel water from the Orta torrent to the city to furnish the local garrison with a sorely needed supply of water. From the square

ramps go up to the massive walls of the Citadelle *(see pp136–7)*.

#### Place du Poilu
In front of the entrance to the bastions of the Citadelle is Place du Poilu, with the house where General Arrighi di Casanova, one of Napoleon Bonaparte's generals, was born. It was here that Napoleon's father lived and that his brother Joseph, who was to become king of Spain, was born in 1768.

The 17th-century **Palais National**, once the residence of the Genoese governors and then of Pascal Paoli, is where Corsican independence was declared. For 14 years (1755–69, *see pp46–7*) this palace was the home of the new Corsican parliament. It now houses the University Institute of Corsican Studies, a separate branch of the University of Corte, which is based in the Citadelle.

**Plaque on the house where Joseph Bonaparte was born**

**VISITORS' CHECKLIST**

Road map C3. 🏠 5,700.
🚌 🚉 04 95 46 00 97. 🛈
*Station Touristique de l'Intérieur, Citadelle (04 95 46 26 70).* 🎭
*Easter Procession (Thu–Good Fri); St Theophilus's Procession (19 May); Festival des Arts Sonnés (second weekend in May); Ballu in Corti (Aug).* 🛒 *Friday.*
**www**.corte-tourisme.com

#### Belvedere
Before visiting the Citadelle, it is worth making time for a walk along the uphill road that skirts its walls. This road leads to the platform of the Belvedere, which offers a magnificent view of the castle, the Nid d'Aigle ("eagle's nest") tower and, below this, the city and the confluence of the Tavignano and Restonica rivers.

From the Belvedere a steep path leads to the banks of the Tavignano river. The reward for making this trek is an impressive panoramic view over the rocky cliffs of the Citadelle.

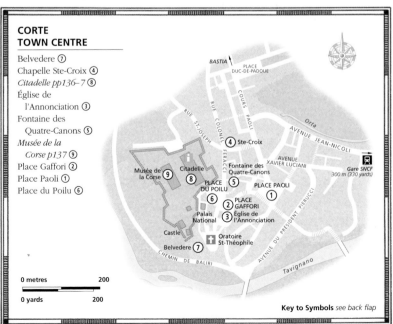

**CORTE TOWN CENTRE**

Belvedere ⑦
Chapelle Ste-Croix ④
*Citadelle pp136–7* ⑧
Église de l'Annonciation ③
Fontaine des Quatre-Canons ⑤
*Musée de la Corse p137* ⑨
Place Gaffori ②
Place Paoli ①
Place du Poilu ⑥

0 metres          200
0 yards           200

**Key to Symbols** *see back flap*

# Corte: the Citadelle

Aleady fortified before the Genoese conquest in the 13th century, the Citadelle was transformed into a true fortress in 1419. After many years of foreign rule, the Citadelle became the symbol of the islanders' struggle for independence, especially when Pascal Paoli established Corsica's first university here. When the French took control of Corsica in 1769, the Citadelle became a military zone. Today it houses the tourist office, a museum, an art institute and many historic archives, located on the lower level. On the upper level is the castle, with the Nid d'Aigle, the tallest tower, overlooking the Restonica and Tavignano valleys. Restoration projects have included the preservation of battlements perched high on the western part of the citadelle.

**★ Castle**
*Built in 1419 on the southern tip of the rocky spur by Vincentello d'Istria, the castle is the oldest part of the Citadelle.*

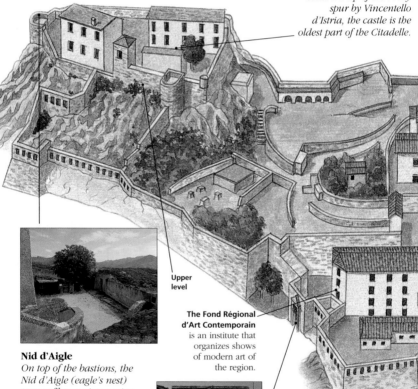

**Upper
level**

**The Fond Régional
d'Art Contemporain**
is an institute that organizes shows of modern art of the region.

**Nid d'Aigle**
*On top of the bastions, the Nid d'Aigle (eagle's nest) tower offers an impressive view of the precipitous walls of the Citadelle.*

**Entrance to
the Citadelle**
*Austere and fortified, as befits a military structure, the entrance portal to the Citadelle is a simple arch surmounted by a tympanum.*

### STAR SIGHTS

★ Musée de la Corse

★ Castle

**Panorama of the Citadelle**
*Perched on a huge rock, the Citadelle can be seen from Corte and the surrounding area. Many people consider it one of the symbols of Corsica.*

**VISITORS' CHECKLIST**

**Musée de la Corse & Citadelle**
**Tel** 04 95 45 25 45. ◯ Tue–Sun (mid-Jun–mid-Sep: daily; Nov–Mar: Tue–Sat). ◐ 1st 2 weeks Jan, 1 May, 24 Dec & pub hols. ◻◻ ◻◻ ◻ ◻ ◻ **Fond Régional d'Art Contemporain Tel** 04 95 46 22 18. ◯ Mon–Fri pm only.
**www**.musee-corse.com

## EXPLORING THE MUSEE DE LA CORSE

*This museum houses a fine anthropological collection, the core of which consists of the objects gathered from the 1950s onwards by abbot Louis Doazan. On display are various relics of the island's past, from the costumes of the confraternities of Corte, Bonifacio and other towns, to farmers' work tools. An interesting feature are the booths where visitors can listen to the traditional religious and secular music of the region. The first floor hosts temporary exhibits, and the museum also organizes concerts of traditional Corsican music here. The Nid d'Aigle tower and its spectacular views can be reached by a short walk after exiting through the first-floor doors.*

**Entrance to Musée de la Corse**
*Entrance to the museum is through a slim gap in the Citadelle bastions.*

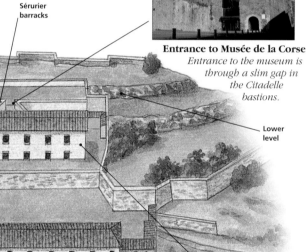

Sérurier barracks

Lower level

★ **Musée de la Corse**
*The exhibition rooms are in the former Sérurier barracks, once used by the Foreign Legion.*

**The bastions** are in keeping with late 18th-century military architecture. The large casemates and terracing accommodated pieces of artillery that made the Citadelle virtually impregnable.

**Padoue barracks**

# A Tour of Bozio ❷

The hilly regions of Bozio and Castagniccia (*see pp146–7*), respectively east and northeast of the town of Corte, have many surprises in store for art lovers. Do not expect grandiose basilicas or majestic bell towers, however. The art in these areas consists of a series of chapels – sometimes in a tiny hamlet, sometimes in open countryside – that require a degree of patience to find, and just as much patience to track down the person with the keys (who is always quite courteous). The Bozio tourist office organizes tours of the chapels with frescoes in the area, many of which benefited from restoration work during 2005 to 2010. The regions east of Corte are worth exploring for their natural landscape, which features hills, gorges and winding valleys. The constant curves and hairpin turns make the average speed on these roads extremely low. However, they do offer beautiful views.

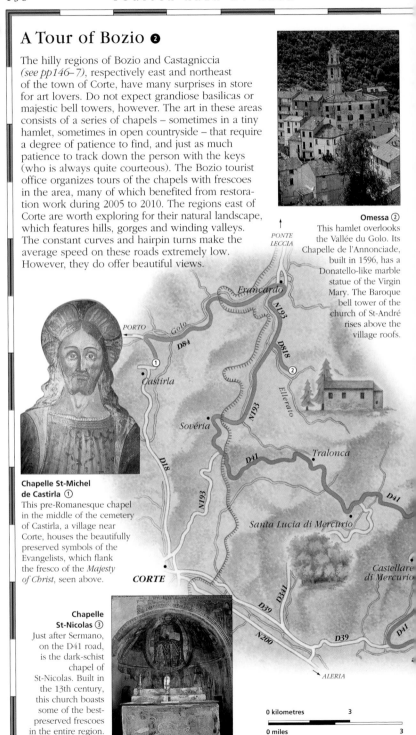

**Omessa** ②
This hamlet overlooks the Vallée du Golo. Its Chapelle de l'Annonciade, built in 1596, has a Donatello-like marble statue of the Virgin Mary. The Baroque bell tower of the church of St-André rises above the village roofs.

**Chapelle St-Michel de Castirla** ①
This pre-Romanesque chapel in the middle of the cemetery of Castirla, a village near Corte, houses the beautifully preserved symbols of the Evangelists, which flank the fresco of the *Majesty of Christ*, seen above.

**Chapelle St-Nicolas** ③
Just after Sermano, on the D41 road, is the dark-schist chapel of St-Nicolas. Built in the 13th century, this church boasts some of the best-preserved frescoes in the entire region.

PONTE LECCIA

Francardo

PORTO

Golo

D84

Castirla

Sovéria

Tralonca

Santa Lucia di Mercurio

Castellare di Mercurio

CORTE

ALERIA

0 kilometres          3

0 miles          3

**Chapelle Ste-Marie** ④
Near Favalello, on a curve along the road, is this tiny chapel, which is usually open on Wednesdays. Its noteworthy frescoes reflect the faith of the Corsican artists who lived five centuries ago.

**KEY**

▬ Tour route

═ Other roads

# Gorges de la Restonica ❸

**Road map** C3. 🚌 *Bus across the length of the valley (Jul–Aug); at these times the last stretch of the D623 might be closed to private cars due to congestion.* ℹ️ *Station Touristique de l'Intérieur, Citadelle, Corte (04 95 46 26 70).*
**Tuani Camping** *Tel 04 95 46 11 65.*

The narrow valley that descends from the seven lakes of Monte Rotondo *(see p24)* towards Corte lies between steep slopes, creating a series of awesome gorges. Despite the terrible fires that, in 2000, damaged the centuries-old forest covering its slopes, this fascinating valley is still very popular among hikers who, from spring onwards, look for relief from the heat along the pebbled shores of the torrent.

After leaving Corte, the Restonica road (D623) goes past the small Hotel Dominique Colonna and up the hills. For certain stretches the gorge becomes deep and seems to be hewn out of the rock. After about 14 km (9 miles) are the Bergeries de Grottelle, which lie 1,375 m (4,511 ft) above sea level. These typical stone-hut complexes house shepherds and sheep in the summer. This is where the motorable road ends and there are some kiosks open in spring and summer. From the Bergeries de Grottelle, a steep path goes over a rocky crest. Here the hardest stretches have metal ladders;

*A Vanessa butterfly, typical of this zone*

**The Restonica, flowing quickly down through the rocks**

should it rain, be careful of the slippery rocks. After about an hour's walk is the first of the small lakes in this area, the Lac de Mélo, at an altitude of 1,711 m (5,613 ft). From the shore of the lake the views encompass the surrounding mountains and the Vallée de la Restonica. Further along the path, at 1,930 m (6,331 ft), is the Lac du Capitellu, a glacial lake surrounded by steep cliffs.

At an altitude of about 2,000 m (6,500 ft), where the forest ends, the landscape is open and impressive: to the left is the 2,622-m (8,602-ft) high Monte Rotondo, and to the right the crest of Capo Chiostro, which reaches 2,295 m (7,529 ft).

The two sides of the valley have many paths leading to lakes and *bergeries*. In summer it is possible to stay at the Tuani camp site, renowned for its delicious pizzas, midway along the D623.

**A breathtaking view of the Gorges de la Restonica**

**One of the many swiftly flowing torrents of inland Corsica** ▷

**Panoramic view of the large Forêt de Vizzavona**

## Forêt de Vizzavona ❹

**Road map** C4. 🚉 *Vizzavona.* 🚌
ℹ️ *Station Touristique de l'Intérieur, Citadelle, Corte (04 95 46 26 70).*

Of all the forests in the large green heart of the island, the Forêt de Vizzavona is one of the most famous and popular. This partly depends on the fact that the area is traversed by the GR20 long-distance path *(see p25)*, and in spring and summer groups of hikers disembark at the small railway station of Vizzavona, 3 km (2 miles) away.

The forest is the home of hazelnut and chestnut trees as well as Corsican pines and other conifers. Ask at the tourist office about local environmental events.

The Forêt de Vizzavona is also crossed by the N193 road linking Ajaccio and Bastia and by the railway line inaugurated in 1894.

## Col de Vizzavona ❺

**Road map** C4. 🚉 *Vizzavona.* 🚌
ℹ️ *Station Touristique de l'Intérieur, Citadelle, Corte (04 95 46 26 70).*

The road linking Bastia and Ajaccio (the N193, one of the main roads on the island) crosses Corsica's inland mountain ranges at the pass of Col de Vizzavona. This mountain, at an altitude of 1,161 m (3,809 ft), marks

the border between Haute-Corse and Corse-du-Sud *(see p49)*. The pass has tables and benches for a stopoff and picnic and is populated by wild pigs that are not disturbed by visitors.

From Col de Vizzavona, which is often quite windy, there is a fine view of the impressive silhouette of the 2,389-m (7,838-ft) high Monte d'Oro.

An easy, uphill path leading north off the N193 road to Bastia stretches for about 400 m (1,300 ft) to the ruins of a Genoese fortification. Many other footpaths cross this area, including the GR20 long-distance path *(see pp22–7)*.

**Delicious hazelnuts**

## Cascade des Anglais ❻

**Road map** C4. 🚉 *Vizzavona.* 🚌
ℹ️ *Station Touristique de l'Intérieur, Citadelle, Corte (04 95 46 26 70).*

One of the most popular walks in this area is the hike along the GR20 long-distance path *(see pp22–7)*, which goes from the road near the hamlet of La Foce to the Cascade des Anglais "waterfall of the English"), a beauty spot much admired by early English visitors to this area. This trip, which is on an easy and well-marked path, takes less than two hours up and back, and follows the course of the Agnone torrent.

Beyond the Cascade des Anglais, which stands 1,100 m (3,600 ft) above sea level, the water has carved a series of deep potholes that are ideal for a swim.

In fair weather, and with adequate equipment, it is possible to continue up to the head of the valley towards the summit of Monte d'Oro. However, this is a strenuous hike of around 7–8 hours from Vizzavona and is only recommended for fit and experienced hill walkers.

The summit of Monte d'Oro overlooks all the main Corsican peaks and from there it is even possible to see the Italian coast.

---

### THE GENOESE BRIDGES

The architectural works that the Genoese bequeathed to the island of Corsica comprise not only buildings, squares, citadels and watchtowers *(see pp29 and 93)*, but also a great many bridges. Over the centuries, these have facilitated communications with the interior, which is traversed by numerous watercourses that more often than not are quite swift. Many of these bridges, which were built from 1284 onwards, are intact and still in use today. They are made of dry-stone, have a single arch and are never more than 20 m (65 ft) long. The bridges are usually supported by two piers that are often reinforced with corner brackets on the upper part; there may be circular openings on the sides of the arch to let the water pass through in case of a flood. Originally quite simple, the bridges began to be decorated only after the Renaissance.

**The Genoese bridge in the Vallée de l'Asco**

# Tour of the Fiumorbo ❼

This area is named after the Fium'Orbu ("blind river" in Corsican). The river starts from the slopes of Monte Renoso and winds its way down through the deep Strette and Inzecca gorges to the east coast, a short distance south of the archaeological site of Aléria. This wild region was one of the last in Corsica to agree to abide by French law, and tales of the battles between the French army and the locals have become legendary. The small villages have not changed much in the last two centuries and are not famous tourist attractions, but a tour of the rugged scenery and isolated hamlets is certainly worthwhile.

## TIPS FOR DRIVERS

ℹ️ *Route Nationale 198, Ghisonaccia (04 95 56 12 38).*
**Length of tour**: *90 km (56 miles).*
**Duration**: *one or two days, depending on the stops.*
**Stopping-off points**: *in the villages.*

**Auberge Vecchia Mina ⑤**
A short distance from Ghisoni is this charming little hotel. To its left is a path that descends towards Ponte a Mela, a lovely Genoese bridge.

**Defilé de l'Inzecca ④**
The D344 road, going from the coast to the village of Ghisoni, crosses the narrow gorge known as Defilé de l'Inzecca, followed by Lac de Sampolo and the Defilé des Strette.

**Pietrapola ②**
Near the village of Pietrapola are the hot springs that were frequented by the ancient Romans who lived in Aléria. They are still in use today.

**Prunelli-di-Fiumorbo ③**
The main village in this region is dominated by an austere fortified church. From here there is a great view of the region and the coast.

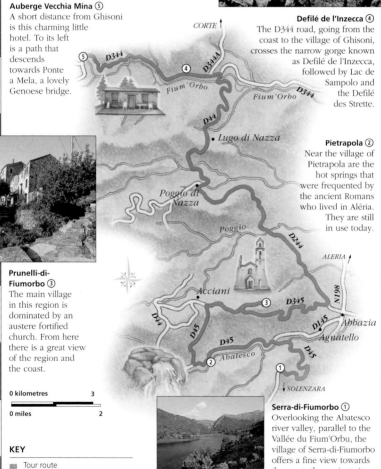

0 kilometres    3

0 miles    2

## KEY

▨ Tour route

═ Other roads

**Serra-di-Fiumorbo ①**
Overlooking the Abatesco river valley, parallel to the Vallée du Fium'Orbu, the village of Serra-di-Fiumorbo offers a fine view towards the coast, the ancient site of Aléria and the small Étang de Palo.

# Aléria ⑧

**Road map** D4. 🏘 *2,500.* 🚉 *Route Nationale 198 (04 95 57 01 51).* **www**.corsica-costaserena.com

The history of the ancient settlement of Aléria, on the marshy east coast of Corsica, began when Greek colonists set up a commercial outpost here around the mid-6th century BC. The outpost, then known as Alalia, served as a strategic base for trade with the populations on the nearby Italian and southern French coasts. For the Greeks, Corsica was also a vital source of raw materials, from timber to lead and copper from the mines inland.

After a period of Carthaginian domination, in 259 BC Alalia was invaded by the Roman troops of consul Lucius Cornelius Scipio. The Romans renamed the settlement Aléria and initiated the conquest of the island, which lasted for more than a century. Aléria was the capital of Corsica in the Imperial Age, and Augustus, Hadrian and Diocletian beautified it with large public works.

**Courtyard of Fort Matra, home of the Musée Jérôme Carcopino**

In the 5th century AD, the increase of malaria and invasion by the Vandals led to the abandonment of the city.

Visits to the archaeological site begin at a Genoese fort, Fort Matra. Built in 1484, it is now the home of the **Musée d'Archéologie Jérôme Carcopino**, named after the great scholar of Corsican origin. The items on display in this archaeological museum illustrate the historic continuity of Aléria and the great number of trade relations it had with the entire Mediterranean region. Greek, Phoenician, Roman, Apulian and Etruscan vases and ceramics were found on the hill where the city rose up. Among the most interesting works are two rhytons (wine vessels) that were made in Attica, Greece, one in the shape of a mule's head, the other representing a dog.

Outside the museum are the ruins of the Roman city. To the left of the Forum is a large temple flanked by two porticoes and, to the right, the Praetorium – the official residence of the governor of the island – and the Capitol. Everything gives the impression of an efficient city with all the typical Roman amenities. In addition, tombs and traces of past civilizations dating as far back as the 6th century BC have been found throughout the area.

🏛 **Musée d'Archéologie Jérôme Carcopino & site of Aléria**
Fort Matra. **Tel** *04 95 57 00 92.* 🔆 *daily.* 🔆 *mid-Oct–mid-May: Sun.* 🔆

## THE RUINS OF ALERIA

Balneum (baths) ⑨
Bastions ⑲
Calidarium
   (steam rooms) ⑩
Capitol ⑮
Chambers ⑪
Decumanus ⑱
Domus cum Domus
   (town house) ③

Domus cum Impluvium
   (water storage) ④
Forum ①
Industrial edifices ⑫
North arch ⑯
North portico ⑦
Pools ⑬

Praetorium (governor's
   residence) ⑭
Shops ⑤
South arch ⑰
South portico ⑥
Temple ②
Thermae (warm baths) ⑧

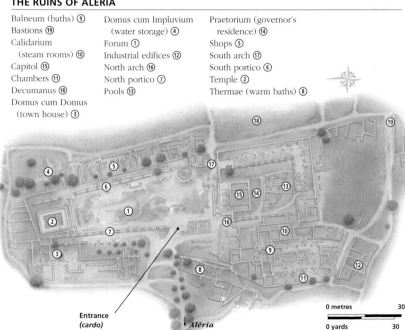

Entrance
**(cardo)**

↓ *Aléria*

0 metres    30
0 yards     30

The Genoese bridge of Altiani, decorated with a series of small blind arches

# Vallée du Tavignano **❾**

**Road map** C3. **ℹ** *Station Touristique de l'Intérieur, Citadelle, Corte (04 95 46 26 70).*

The Vallée du Tavignano is traversed by one of the oldest roads on the island, the N200, connecting Aléria and Corte.

Travelling from Aléria along the course of the Tavignano river, which begins at Lac de Nino, in the middle of Corsica, there are many narrow gorges.

On the north side of the valley, the narrow D14 road leads to villages typical of the region, perched halfway up the hills in panoramic positions. One of these, **Piedicorte di Gaggio**, offers a fine view towards the coast and has an ancient Roman architrave in the wall of the parish-church bell tower.

A Genoese bridge still stands at **Altiani**, as promised by its engineers, who guaranteed the bridge would remain standing in all circumstances "save a deluge".

The village of **Erbajolo**, towering over the canyon

The village of Piedicorte, in the Vallée du Tavignano

carved by the Tavignano river, offers a breathtaking view of the profiles of Monte Renoso and Monte d'Oro. On the belvedere square is a plaque indicating interesting natural and historic attractions.

# Gorges du Tavignano **❿**

**Road map** C3. **ℹ** *Station Touristique de l'Intérieur, Citadelle, Corte (04 95 46 26 70).*

While, east of Corte, the lower course of the Tavignano river extends to Aléria and the sea, its upper course consists of a narrow valley. Here are fascinating gorges that can be reached only by walking along easy paths paved for much of their length in original medieval cobbles and steeped in nature.

One of these paths starts off from below Corte's Citadelle and leads to the Arche de Corte (also known as Arche de Padule), a rocky crest surrounded by *bergeries* lying at an altitude of 1,500 m (4,921 ft). The path passes through chestnut groves in the hilly zone and then, above 1,000 m (3,300 ft), through conifer woods. Strenuous rather than difficult, it

entails a walk of over five hours each way. Looking back from the gorges, the impressive rock of the Citadelle can be seen, still seeming to have control over the entire region.

# Sovéria **⓫**

**Road map** C3. **🚊** *Sovéria.* **ℹ** *Station Touristique de l'Intérieur, Citadelle, Corte (04 95 46 26 70).*

Not far from Corte is the pretty village of Sovéria, located high over the Vallée du Golo, a stone's throw away from the Vallée de l'Asco and the regions of Bozio and Castagniccia. Sovéria is appreciated for the harmonious architecture of its houses.

In antiquity the countryside around Sovéria was given over to vineyards and winemaking. The landscape has changed, however, and today the soft hills are covered with oak and chestnut groves; the area is renowned for its production of excellent nougat.

Niche with statue, Santa Mariona

Along the D18 road, just outside Corte, is the 10th-century Romanesque church of **Santa Mariona**. The only remaining original parts of this church are the twin apses made up of grey stone from the local schist mountains.

# A Tour of Castagniccia ⑫

With its rolling green hills, the region east of Corte offers quite a different landscape from Corsica's mountainous interior. Named after its numerous chestnut *(castagna)* groves, Castagniccia was one of the first areas on the island to be inhabited. The highlights of a journey through this region include small villages, 16th-century Baroque chapels with impressive frescoes, many of which were restored between 2005 and 2010, and the complex 18th-century architecture of the churches of La Porta and Piedicroce. Castagniccia also played a significant role in the history of Corsica – Morosaglia was the birthplace of independence hero Pascal Paoli, and the region became the centre of a thriving arms industry during the Corsican revolution.

**San Tommaso di Pastoreccia ①**
This chapel has survived excessive restoration that, in the 1930s, destroyed half of its original structure. In the apse, above the hieratic image of *Christ Pantocrator*, is an *Annunciation*; on the walls are the remains of a *Last Judgment*.

**Morosaglia ②**
Corsicans attach special importance to this village where Pascal Paoli, the national hero during the period of independence *(see pp46–7)*, was born. His ashes are interred here. A short walk from Paoli's house-museum is the small church of Santa Reparata, decorated with sculptures that reveal its Romanesque origin.

**San Pantaleo ③**
The small church of San Pantaleo is on the D639 road going down from Morosaglia in the direction of the village of Saliceto. It is worth a visit for the splendid apse that was frescoed in the 15th century.

*N193*

*PONTE LECCIA*

*D15-B*

*D71*

*D71*

*Quercitello*

**CORTE**

*D639*

*Saliceto*

*Nocari*

*D39*

**San Quilico ④**
On the D639 road is the Pisan chapel of San Quilico, the lovely tympanum of which is sculpted with Adam and Eve being tempted by the serpent, and with a bas-relief of a man fighting a dragon with his bare hands.

**KEY**

▬ Tour route

═ Other roads

| 0 kilometres | | 5 |
| 0 miles | | 3 |

**La Porta ⑤**
A masterpiece of Corsican Baroque architecture, the church of St-Jean-Baptiste towers over the hamlet of La Porta with its tall bell tower, to the left of the façade.

**Piedicroce ⑥**
At Piedicroce, the Baroque church of Sts-Pierre-et-Paul dominates a soft landscape of rolling green hills. Built in 1691, its light-coloured façade is decorated with white pilasters and friezes. Inside are frescoes and Rococo decorations.

**Couvent d'Orezza ⑦**
An assembly met in this large monastery in the outskirts of Piedicroce in 1751 and conferred military and executive power on Jean-Pierre Gaffori *(see p134).* The monastery was reduced to ruins during World War II.

## La Porta ⑬

**Road map** *D3.* 🚗 *250.*
**i** *Mairie (04 95 39 21 48).*
**St-Jean-Baptiste** ☐ *daily.*

Situated in a fertile area covered in woods, the village of La Porta ("the door") owes its name and prosperity to its location – in the past this village was the only access route to the region of Castagniccia.

Today La Porta is famous because of the beautiful church of **St-Jean-Baptiste**, which, together with its imposing bell tower, stands out among the slate roofs of the village. It is considered to be the most complete work of Baroque architecture in Corsica. Construction of the church began in 1648 and continued for nearly half a century under the Italian architect Domenico Baina. The façade was completed in 1707, although it had later alterations. It has recently been restored to its original ochre colour, which, combined with the vertical white pilasters, gives quite a spectacular impression.

The lower part of the façade is rather austere, with tall pilasters forming a strict pattern. This is broken up by the upper level's elaborate Baroque elements with hints of Rococo, in the shape of pilaster strips,

*Pulpit, St-Jean-Baptiste*

swirly volutes and cartouches. The Baroque influence is also predominant around the entrance, which is surmounted by friezes. The excesses of the Italian Baroque style have been avoided through this juxtaposition of the plain base with detailing on the higher parts, while the overall harmony of the building has been maintained. The 45-m (147-ft) bell tower next to it shares the same pattern of design: simpler at the base and growing more elaborate for each of its five storeys.

The interior has a single nave flanked by side chapels separated from one another by columns with Corinthian capitals. The walls and ceiling are decorated with late 19th-century stucco work and trompe l'oeil by the artist Girolamo da Porta. Above the entrance is a magnificent monumental organ used in concerts. Other interesting works here include the high altar, made of white Carrara marble, with the altarpiece framed by two small columns, and the pulpit.

The interior contains many fine works of art. Among these are a *Decapitation of St John the Baptist*, to the right of the choir, and two 17th-century wooden sculptures representing Christ and the Virgin Mary.

**The village of La Porta, dominated by the Baroque bell tower**

# Vallée d'Alesani ⑭

**Road map** D3. 🏠 *190.*
ℹ️ *Tourist office, Piedicroce-Castagniccia (04 95 35 82 54).*

This area consists of a group of hamlets scattered on the upper course of the Alesani river. The region is known for the circumstances linked to the rise and fall of Theodor von Neuhof, the first and only king of Corsica *(see p46)*, who was crowned in the **Couvent St-François d'Alesani** in 1736 at Perelli. The monastery was founded in 1236, but the current Baroque building dates to 1716. One of the side chapels has the *Virgin of the Cherry* (1450), an oil painting on a wooden panel attributed to Sano di Pietro, an artist from Siena.

This hamlet was also the home of the legendary Grosso-Minuto.

The bell tower of Ste-Marie-et-St-Erasme at Cervione

# Cervione ⑮

**Road map** D3. 🏠 *1,350.*
ℹ️ *Tourist office, Piedicroce-Castagniccia (04 95 35 82 54).*

At the foot of Monte Castello and in the easternmost part of Castagniccia, Cervione lies in a beautiful location surrounded by vineyards, olive orchards and chestnut groves. After the destruction of Aléria, Cervione became a bishopric and, for that occasion, the cathedral of St-Erasme was built.

In 1714 the original church was replaced by a new complex, **Ste-Marie-et-St-Erasme**, the present-day cathedral. The Bishop's Palace and the seminary – now the home of a small ethnographic museum – were also built in this same period. Cervione is the starting point of the panoramic D330 road, also called **Corniche de la Castagniccia**. About 2 km (1 mile) from the town, along this route, is the 9th-century Chapelle Ste-Christine, with twin apses and some frescoes.

**Detail of a frieze, La Canonica**

# La Canonica ⑯

**Road map** D2. ℹ️ *Tourist office, Lucciana Porretta, Lieu-dit Crucetta (04 95 38 43 40).* 🕐 *Summer: daily.*

During the period of the Roman conquest (c.259 BC), various colonies were founded in Corsica. While the main colonial city was Aléria *(see p144)*, another one, Mariana, lay nearer to present-day Bastia. It was named after the Roman general Marius, who in 100 BC founded a colony for the veterans of his army near the waters of the Étang de Biguglia.

Mariana, where Augustus had a port built on the Golo river, was the base for the conquest of nearby Cap Corse and for the reclamation and cultivation of the entire plain surrounding the city.

Destroyed by the Vandals in the 5th century AD, as was Aléria, Mariana was dealt its final blow by the malaria epidemics that struck the inhabitants of the coastal plains in medieval times.

The Pisans built one of their cathedrals nearby, La Canonica, which was consecrated in 1119 by the archbishop of Pisa. He resided in the nearby bishop's palace, of which only traces of the foundations remain. Known by its original name, even though it was dedicated to Santa Maria Assunta, this church was abandoned for reasons of health and security two centuries later, when the bishop moved to the hills of nearby Vescovato. This church is considered the prototype of

The austere Romanesque church La Canonica

all the Pisan churches in Corsica. The nave is divided into three sections and ends in a semicircular apse; its elegance is created by the colours of the stone (from the Cap Corse quarries) and by few architectural decorative elements. Above the main portal are friezes representing griffons, a lamb, a wolf and a deer being chased by a dog. The series of holes on the outer walls of the church have sometimes been said to have originally contained multicoloured stone inlays, but they are in fact damage caused by scaffolding.

## Vescovato ⑰

**Road map** D2. 𝕄 *2,350.*
 Mairie (04 95 36 70 19).

On a mountainside at the northern end of the Castagniccia region, the town of Vescovato was founded by refugees who had abandoned the city of Mariana, which had proved too vulnerable to invasions and malaria.

For centuries, Vescovato was the capital of the small hilly region of Casinca, which lies between the Golo river and the Vallée du Fium'Alto and which, thanks to its fertile soil, for a long period had the largest population on the island. Formerly called Belfiorito, it was later renamed Vescovato ("bishopric") because it was the bishop's seat from 1269 to 1570, when it was replaced by Bastia.

The fountain in the square of Vescovato

To make the best of a visit here, it is advisable to park at the only tree-lined square and walk through the alleys. In the middle of the village is the Baroque church of **San Martino**, with a 16th-century tabernacle sculpted by the Italian Antonello Gagini. Next to the church, a vaulted passageway leads to the main square, which has a handsome fountain guarded by an eagle.

There are three other churches in town, reminders that this was once a bishopric: the church of the Capuchin monastery, the chapel of the Ste-Croix Confraternity and the Romanesque Chapelle San Michele.

The coast east of Vescovato is lined by increasingly popular sandy beaches and tourist resorts.

View of Vescovato, formerly a bishopric

The famous Ponte-Novo, site of a battle between Corsicans and French

## Ponte-Novo ⑱

**Road map** D2. Along the N193 road, 8 km (5 miles) northeast of Ponte Leccia.  Station Touristique de l'Intérieur, Citadelle, Corte (04 95 46 26 70).

This locality was named after a bridge built by the Genoese, but its fame throughout the island is due to the battle fought on the banks of the Golo river between the French troops commanded by Count de Vaux and the Corsican patriots led by Pascal Paoli *(see pp46–7)*.

On 8 May 1769 the invading French troops, who had been defeated the year before at Borgo, were trying to find an entry point to the interior of the island, which was under the control of the independence fighters. The 2,000 Corsican patriots were driven back by the French and retreated along the bridge, where they were quickly overcome. After this defeat, Paoli was forced to abandon the struggle against the French and, in June 1769, left the island for England. Thus ended the Corsicans' dream of independence and freedom.

Today the original bridge is in ruins because of bombardments during World War II. A new bridge was built over the river, but the battle is commemorated by a monument and a plaque, accompanied by flags with a Moor's head, the symbol of the Corsican nation *(see p47)*. A visit here offers a great insight into the spirit of the Corsicans.

Cirque de Trimbolocciu, in the Haut-Asco region

## Vallée de l'Asco ⓳

**Road map** C2–C3. ℹ Station
Touristique de l'Intérieur, Citadelle,
Corte (04 95 46 26 70).

The long, diagonal Vallée de
l'Asco – which runs for 30 km
(18 miles) southwest of Ponte
Leccia – is one of the most
isolated areas in Corsica. The
road that traverses it follows
the winding course of the
river Asco up to Corsica's
most striking range of
mountains, dominated by the
dark profile of **Monte Cinto**,
the highest peak on the
island at 2,706 m (8,878 ft).
Along the road is the
spectacular **Cirque de
Trimbolocciu**, near Monte
Cinto, at the head of the
Vallée de l'Asco.
　In an open area of the valley
is the village of **Asco**, which
in the 16th century was one
of the centres of the Corsican
resistance against the Genoese
troops. An unsurfaced road
full of hairpin bends drops
down from Asco towards the
banks of the river and then to
a marvellous Genoese bridge
with the typical arched span.
　As the valley rises, the
vegetation changes, and the
shrubs give way to the pines
and larches of the **Forêt de
Carozzica**. After this forest, the
road ends in the small ski
resort of **Haut-Asco**. At an
altitude of 1,450 m (4,757 ft),
this resort is one of the
favourite starting points for
hikers on their way towards
Monte Cinto (eight hours up
and back) or for those who

follow the GR20 long-distance
path (see p22), which crosses
the Haut-Asco area, passes
near the 2,556-m (8,385-ft) high
Punta Minuta and arrives at the
Tighjiettu refuge (see p23).

The Genoese bridge crossing the
river near Asco

## St-François
de Caccia ⓴

**Road map** C2. Castifao. ℹ Office
de Tourisme, Ghjunssani (04 95
47 22 06).

At the beginning of the Vallée
de l'Asco, leaving the D47
road in the direction
of Moltifao, a detour of
about 4 km (2 miles)
leads to the ruins of
the monastery of St-
François de Caccia, near
the village of Castifao.
　Founded in the early
16th century and
destroyed by the Genoese
in 1553, the monastery
and its church were
reconstructed thanks
to the efforts of friar
Augustinu da Populasca
and then entrusted to
a group of Franciscan
monks. The church, built

in 1569 and rebuilt in 1750,
collapsed in 1782. Here, in
1755, Pascal Paoli (see p47)
took part in the assembly of
Corsican deputies who drew
up the island's constitution.

## Scala di Santa
Regina ㉑

**Road map** C3. ℹ Office de
Tourisme, 29B Ave Valdoniello, Niolu
(04 95 47 12 62).

The Vallée du Golo has always
been an important communication link between the interior
and the west coast of Corsica.
　Following the course of the
Golo river leads to the highest
motorable pass on the island,
the Col de Verghio, at 1,464 m
(4,803 ft) above sea level.
From here one can descend
towards Porto and Ajaccio.
　Along the valley, on the
right-hand side of the road,
is the Scala di Santa Regina
gorge, which, according to
popular tradition, was created
thanks to the intervention of
the Virgin Mary at the end of
a fierce battle between St
Martin and Satan. With the
brilliant reddish hues of the
local granite, this narrow
gorge is an impressive sight
from the road, stretches of
which are often cut from the
steep rock.
　Parts of a narrow mule track
along which commercial
traffic travelled in the past are
still visible from the paved
road on the opposite slope of
the valley.

The impressive gorges known as
Scala di Santa Regina

**Wild horses near Calacuccia**

## Calacuccia ㉒

**Road map** C3. 🏔 *350.* 🛈 *Office de Tourisme, 29B Ave Valdoniello, Niolu (04 95 47 12 62).*

The main town in the Niolo mountain region and in the pass that leads to the Col de Verghio, Calacuccia stands 1,000 m (3,300 ft) above sea level. It is famous for its superb position on the banks of the lake created by a dam that blocks the flow of the Golo river. Small hotels and restaurants that are quite crowded in summer provide relaxation and magnificent views of Monte Cinto to the northwest *(see p23)* and Capo Tafonato, which rises up next to Col de Verghio.

From Albertacce, 5 km (3 miles) southwest of Calacuccia, orange waymarks lead from opposite a large white crucifix on the western edge of the village to the **Pont de Muricciolu**, an old Genoese footbridge overlooking natural pools that are popular bathing spots.

On the south bank of the artificial lake is the hamlet of Casamaccioli, and going up towards the 1,592-m (5,223-ft) high **Bocca di l'Arinella** pass, an unpaved road offers breathtaking views of the lake and surrounding mountains.

## Casamaccioli ㉓

**Road map** C3. 🏔 *90.* 🛈 *Station Touristique de l'Intérieur, Citadelle, Corte (04 95 46 26 70).* 🎌 *Nativity of the Virgin (7–10 Sep).*

Opposite Calacuccia, across the artificial lake and at an altitude of 850 m (2,800 ft), is Casamaccioli, a hamlet with fewer than 100 permanent inhabitants. Besides offering a marvellous view of the lake, the Monte Cinto massif and the surrounding chestnut forests, this village has an interesting tradition that always attracts visitors. In the Nativité parish church, beside a wooden statue of St Roch, there is one of the Virgin Mary, or "La Santa", as she is called in Corsica. On 7–10 September this statue is carried in the Nativity of the Virgin procession *(see p34)* during the festivities in her honour.

## Forêt de Valdu-Niellu ㉔

**Road map** C3. 🛈 *Office de Tourisme, 29B Ave Valdoniello, Niolu (04 95 47 12 62).*

Southwest of Casamaccioli, on the left-hand side of the road is this forest, the largest in Corsica. Although severely damaged by fires over the past decade, the forest covers a surface area of more than 46 sq km (18 sq miles) in a mountain zone at an altitude of about 1,000–1,600 m (3,300–5,250 ft). The forest is dominated by birch and beech trees as well as Laricio pines, trees found only on the island of Elba, in parts of the Italian region of Calabria and here in Corsica. At Valdu-Niellu there are Laricio pines as much as 500 years old.

The forest offers many activities, including hiking paths of several levels of difficulty. There is one that takes an hour, going from the Popaja rangers' house to the heart of the forest and then to the Bergeries de Colga. A harder path goes to the 1,743-m (5,718-ft) high glacial Lac de Nino (a walk of 3½ hours), the source of the Tavignano river *(see p24)*. The descent to the Cascades de Radule takes a further 90 minutes.

## Col de Verghio ㉕

**Road map** C3. 🛈 *Station Touristique de l'Intérieur, Citadelle, Corte (04 95 46 26 70).*

The road towards Porto (D84) passes over the Col de Verghio, the highest point in the island's road network. Just east of the Col de Verghio pass, along this route is the small winter sports resort of **Verghio**, which is a favourite with hikers in the summer.

Here it is possible to make the ascent to the small Lac de Nino *(see p24)*, the grassy basin of which is grazing land for small herds of wild horses during the summer.

Beaten by the wind and extremely wild, Col de Verghio is part of the itinerary of the GR20 long-distance path *(see p22)*, which, heading north, passes by the Cascades de Radule and then heads up to the Ciuttulu di i Mori refuge at the foot of the majestic Capo Tafonato mountain and the nearby peak of Paglia Orba.

**A humid meadowland area near the Col de Verghio**

# TRAVELLERS' NEEDS

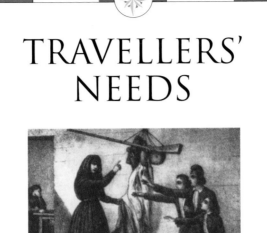

# WHERE TO STAY

From holiday villages along the coast to farm holiday establishments in the mountains, Corsica has about 400 places to stay. They are mostly concentrated in the gulfs of Ajaccio, Calvi, Porto-Vecchio and Bonifacio, and on the coast. Luxury establishments with a swimming pool or private beach tend to be located near the main seaside resorts. It is also possible to rent flats in residences or holiday homes, most of which are located in the southern part of the island. The many camp sites both in the interior and on the coast offer an economic alternative for those who prefer to stay in contact with nature. Another accommodation option consists of the *gîtes ruraux*, or farm holidays. These are small, family-run establishments that enable visitors to become better acquainted with Corsican people and their customs.

**The Gîtes de France logo**

## GRADING

As in the rest of Europe, hotels in Corsica are graded with a star-rating system. One star is for inns with only the most essential comforts and service, while four stars are awarded to first-class hotels that offer high-quality service.

The highest rating bracket is reserved for luxury hotels, such as La Villa *(see p159)* in Calvi, the Dolce Vita *(see p161)* in Ajaccio, the Genovese *(see p163)* in Bonifacio and Le Goéland *(see p164)* in Porto-Vecchio.

Three-star hotels often offer surprisingly good value for money. They include the Centre Nautique *(see p163)* in Bonifacio, the Castel Brando *(see p159)* in Erbalunga and the Dolce Notte *(see p160)* in St-Florent.

**The pool in the Hotel Pietracap *(see p158)* in Bastia**

All the four-star and most of the three-star hotels in resorts along the coastline have either a swimming pool or, when they are located on the seaside, private access to a beach.

Pleasant accommodation can also be found in two-star establishments, such as the Splendid Hôtel *(see p159)* in L'Île Rousse or the Hôtel Rossi *(see p165)* in Sartène.

Rarely will you find single rooms in the hotels so, should you be travelling alone, you will probably have to pay the price for a double room. Conversely, any extra bed in your room must be paid for separately.

Only in the recently built or remodelled hotels has attention been paid to the needs of the disabled so, if you have any special requests, it is advisable to make enquiries beforehand.

A good number of hotels in Corsica welcome pets.

## PRICES

French law requires hotels to post, both outside the premises and in each room, a price list. This list shows the maximum prices TTC, or *Toutes Taxes Comprises* ("including all taxes"), for each season. The prices shown (or quoted when you book a room) also include service. It is illegal to exceed the listed prices.

In the summer, hotels along the coast often quote a rate for obligatory half board.

Not all hotels have their own restaurant, and usually breakfast is not included in the price. The same applies for drinks during your meal, food or drinks served in your room, beverages taken from the minibar and telephone calls. Phone calls are usually quite expensive, so, unless it is absolutely necessary, it is better to use public phones.

**Main entrance to the Hostellerie de l'Abbaye *(see p159)* in Calvi**

◁ **Outdoor cafés and restaurants, a feature of Corsican towns**

## THE HOTEL SEASON AND BOOKING

Most hotels in Corsica are run on a seasonal basis and are open from April to October. High season corresponds to the summer months, in particular July and August. Should you decide to visit the island's seaside resorts during these months, it is vital that you arrange accommodation well in advance since many hotels are booked up for the high season.

From November to March, finding any accommodation at all, especially in the smaller tourist resorts, may also prove difficult. However, hotels in the main cities tend to stay open all year round.

When you book your room, you may be asked either to send a certain amount of money as a deposit or to supply your credit card details.

A room in the Casa Musicale *(see p160)* in Pigna

sports activities, including tennis, windsurfing, diving or sailing. Some clubs even provide the option of using a baby-sitting service.

Among the best such complexes are the Club Med holiday villages at Cargèse and Sant'Ambroggio, both not far from Calvi.

Some villages offer all-inclusive packages, in which everything, even drinks at the bar, is included in the price. The prices of these packages are quoted on a weekly basis. Other clubs allow you to rent an apartment and leave you free to choose whether you want to make use of the services, activities and entertainment.

Those staying in Corsica for one week or longer could consider renting a house, an option that affords the convenience of modern facilities while maintaining a degree of independence.

For information on holiday villages, contact your travel agency or the tour operator who manages the establish-

ments. For information on residences, call the **Syndicat National des Résidences de Tourisme** in Paris, or ask the **Agence de Tourisme de la Corse** for a brochure. Local tourist offices also publish lists of private houses and apartments to let in their areas.

## CAMPING

Staying at a camp site is an inexpensive way to spend your holiday. There are about 200 camp sites in Corsica, most of which are between Bonifacio and Porto-Vecchio, along the coast of the Balagne region and in the Golfe d'Ajaccio. Most sites are open from Easter to October, while very few are open all year round.

The standard of services and facilities varies quite a lot. Some camp sites are mere plots of land with modest facilities, few bathrooms and some trees for shade. Others have swimming pools, organize sports activities and have many facilities, including food stores, pizzerias (and, occasionally, restaurants) and laundry rooms. Some even rent bungalows for two to four people, with a private bathroom and kitchenette.

For a small fee, some farmers allow tents to be pitched in their farmyards. This type of camping also includes the use of the farm's bathing facilities.

It is forbidden to pitch tents outside camp sites or sleep on the beach. To camp on private land, you must ask the owner's permission.

As with hotels, it is best to book well in advance, especially for long stays.

A panoramic terrace at the Dolce Vita *(see p161)* in Ajaccio

## HOLIDAY VILLAGES AND RÉSIDENCES

Along the seaside, holiday villages and *résidences* (holiday homes) offer visitors a less formal atmosphere than that found in a hotel. The level of accommodation in these establishments varies according to the needs of the guest: from simple rooms in a bungalow with restaurant service and entertainment, to self-catering apartments.

All the holiday villages offer entertainment, one or more pools and a wide range of

Staying at a camp site: an economic way to spend a holiday

## SELF-CATERING

Whether it is a mini-apartment in Bonifacio, or a villa with a garden and swimming pool in Balagne, a self-catering apartment (*location saisonnière*) is an inexpensive solution for a family or a group of friends, and certainly an option worth considering when there are small children in your party.

This type of accommodation is particularly convenient for holidays of two weeks or more. Self-catering for only one week is a less valid option, partly because fixed expenses, such as cleaning, may be the same for a short or long period.

Corsica offers a great many houses and apartments for rent, but it is always advisable to make your reservations in advance. Local tourist offices provide lists of houses for rent; alternatively estate agents sometimes offer flats and villas for short periods as well.

Before agreeing to rent a place, ask for a detailed description of the house or apartment, its location and amenities, as well as the services and facilities in the area. Sometimes one discovers too late that the sea is quite a distance from the house or that some beds in the house are mere makeshift arrangements. It is a good idea to find out whether the

One of the many mountain refuges offering shelter to hikers

gas and electricity expenses are included in the rent or are considered extras. Enquiries should also be made about all the amenities, even the swimming pool or garden, in order to avoid having to pay for unexpected maintenance expenses.

## CHAMBRES D'HÔTES

Much like the British bed and breakfast, *chambres d'hôtes* are rooms rented in private homes. They include breakfast and are ideal for visitors who plan to travel a lot. They are also a good way to get to know Corsican people first-hand. To find a *chambre d'hôtes* in Corsica, contact a local tourist office.

## REFUGES AND HOSTELS

Corsica offers 16 mountain refuges and many more *gîtes d'étapes* (shelters). They are located mostly along the GR20 long-distance path *(see pp22–7 and 188)* and all are marked on IGN maps. Both refuges and *gîtes d'étapes* tend to be small, with 20–50 bed spaces, often in a dorm, and with only one communal shower room. *Gîtes d'étapes* also have self-catering facilities.

Refuges are staffed from June to September. In the high season it may be hard to find a place to stay, since it is not possible to book in advance, but for those who cannot find a bed there is always an area with facilities for camping.

A comfortable, family-run farm-holiday establishment in the Corsican interior

A handful of refuges also have food available, such as cheese and charcuterie, and drinks.

There are only two youth hostels (*relais de jeunesse*) in Corsica providing beds at low prices; both are in Calvi.

## FARM HOLIDAYS

For simple accommodation in exceptionally beautiful settings try the *gîtes ruraux*. Although there are not many of these farms on the island, they are a pleasant and economic solution allowing an opportunity to become acquainted with the local traditions and life.

The grading of the *gîtes* is based not on stars, like hotels, but on ears of wheat (from one to four), and they are guaranteed by the **Maison des Gîtes de France**.

As well as rooms, which usually have a private bathroom and include breakfast, there are many small flats with a kitchenette and private bathroom, usually in converted stables or rooms where wine was once made.

All the guests eat at the same table, so if you like your privacy this is not the solution for you. However, it is ideal for those who want to relax without being tied down to a hotel routine, and for families with children, who will have plenty of space to play in. The price categories you will be quoted indicate the maximum price for a double room with breakfast, including tax and service.

# DIRECTORY

## TOURIST OFFICES

**Agence de Tourisme de la Corse**
17 Blvd du Roi Jérôme, Ajaccio.
*Tel 04 95 51 00 00.*
www.visit-corsica.com

## RESIDENCES

**Arinella**
Route du Bord de Mer, Lumio.
*Tel 04 95 60 60 60.*

**Baies des Voiles**
Santa Manza, Bonifacio.
*Tel 04 95 73 03 55.*

**Belvédère de Palombaggia**
Route de Palombaggia, Porto-Vecchio.
*Tel 04 95 70 95 70.*

**Carole Leandri**
Pian di Leccia, Baracci, Propriano.
*Tel 04 95 76 19 48.*

**Les Pins**
Route de Porto, Calvi.
*Tel 04 95 65 28 20.*

**Sarl Immobilière de Balagne**
Cocody Village, Baie de Sant'Ambroggio, Lumio.
*Tel 04 95 60 72 76.*

**Syndicat National des Résidences de Tourisme**
Paris.
*Tel 01 47 38 35 60.*
www.snrt.fr

**Le Thyrrénéen**
Solenzara.
*Tel 04 95 57 47 59.*

## CAMPING

**Arinella Bianca**
Ghisonaccia.
*Tel 04 95 56 04 78.*
www.arinellabianca.com

**Barbicaja**
Route des Sanguinaires, Ajaccio.
*Tel 04 95 52 01 17.*

**Belgodère**
Camping Campéole, Hameau Lozari.
*Tel 04 95 60 20 20.*

**Benista**
Pisciatello, Porticcio.
*Tel 04 95 25 19 30.*

**Le Clos du Mouflon**
Route de Porto, Calvi.
*Tel 04 95 65 03 53.*

**Dolce Vita**
Route Nationale 197, Calvi.
*Tel 04 95 65 05 99.*

**Kallisté**
Route de la Plage, St-Florent.
*Tel 04 95 37 03 08.*

**Kalypso**
Route Nationale 198, Santa Maria, Poghju.
*Tel 04 95 38 56 74.*

**Marina d'Aléria**
Boîte Postale 11, Aléria.
*Tel 04 95 57 01 42.*

**Les Oliviers**
Porto (Ota).
*Tel 04 95 26 14 49.*

**Ostriconi**
Palasca. *Tel 04 95 60 10 05.*

**La Pinède**
Lieu-dit Serrigio, St-Florent.
*Tel 04 95 37 07 26.*

**Torraccia**
Baghiuccia, Cargèse.
*Tel 04 95 26 42 39.*

**U Prunelli**
Pont du Prunelli, Porticcio.
*Tel 04 95 25 19 23.*

## ESTATE AGENCIES

**Agence du Golfe**
111 Cours Napoléon, Ajaccio.
*Tel 04 95 22 19 09.*

**Agence Sud Corse Immobilier**
6 Route de la Corniche, Propriano.
*Tel 04 95 70 30 69.*

**Bastia Immobilier**
45 Blvd Paoli, Bastia.
*Tel 04 95 32 78 49.*

**Calvi Balagne**
8 Blvd Wilson, Calvi.
*Tel 04 95 65 11 40.*

**Immobilier Alias**
Marina di Fiori, Porto-Vecchio.
*Tel 04 95 70 21 30.*

**Millénaire Immobilier**
12 Rue St-Jean-Baptiste, Bonifacio.
*Tel 04 95 73 59 51.*

## CHAMBRES D'HOTES

**Alberte Bartoli**
L'Orca di San Gavinu, Figari. *Tel 04 95 71 01 29.*

**A Pignata**
Route du Pianu, Levie.
*Tel 04 95 78 41 90.*

**A Tinedda**
Sartène.
*Tel 04 95 77 09 31.*

**Jean-Jacques Bartoli**
Tasso.
*Tel 04 95 24 50 54.*

**Kyrn Flor**
Route Nationale 193, U San Gavinu, Corte.
*Tel 04 95 61 02 88.*

**Stéphane Natalini**
Ferme Auberge, Altu Pratu, Erbajolo.
*Tel 04 95 48 80 07.*

## YOUTH HOSTELS

**BJV Corsotel**
43 Ave de la République, Calvi.
*Tel 04 95 65 14 15.*

**U Carabellu**
Route de Pietramaggiore, Calvi.
*Tel 04 95 65 14 16.*

## FARM HOLIDAYS

**Gîtes de France Corse**
77 Cours Napoléon, Boîte Postale 10, Ajaccio.
*Tel 04 95 10 06 14.*
www.gites-corsica.com

**Maison des Gîtes de France et du Tourisme Vert**
Paris.
*Tel 01 49 70 75 75.*
www.gites-de-france.fr

# Choosing a Hotel

Hotels have been selected across a wide price range for their quality, service and location. All rooms have private bath or shower. Wheelchair users should assume hotels in Corsica do not offer adequate facilities and are advised to make further enquiries *(see p197)*. For map references refer to the road map of Corsica on the back endpaper.

**PRICE CATEGORIES**
Price categories for a standard double room with bath or shower per night in high season including tax and service but not breakfast:
€ Under €65
€€ €65–€100
€€€ €100–€150
€€€€ €150–€200
€€€€€ Over €200

## BASTIA AND THE NORTH

### ALGAJOLA Hôtel Beau Rivage
€€€

*29 Rue A. Marina, Algajola, 20220* **Tel** *04 95 60 73 99* **Fax** *04 95 60 79 51* **Rooms** *36*    **Map** *C2*

With a terrace literally on the sandy Algajola beach, the Beau Rivage has fairly standard rooms, though each one has its own balcony. The hotel restaurant serves up meals with amazing sea views. Enjoy the silence – Algajola is still a fairly sleepy seaside town where visitors can get a taste of true local culture. **www.hotel-beau-rivage.com**

### ARGENTELLA Auberge Ferayola
€€€

*Argentella, 20260* **Tel** *04 95 65 25 25, or mob 06 10 82 07 33* **Fax** *04 95 65 20 78* **Rooms** *10*    **Map** *B2*

Between Calvi and Porto, Auberge Ferayola is one of only a handful of hotels on the winding stretch of this western coastal road. Book a room or a chalet, and take advantage of the peace and quiet, far from the summer hordes. The magnificent Argentella beach is a ten-minute walk away. Closed end Sep–Nov. **www.ferayola.com**

### BASTIA Hôtel Central
€€

*3 Rue Miot, 20200* **Tel** *04 95 31 71 12* **Fax** *04 95 31 82 40* **Rooms** *22*    **Map** *D2*

Charm, history, excellent location and friendly smiles – the Hôtel Central has it all. Rooms blend classic French decor, like original terracotta tiles and patterned wallpaper, with space-saving modern touches, like mirrored panels in the bathroom doors. Breakfast is served in a cosy room on the first floor. **www.centralhotel.fr**

### BASTIA Hôtel Pietracap
€€

*Route San Martino, San Martino di Lota, 20200* **Tel** *04 95 31 64 63* **Fax** *04 95 31 39 00* **Rooms** *39*    **Map** *D2*

This supremely comfortable hotel can be found in a beautiful setting along the coastal road from Bastia. A large park with 100-year-old olive trees separates the hotel from the sea. One of the highlights is a large outdoor swimming pool, with pool-side snacks available. Private parking. Closed Dec–Mar. **www.hotel-pietracap.com**

### BASTIA Hôtel Posta Vecchia
€€

*Quai des Martyrs de la Libération, 20200* **Tel** *04 95 32 32 38* **Fax** *04 95 32 14 05* **Rooms** *49*    **Map** *D2*

Conveniently situated in the heart of the city, this popular hotel is next to the bustling, colourful old port, with its lively restaurants and cafés. Ask for a room at the front, to watch the town's population take their evening stroll along the pretty tree-lined quay. Public parking is available. **www.hotel-postavecchia.com**

### BASTIA Les Voyageurs
€€

*9 Avenue Maréchal Sébastiani, 20200* **Tel** *04 95 34 90 80* **Fax** *04 95 34 00 65* **Rooms** *24*    **Map** *D2*

Just steps away from Bastia's train station, Les Voyageurs prides itself on offering uncluttered, bright rooms. Curved wooden furniture is painted white, and rooms are relatively spacious. The lobby makes a good meeting place for business in a city where most hotels do not offer adequate communal areas. **www.hotel-lesvoyageurs.com**

### BASTIA Hôtel Ostella
€€€

*Avenue Sampiero Corso, Sortie Sud Bastia, 20600* **Tel** *04 95 30 97 70* **Fax** *04 95 33 11 70* **Rooms** *52*    **Map** *D2*

Located in the industrial area on the outskirts of Bastia, the Ostella may lack some historic and aesthetic charm, nevertheless, it does offer the highest levels of comfort, including a hammam, fitness centre, pool and an outstanding restaurant. Rooms are sunny and bright, with balconies, and were renovated in 2009. **www.hotel-ostella.com**

### CALENZANA A Flatta
€€€

*Calenzana, 20214* **Tel** *04 95 62 80 38* **Fax** *04 95 62 86 30* **Rooms** *5*    **Map** *C2*

From Calenzana, follow the signs along the 3-km (2-mile) track to this isolated hideaway. You won't be disappointed with A Flatta. With a pool that offers spectacular views over the surrounding countryside, and an excellent restaurant to boot, you may well spend most of your holiday in the immediate vicinity. **www.aflatta.com**

### CALVI Hôtel Les Aloes
€€

*Lieu-dit Poggiale, Quartier Donateo, 20260* **Tel** *04 95 65 01 46* **Fax** *04 95 65 01 67* **Rooms** *21*    **Map** *B2*

At the end of a no-through road, the Hôtel Les Aloes is located in a fragrant garden of large aloes and climbing vines. A simple terrace dotted with striped parasols overlooks Calvi and the coast, and staff are friendly. The private library and quiet, remote location make this an excellent place to relax. Closed mid-Oct–Apr. **www.hotel-les-aloes.com**

**Key to Symbols** *see back cover flap*

### CALVI Les Clos des Amandiers

⊞ ☷ ▼ ⏿ €€ · Map B2

*Route de Pietramaggiore, 20260* **Tel** *04 95 65 08 32* **Fax** *04 95 65 37 76* **Rooms** *24*

A peaceful haven close to Calvi centre, Les Clos des Amandiers boasts a large pool and terrace shaded by almond trees, where dinner can be taken. Although somewhat rustic, the Clos is easily accessible for those without a vehicle, just a ten-minute walk from the city centre and Avenue Christophe Colomb. **www.clos-des-amandiers.com**

### CALVI Hostellerie l'Abbaye

▣ ▤ ▼ €€€ · Map B2

*Route Santore, 20260* **Tel** *04 95 65 04 27* **Fax** *04 95 65 30 23* **Rooms** *43*

This pretty ivy-covered hotel was built on the walls of a 16th-century abbey. Ideally positioned on a slight incline just above the port, it is set back from the road and surrounded by an immaculate garden. A five-minute walk takes you to the town centre. Closed in winter. **www.hostellerie-abbaye.com**

### CALVI Hôtel Balanea

▣ ▤ €€€ · Map B2

*6 Rue Clemenceau, 20260* **Tel** *04 95 65 94 94* **Fax** *04 95 65 29 71* **Rooms** *38*

Located in the town centre on the quayside, this comfortable hotel enjoys an uninterrupted view across the bay to the mountains. Rooms are spacious and well decorated, with large bathrooms. At night, you can join the cosmopolitan crowd at one of the many restaurants in the port area. Closed Sep–Oct. **www.hotel-balanea.com**

### CALVI Hôtel Christophe Colomb

▣ ⊞ ▤ ▼ €€€ · Map B2

*Place Christophe Colomb, 20260* **Tel** *04 95 65 06 04* **Fax** *04 95 65 29 65* **Rooms** *25*

This hotel faces Calvi's citadel, and is a few minutes' walk from the port. With its sunny rooms, colourful artworks and old photos on the walls, and a lobby littered with international magazines, the Christophe Colomb is a cheerful home away from home. Closed Nov–Mar. **www.hotelchristophecolomb.com**

### CALVI Hôtel Le Magnolia

⊞ ▤ ▼ ⏿ €€€ · Map B2

*Rue Alsace Lorraine (Place du Marché), 20260* **Tel** *04 95 65 19 16* **Fax** *04 95 65 34 52* **Rooms** *11*

Le Magnolia is a beautiful 19th-century mansion in the heart of Calvi. Romantic and elegant, it is at its best in late spring, when the massive 100-year-old magnolia tree in the garden is in bloom. Rooms may be small for some tastes, and due to its central location, some can be noisy. Closed Nov–Apr. **www.hotel-le-magnolia.com**

### CALVI Château Hôtel La Signoria

⊞ ☷ ▤ ▼ ⏿ €€€€€ · Map B2

*Route de la Forêt de Bonifato, 20260* **Tel** *04 95 65 93 00* **Fax** *04 95 65 38 77* **Rooms** *24*

Pamperingly high-end, La Signoria is positioned between St-Catherine airport and the town itself, making your own transport essential. Spend your time in the eucalyptus-filled garden, the pool, the hammam or the gourmet restaurant, or with the resident masseur. Private beach. Closed mid-Jan–Mar. **www.auberge-relais-lasignoria.com**

### CALVI La Villa

▣ ⊞ ☷ ▤ ▼ ⏿ €€€€€ · Map B2

*Chemin Notre Dame de la Serra, 20260* **Tel** *04 95 65 10 10* **Fax** *04 95 65 10 50* **Rooms** *53*

Fancy lounging by the infinity pool, dining with an uninterrupted view of Calvi's citadel, or maybe renting your own private villa and swimming pool? For utter luxury, head to La Villa, located in the foothills above Calvi. This chic little haven even goes so far as to discourage mobile-phone use in common areas. **www.hotel-lavilla.com**

### CALVI The Manor (Chambres d'hôtes)

⊞ ☷ ▤ ⏿ €€€€€ · Map B2

*Chemin Saint-Antoine, 20260* **Tel** *04 95 62 72 42* **Fax** *04 95 62 72 42* **Rooms** *4*

A beautifully restored stone house, The Manor is set on five acres of land, 1.5 km (1 mile) outside of Calvi. Two of the rooms can be linked to make a suite, and there are vast amounts of space to wander in. Alternatively, you can rent the whole house (staff included); see the website for details. Breakfast is included. **www.manor-corsica.com**

### CENTURI Le Vieux Moulin

⊞ ▤ ▼ ⏿ €€€ · Map D1

*Centuri Port, 20238* **Tel** *04 95 35 60 15* **Fax** *04 95 35 60 24* **Rooms** *22*

Located in the tiny fishing village of Centuri, in the northwest corner of Cap Corse, Le Vieux Moulin is a converted 19th-century American-style home, with spectacular views over the port. Don't miss their renowned *haute-cuisine* restaurant *(see p173)*, one of the best on the peninsula. **www.le-vieux-moulin.net**

### ERBALUNGA Hôtel Demeure Castel Brando

☷ ▤ ▼ ⏿ €€€ · Map D1

*Erbalunga, 20222* **Tel** *04 95 30 10 30* **Fax** *04 95 33 98 18* **Rooms** *45*

One of the most charming hotels in Corsica, in one of the most charming towns on the island. The walled garden encourages a lingering breakfast under the olive trees; the beach is a five-minute walk away. The decor blends elegance and comfort for a unique and relaxing base for your holiday. Closed end Sep–Oct. **www.castelbrando.com**

### L'ÎLE ROUSSE Hôtel Le Grillon

⊞ ▤ ▼ € · Map C2

*10 Avenue Paul Doumer, 20220* **Tel** *04 95 60 00 49* **Fax** *04 95 60 43 69* **Rooms** *16*

An excellent budget option in the pretty resort town of L'Île Rousse, Le Grillon is located a mere five minutes' walk from the town's main square. Staff are friendly, and the rooms simple and clean – if possible, opt for one of the lodgings at the back, since these are the quietest. Closed Nov–Feb. **www.hotel-grillon.net**

### L'ÎLE ROUSSE Splendid Hôtel

▣ ⊞ ☷ ▼ ⏿ €€ · Map C2

*Avenue Comte Valéry, 20220* **Tel** *04 95 60 00 24* **Fax** *04 95 60 04 57* **Rooms** *51*

This hotel's most splendid feature is its ample swimming pool. The thatched-roof of the pool-side bar, nestled between palm trees, reconfirms the exotic-island ambience. Rooms are modest, with pale walls and large windows. Breakfast is included in the price. Closed Nov–Mar. **www.le-splendid-hotel.com**

## L'ÎLE ROUSSE Hôtel Santa Maria

*Route du Port, 20220* **Tel** *04 95 63 05 05* **Fax** *04 95 60 32 48* **Rooms** *56*     **Map**C2

Superbly situated on the road to L'Île Rousse, this charming hotel has its own little beach and is just a short walk to the main town square, with its shops and restaurants. All rooms have a terrace with mountain or sea views. The restaurant serves lunch in the months of July and August. Dinner by reservation. **www.hotelsantamaria.com**

## L'ÎLE ROUSSE L'Escale Hôtel Côté Sud

*22 Rue Notre Dame, 20220* **Tel** *04 95 63 01 70* **Fax** *04 95 39 22 10* **Rooms** *12, plus 5 suites*     **Map** C2

L'Escale, located upstairs from the eponymous restaurant and cocktail bar, blends modern colours and edgy design for a truly contemporary feel. Plate-glass windows overlook the sea, just metres away, and are perfectly positioned for amazing sunrises. Staff are relaxed and willing to help with special requests. **www.hotel-ilerousse.com**

## L'ÎLE ROUSSE Hôtel Napoléon Bonaparte

*3 Place Paoli, 20220* **Tel** *04 95 60 06 09* **Fax** *04 95 60 11 51* **Rooms** *92*     **Map** C2

The Napoléon Bonaparte was the former home of Mohammed V, exiled sultan of Morocco. Paul Theroux stayed here in 1978, while travelling around the island. Situated directly on Place Paoli, the hotel still exudes an air of grandeur, although it caters mainly to package tours nowadays. Call directly for availability. Closed Oct–Dec.

## MACINAGGIO U Libecciu

*Route de la Plage, 20248* **Tel** *04 95 35 43 22* **Fax** *04 95 35 46 08* **Rooms** *30, plus 10 apartments*     **Map** D1

Located just behind Macinaggio's port, U Libecciu is an excellent base for exploring the northernmost part of Cap Corse. While the decor feels a little outdated, the infinity pool and private beach definitely add a ultra-modern touch. The concierge can organize a wide range of outdoor activities. Closed Nov–end Mar. **www.u-libecciu.com**

## NONZA Casa Lisa (Chambres d'hôtes)

*Paule Patrizi Olmeta, 20217* **Tel** *04 95 37 83 52, or mob 06 11 70 45 73* **Rooms** *5*     **Map** D1

A truly unmissable village, Nonza is set high above a sprawling black sand beach. Make sure to book well ahead to secure one of the popular west-facing rooms at Casa Lisa, so you can watch the sun set over the water. The same spectacle is available from the terrace, where guests can enjoy a pleasant evening drink. **casalisa.free.fr**

## PATRIMONIO U Lustincone

*Route de Cap, 20253* **Tel** *04 95 37 15 28* **Fax** *04 95 37 15 28* **Rooms** *9*     **Map** D2

If wine is your passion, a visit to Corsica's Patrimonio region is essential. Base yourself at U Lustincone, a friendly spot with an outstanding restaurant, and visit the nearby wineries. Most are happy to offer tours and will organize the transport of your favourite bottles back home for you. Closed Oct–Apr. **www.u-lustincone.com**

## PIETRACORBARA Macchia e Mare

*Marine de Pietracorbara, 20233* **Tel** *04 95 35 21 36* **Fax** *04 95 36 67 25* **Rooms** *8*     **Map** D1

Located just a short stroll away from Pietracorbara's vast sandy beach, Macchia e Mare offers its guests the choice of rooms with a terrace or a small private garden. The town is relatively quiet most of the year, and the seaside location makes this hotel an excellent base for passionate hikers. Breakfast is included. **www.macchia-e-mare.com**

## PIGNA Casa Musicale

*Pigna, 20220* **Tel** *04 95 61 77 31* **Fax** *04 95 61 74 28* **Rooms** *7*     **Map** C2

In the 1960s, Pigna was the first of the Balagne villages to actively preserve its cultural heritage. It is therefore apt that Festivoce, a seasonal Corsican music festival, takes place annually at this small hotel that doubles as Pigna's cultural centre. Each room is named after a singing range. Closed Jan–mid-Feb. **www.casa-musicale.org**

## SAINT-FLORENT Hôtel Maxime

*Route La Cathédrale, 20217* **Tel** *04 95 37 05 30* **Fax** *04 95 37 13 07* **Rooms** *19*     **Map** D2

Set back from the street on the way to the 12th-century cathedral of Santa Maria Assunta, this converted villa is an oasis of calm only five minutes' walk from the hurly-burly of the fashionable port of Saint-Florent. The pleasant, airy rooms on the top floor boast spectacular sea views. Closed end Oct–Dec.

## SAINT-FLORENT Hôtel de l'Europe

*Place des Portes, 20217* **Tel** *04 95 37 00 03* **Fax** *04 95 37 17 36* **Rooms** *17*     **Map** D2

Although not the cheapest in town, the Hôtel de l'Europe is a family-run establishment. Rooms ooze character, with terracotta floors, white linens and dark wooden furniture. The excellent restaurant L'Auberge *(see p175)* is just downstairs. Opt for one of the rooms facing the picturesque port. Closed mid-Nov–Feb. **www.hotel-europe2.com**

## SAINT-FLORENT Hôtel du Centre

*Rue du Centre, 20217* **Tel** *04 95 37 00 68* **Fax** *04 95 37 41 01* **Rooms** *12*     **Map** D2

The Hôtel du Centre is a bargain spot in Saint-Florent's old town. Rooms tend to be rather on the small side, but the central location, as promised by the name, is unbeatable for quick and easy access to the town's myriad bars and restaurants. Closed Nov–mid-Mar.

## SAINT-FLORENT Dolce Notte

*Plage de l'Ospedale, Route de Bastia, 20217* **Tel** *04 95 37 06 65* **Fax** *04 95 37 10 70* **Rooms** *20*     **Map** D2

Set slightly out of town in the direction of Cap Corse, the Dolce Notte is definitely the place to stay for hard-core sun worshippers, with less than a ten-second walk separating the rooms from the beach. Ground-floor accommodation features a private terrace. A great place to watch the sun set. Closed end Oct–end Mar. **www.hotel-dolce-notte.com**

**Key to Price Guide** *see p158* **Key to Symbols** *see back cover flap*

# AJACCIO AND THE WEST COAST

### AJACCIO Hôtel du Palais

*5 Avenue Bévérini Vico, 20000* **Tel** *04 95 22 73 68* **Fax** *04 95 20 67 11* **Rooms** *14*    **Map** *B4*

A budget option approximately ten minutes' walk from Ajaccio's old town, the discreet Hôtel du Palais is the epitome of cheap and cheerful. Take advantage of the hotel's position to explore the surrounding neighbourhood, in order to get a feel for the true local goings-on in the city. Breakfast is included. **www.hoteldupalaisajaccio.com**

### AJACCIO Hôtel Fesch

*7 Rue Cardinal Fesch, 20000* **Tel** *04 95 51 62 62* **Fax** *04 95 21 83 36* **Rooms** *77*    **Map** *B4*

This long-established hotel is situated on a pedestrian street in the centre of town. It provides a good base for visiting historic sites in the surrounding area, with Napoleon Bonaparte's house and the Fesch Museum just a five-minute walk away. The rooms are large, with solid furnishings. Closed mid-Dec–mid-Jan. **www.hotel-fesch.com**

### AJACCIO Hôtel Kallisté

*51 Cours Napoléon, 20000* **Tel** *04 95 51 34 45* **Fax** *04 95 21 79 00* **Rooms** *48*    **Map** *B4*

Although located right in the middle of the busy Cours Napoléon, the clean and well-run Kallisté offers surprisingly quiet rooms. Wrought-iron banisters and exposed-stone walls add a rustic touch to the building, which dates back to 1864 and is situated just a few minutes' walk from the train and bus stations. **www.hotel-kalliste-ajaccio.com**

### AJACCIO Hôtel Marengo

*2 Rue Marengo, 20000* **Tel** *04 95 21 43 66* **Fax** *04 95 21 51 26* **Rooms** *18*    **Map** *B4*

One of the friendliest places in town, with a tiny fruit- and flower-laden garden to gaze upon or sit in. Located just one kilometre (half a mile) to the west of Ajaccio's old town, the Marengo has long been a favourite for budget tourists in the know. Not far from the beach, this hotel feels pleasantly secluded. **www.hotel-marengo.com**

### AJACCIO Hôtel du Golfe

*5 Boulevard Roi Jérôme, 20000* **Tel** *04 95 21 47 64* **Fax** *04 95 21 71 05* **Rooms** *50*    **Map** *B4*

If a city break is what you are after, there is no better spot than the Hôtel du Golfe, in the centre of Ajaccio. Across the street from the daily produce market, the hotel affords views over the city's busy port. It is an excellent place for travellers on foot, since transport connections are easily accessible. Closed Nov–mid-Mar. **www.hoteldugolfe.com**

### AJACCIO Hôtel Napoléon

*4 Rue Lorenzo Vero, 20181* **Tel** *04 95 51 54 00* **Fax** *04 95 21 80 40* **Rooms** *62*    **Map** *B4*

Although somewhat dated, this hotel boasts an excellent location – directly in the city centre, close to the port and the casino, just behind the main post office – and truly friendly, helpful staff. Ask for one of the rooms facing the picturesque citrus garden, if they are available. Free WiFi connection. **www.hotelnapoleonajaccio.fr**

### AJACCIO Hôtel San Carlu

*8 Boulevard Danielle Casanova, 20000* **Tel** *04 95 21 13 84* **Fax** *04 95 21 09 99* **Rooms** *40*    **Map** *B4*

Rooms at the San Carlu may be a little on the small side, but the hotel's location is unbeatable: on the very edge of Ajaccio's old town and a two-minute stroll from the birthplace of Napoleon Bonaparte. Guests can gaze out over the sea and the city's imposing 15th-century citadel. Closed mid-Dec–Jan. **www.hotel-sancarlu.com**

### AJACCIO Stella di Mare

*Route des Îles Sanguinaires, 20000* **Tel** *04 95 52 01 07* **Fax** *04 95 52 08 69* **Rooms** *60*    **Map** *B4*

An affordable option on the Route des Îles Sanguinaires, the Stella di Mare is located directly on the sandy beach. Visit the pool or linger over an aperitif at the terraced bar while watching the sunset turn the Îles Sanguinaires their famous blood-red hue. **www.hotel-stelladimare.com**

### AJACCIO Hôtel Palazzu u Domu

*17 Rue Bonaparte, 20000* **Tel** *04 95 50 00 20* **Fax** *04 95 50 02 19* **Rooms** *45*    **Map** *B4*

One of the few hotels in Ajaccio's old town, Palazzu u Domu is all about understated elegance and luxury. Each unique room is absolutely awe-inspiring, featuring stone floors and muted, natural tones. The building itself is steeped in history, since it was formerly the ancestral home of the Duke Pozzo di Borgo. **www.palazzu-domu.com**

### AJACCIO Eden Roc

*Route des Îles Sanguinaires, 20000* **Tel** *04 95 51 56 00* **Fax** *04 95 52 05 03* **Rooms** *40*    **Map** *B4*

An exquisite hotel, the Eden Roc lives up entirely to the promise of its idyllic name. Rooms face the Gulf of Ajaccio and the Îles Sanguinaires, and guests can choose to spend lazy days by the landscaped pool or on the hotel's private beach. Pamper yourself in the spa, Jacuzzi or hammam. **www.edenroc-corsica.fr**

### AJACCIO Hôtel Dolce Vita

*Route des Îles Sanguinaires, 20000* **Tel** *04 95 52 42 42* **Fax** *04 95 52 07 15* **Rooms** *32*    **Map** *B4*

A favourite with French VIPs in the 1970s, the Dolce Vita has long been synonymous with luxury and elegance. Dine on the terrace overlooking the sea, or sip a cocktail under a striped parasol on the paved terraces, between the sheltering rocks of the shoreline. Price includes obligatory half-board. **www.hotel-dolcevita.com**

### CARGÈSE Le Continental
*Route de Piana, 20130* **Tel** *04 95 26 42 24* **Fax** *04 95 26 42 24* **Rooms** *8*     **Map** *B3*

Set in the higher area of the tiny fishing village of Cargèse, this is a welcoming establishment with knockout views over the sea and the nearby Plage du Péro. Rooms are basic, but staff are the friendliest you are likely to find, and the restaurant's specials are tasty and filling. The best option in Cargèse's town centre. **continentalhotel.free.fr**

### CARGÈSE Hôtel Résidence Hélios
*Menasina, 20130* **Tel** *04 95 26 41 24, or mob 06 71 00 89 95* **Fax** *04 95 26 47 19* **Rooms** *17*     **Map** *B4*

Dripping with flowers, this residence on the edge of a bay near Cargèse is usually fully booked by February, and it is easy to see why. The self-catering apartments have private terraces and shared gardens, making it an ideal spot for a family holiday. Apartments are offered by the week. Book well in advance. **www.locations-corse-cargese.com**

### CARGÈSE Motel Ta Kladia
*Plage du Péro, 20130* **Tel** *04 95 26 40 73* **Fax** *04 95 26 41 08* **Rooms** *30*     **Map** *B3*

Enjoy a laid-back dinner under tropical palm trees, while taking in the views over the adjacent sandy beach. Located 3 km (2 miles) from Cargèse's town centre, Motel Ta Kladia is the northernmost hotel on the stunning Plage du Péro, and one of the most special spots in the area. The studios are equipped for four people. **www.motel-takladia.com**

### GALÉRIA L'Auberge
*Centre du village, 20245* **Tel** *04 95 62 00 15, or mob 06 03 29 11 44* **Rooms** *6*     **Map** *B3*

In the heart of Galéria's old town, the family-run L'Auberge is a tiny hotel set among stone buildings and terraced gardens. The simple yet pretty rooms make for a pleasant stay. Be sure to partake in a hearty meal at the restaurant, which produces excellent local specialities. **www.auberge-corse.com**

### PIANA Hôtel Continental
*Piana, 20115* **Tel** *04 95 27 89 00* **Fax** *04 95 27 84 71* **Rooms** *17*     **Map** *B3*

Owned and run by the same family since 1912, the Continental offers a warm welcome all year round. You can choose between staying at the hotel, in the town centre (shared bathrooms only), or in the slightly more expensive annexed building (1 km/0.6 mile away). Breakfast in the lush garden is included in the price. **www.continentalpiana.com**

### PIANA Hôtel des Calanches
*Entrée Village, 20115* **Tel** *04 95 27 82 08* **Rooms** *17*     **Map** *B3*

Accommodation at the Hôtel des Calanches is clean and basic, and best suited to active guests who will be spending most of their time outside. The breathtaking Calanches are a UNESCO World Heritage site, and accordingly, this area of Corsica is packed in summer so book well in advance. Closed mid-Oct–Mar. **www.hotel-des-calanches.com**

### PIANA Les Roches Rouges
*Route Porto, 20115* **Tel** *04 95 27 81 81* **Fax** *04 95 27 81 76* **Rooms** *30*     **Map** *B3*

Built in 1912, this splendid hotel retains all the charm of that era. Large, simply furnished rooms look out on to the bay of Porto, which has been nominated by UNESCO as one of the world's five most beautiful bays. There are also excellent dining facilities, a pretty terrace and a garden. Closed Nov–Mar. **www.lesrochesrouges.com**

### PORTO Bella Vista Hôtel
*Route de Calvi, 20150* **Tel** *04 95 26 11 08* **Fax** *04 95 26 15 18* **Rooms** *18*     **Map** *B3*

A friendly hotel at the north end of town, the Bella Vista lives up to its name and does indeed have beautiful views over the harbour and town of Porto. Don't miss the copious breakfast (€11 per person), which features local meats and cheeses, as well as delicious quiches and home-made breads. Closed Nov–Mar. **www.hotel-bellavista.net**

### PORTO Hôtel Le Colombo
*Route de Calvi, 20150* **Tel** *04 95 26 10 14* **Fax** *04 95 26 19 90* **Rooms** *16*     **Map** *B3*

Although all the rooms at Le Colombo share a nautical theme, each one is uniquely decorated. Shells abound, and you definitely won't forget that you are just a short distance from the sea. The hotel offers an ample Corsican breakfast (included in the price), along with great views over Porto. Closed Nov–Mar. **www.hotel-colombo-porto.com**

### PORTO Le Subrini
*La Marine de Porto, 20150* **Tel** *04 95 26 14 94* **Fax** *04 95 26 11 57* **Rooms** *23*     **Map** *B3*

Located directly in Porto's marina, just 20 metres from the sea, Le Subrini is the place to choose if you're hankering to be at the heart of the local action. Opt for one of the rooms facing the seafront, both for the gorgeous views and the addictive people-watching. Breakfast is included. **www.hotels-porto.com/hotel-subrini**

### PORTO Le Maquis
*Porto, 20150* **Tel** *04 95 26 12 19* **Fax** *04 95 26 18 55* **Rooms** *6*     **Map** *B3*

Le Maquis is a quiet family-run hotel on the outskirts of town, on the coastal road to Calvi. In addition to dramatic views over the mountains, it offers comfortable rooms and a pretty garden. For such an unpretentious establishment, the charming restaurant produces a surprisingly sophisticated menu. Parking available. **www.hotel-lemaquis.com**

### SAGONE Hôtel Cyrnos
*Sagone, 20118* **Tel** *04 95 28 00 01* **Fax** *04 95 28 00 77* **Rooms** *24*     **Map** *B4*

Sagone has all the feel of a classic resort town in summer – lively, teeming with people and fun. The Cyrnos is located in the absolute centre of the action. You can stroll out of your room directly on to the beach, or take advantage of one of the hotel's many arranged sailing or diving trips. Closed mid-Oct–Jan. **www.hotelcyrnos.com**

**Key to Price Guide** *see p158* **Key to Symbols** *see back cover flap*

### SERRIERA Hôtel Stella Marina

*Plage de Bussaglia, 20147* **Tel** *04 95 26 11 18* **Fax** *04 95 26 12 74* **Rooms** *20*  **Map** *B3*

Although not on the standard Corsican tourist trail, the Plage de Bussaglia is worth seeking out. Cows meander past while you snack in one of the two beach restaurants. The Stella Marina is just down the road (five minutes' walk) and makes an excellent choice for exploring the Calanques or the nearby city of Porto. **www.hotel-stella-marina.com**

### SERRIERA Eden Park

*Golfe de Porto, 20147* **Tel** *04 95 26 10 60* **Fax** *04 95 26 14 74* **Rooms** *35*  **Map** *B3*

Truly a little Eden on the edge of Porto. Hanging vines, the perfume of fig trees, the swimming pool and the spa all make a stay here feel exclusive and relaxing. Treat yourself to a gourmet meal at the hotel's restaurant, and end the evening with drinks at the piano bar. Breakfast is included. Closed mid-Oct–mid-Apr. **www.hotels-porto.com**

# BONIFACIO AND THE SOUTH

### BONIFACIO Hôtel des Etrangers

*Avenue Sylvère Bohn, 20169* **Tel** *04 95 73 01 09* **Fax** *04 95 73 16 97* **Rooms** *31*  **Map** *C6*

On the northern edge of town, just past the port, this is the best of the budget options in a city renowned for its wealthy summer crowd. The staff are exceptionally friendly and seem to truly enjoy interacting with all the different nationalities. The no-frill rooms are clean, and the breakfast is tasty. **hoteldesetrangers.ifrance.com**

### BONIFACIO Hôtel du Roy d'Aragon

*13 Quai Comparetti, Port de Plaisance, 20169* **Tel** *04 95 73 03 99* **Fax** *04 95 73 07 94* **Rooms** *31*  **Map** *C6*

Probably the cheapest of the hotels on the Quai Comparetti, the Roy d'Aragon has basic but relatively spacious rooms. If possible, opt for one of the two top-floor rooms, each of which has a breathtaking terrace overlooking the harbour. For those on a budget, cheaper rooms are available, although views won't be. **www.royaragon.com**

### BONIFACIO La Caravelle

*35–37 Quai Comparetti, 20169* **Tel** *04 95 73 00 03* **Fax** *04 95 73 00 41* **Rooms** *28*  **Map** *C6*

Hotel, restaurant, piano bar: La Caravelle offers a range of options at any time of day. Rooms are classically French, with floral bedspreads and patterned curtains; fresh flowers abound. On the lively Quai Comparetti, so a wide selection of bars and restaurants is right on its doorstep. Closed Nov–Mar. **www.hotel-caravelle-corse.com**

### BONIFACIO Hôtel A Trama

*Cartarana, Route de Santa Manza, 20169* **Tel** *04 95 73 17 17* **Fax** *04 95 73 17 79* **Rooms** *25*  **Map** *C6*

Pull into the round drive at the A Trama, and the first thing you'll notice is the ranch-style layout of the rooms. Quirky, but then, this establishment is pleasantly quirky itself. Located en route to the beautiful beaches of Corsica's southeast coast, this little hotel is an ideal spot for travellers with their own transport. **www.a-trama.com**

### BONIFACIO Hôtel du Golfe

*Lieu-dit Santa Manza, 20169* **Tel** *04 95 73 05 91* **Fax** *04 95 73 17 18* **Rooms** *12*  **Map** *C6*

Facing the sandy beaches of the Gulf of Santa Manza, this is a quiet establishment in the outskirts of Bonifacio. Rooms are basic, but the hotel is an excellent spot for nature-lovers with their own transport. The restaurant is well known for its delicious bouillabaisse (fish soup). Price includes obligatory half-board. **www.hoteldugolfe-bonifacio.com**

### BONIFACIO Hôtel Restaurant Centre Nautique

*Quai Nord – BP 65, 20169* **Tel** *04 95 73 02 11* **Fax** *04 95 73 17 47* **Rooms** *11*  **Map** *C6*

A boutique hotel on the far side of the port, the Centre Nautique affords perfect views of Bonifacio's old town, as well as easy access to the hopping bars and restaurants lining Quai Comparetti. The hotel has a nautical theme (as expected), and rooms are duplexes. The best ones are on the first floor port-side. **www.centre-nautique.com**

### BONIFACIO Hôtel Santa Teresa

*Quartier Saint-François, 20690* **Tel** *04 95 73 11 32* **Fax** *04 95 73 15 99* **Rooms** *48*  **Map** *C6*

Built in 1897 and spectacularly situated at the top of the cliffs, this imposing hotel was originally a police garrison. Several of the elegant rooms have balconies from which you can enjoy the magnificent sea views reaching all the way to Sardinia. Private parking is available. Closed Nov–Mar. **www.hotel-santateresa.com**

### BONIFACIO Hôtel A Cheda

*Cavallo Morto – BP 3, 20169* **Tel** *04 95 73 03 82* **Fax** *04 95 73 17 72* **Rooms** *15*  **Map** *C6*

A cross between a Spanish *hacienda* and an African-inspired abode, with a little southeast Asian decor thrown in, the A Cheda is just a couple of kilometres north of Bonifacio, on the way to Porto-Vecchio. Each room is uniquely designed and furnished, and days can be spent lazing by the pool or in the lush gardens. **www.acheda-hotel.com**

### BONIFACIO Le Genovese

*Quartier de la Citadelle, Rue Prosper Mérimée, 20169* **Tel** *04 95 73 12 34* **Fax** *04 95 73 09 03* **Rooms** *18*  **Map** *C6*

The sister hotel to the Centre Nautique *(see above)*, Le Genovese is the place to stay if you are looking for an establishment that's wildly out of the ordinary. Rooms are definitely lavish here. If you can't afford to bed down for the night, stop in to check out the views while indulging in a fabulous drink. **www.hotel-genovese.com**

### LECCI (PORTO-VECCHIO) Grand Hôtel de Cala Rossa 🎇🛏🎬🍽🛎 €€€€€

*Route de Cala-Rossa, 20137* **Tel** *04 95 71 61 51* **Fax** *04 95 71 60 11* **Rooms** *48* *Map D5*

Often cited as the best hotel in Corsica, the Grand Hôtel de Cala Rossa is located across the bay from Porto-Vecchio. It offers its guests everything from yoga and mud wraps to fishing on a wooden pontoon boat. Utter extravagance but non-pretentious. Price includes obligatory half-board (mid-Jun–mid-Sep). Closed Jan–Mar. **www.cala-rossa.com**

### PINARELLO (SAINTE-LUCIE DE PORTO VECCHIO) Hôtel Le Pinarello 🎇🛜🍽🎬🛎 €€€€€

*Pinarello, 20144* **Tel** *04 95 71 44 39* **Fax** *04 95 70 66 87* **Rooms** *14, plus 10 suites* *Map D5*

A modern boutique hotel, Le Pinarello is located directly on the beach, just north along the coast from Porto-Vecchio. Tthis hotel is perfect for a pampered yet health-conscious break – kayaks and motorboats can be rented, and the nearby beaches teem with outdoor activities in the summer. Closed mid-Oct–mid-Apr. **www.lepinarello.com**

### PORTO-POLLO Hôtel Les Eucalyptus 🎬🍽🛎 €€€

*Porto-Pollo, 20140* **Tel** *04 95 74 01 52* **Fax** *04 95 74 06 56* **Rooms** *32* *Map B5*

Situated on the Golfe de Valinco in Porto-Pollo, Les Eucalyptus is just a few minutes' walk from the bay's huge sandy beach. Located approximately 10 km (6 miles) from Corsica's prehistoric site of Filitosa, this simply designed hotel makes an excellent base for ancient-history buffs. Breakfast is included. Closed Nov–Mar. **www.hoteleucalyptus.com**

### PORTO-VECCHIO Chez Franca 🎬 €€€

*Route de Bonifacio, 20137* **Tel** *04 95 70 15 56* **Fax** *04 95 72 18 41* **Rooms** *14* *Map C6*

This modern hotel is conveniently situated between the town and the port. A lot of care has evidently gone into the renovation of the rooms. The superb beaches of Santa Giulia and Palombaggia are a few miles away, and Chez Franca also makes a good base for excursions to Zonza and Bavella. Closed Dec. **www.francahotel.com**

### PORTO-VECCHIO Hôtel Holtzer 🛜🎇🎬🍽 €€€

*12 Rue Jean Jaurès, 20137* **Tel** *04 95 70 05 93, or mob 06 10 35 61 80* **Fax** *04 95 70 47 82* **Rooms** *30* *Map C6*

The most reasonably priced option in Porto-Vecchio, the Holtzer is located just outside the old town. The more adventurous can sign up for the "Sea and Mountain" tour, an eight-day trip around the island, interspersed with meals and evenings in Porto-Vecchio. Breakfast is included. Half-board is obligatory in August. **www.corse-eternelle.com**

### PORTO-VECCHIO Hôtel Ranch Campo 🏇🎇🎬🍽🛎 €€€

*Route de Palombaggia, 20137* **Tel** *04 95 70 13 27* **Fax** *04 95 70 67 90* **Rooms** *18* *Map C6*

If you dream of horse riding on a sandy beach, this hotel can make it happen. Just 1 km (0.6 mile) from the sandy white Palombaggia Beach, the Ranch Campo is actually a working ranch. For a special stay, choose one of the mini-villas, which are fully equipped and have their own terraces and gardens. Closed Nov–Feb. **www.ranchcampo.com**

### PORTO-VECCHIO Hôtel San Giovanni 🎇🛎 €€€

*Route d'Arca, 20137* **Tel** *04 95 70 22 25* **Fax** *04 95 70 20 11* **Rooms** *30* *Map C6*

A short drive east of Porto-Vecchio, the San Giovanni is a comfortable family-run establishment, set in five hectares of flowering woodlands. The hotel offers true rest and relaxation, and guests can enjoy the heated pool, the Jacuzzi, excellent meals and, even during the summer season, blissful silence. Closed Nov–Feb. **www.hotel-san-giovanni.com**

### PORTO-VECCHIO Kilina 🎬🎇🍽🎇🛎 €€€€

*Route de Cala Rossa, 20137* **Tel** *04 95 71 60 43* **Fax** *04 95 71 68 21* **Rooms** *61* *Map C6*

The Kilina has the feel of a holiday village: nine buildings are dotted around the hotel's ample land, and they surround two large swimming pools. The hotel arranges activities in high season, such as "family hours" on the beach and a kids' club. Closed Oct–mid-Apr. **www.kilina.net**

### PORTO-VECCHIO Hôtel E Casette 🎇🎬🍽🛎 €€€€

*Route de Palombaggia, 20137* **Tel** *04 95 70 13 66* **Fax** *04 95 70 46 97* **Rooms** *11* *Map C6*

Perched across the Golfe de Porto-Vecchio, the E Casette offers unbelievable sunset views over the gorgeous old town. Contemporary rooms nestle into the Corsican hillside. All bathrooms are kitted out with a shower and a Jacuzzi, and open on to private terraces, making this hotel one of the area's most romantic options. **www.ecasette.com**

### PORTO-VECCHIO Le Goéland 🎇🎬🍽🛎 €€€€€

*La Marine, 20137* **Tel** *04 95 70 14 15* **Fax** *04 95 72 05 18* **Rooms** *30* *Map C6*

Le Goéland is a truly unique establishment, set on a small piece of land jutting into the sea, and just down the road from Porto-Vecchio's port. The hotel is airy and tastefully decorated, and it offers both a private beach and a private port (for those arriving by sea). Price includes obligatory half-board (May–Sep). **www.hotelgoeland.com**

### PROPRIANO Le Bellevue 🍽 €€

*9 Avenue Napoleon, 20110* **Tel** *04 95 76 01 86, or mob 06 87 78 69 23* **Fax** *04 95 76 38 94* **Rooms** *16* *Map B5*

Located on Propriano's main seafront road, amid various other hotels, restaurants and bars, Le Bellevue is an excellent choice for the young and energetic. Everything happens within steps of the hotel's doorway. Rooms are somewhat austere, but the best have sea-facing balconies. **www.hotels-propriano.com**

### PROPRIANO Grand Hôtel Miramar 🎇🎇🎬🍽🛎 €€€€€

*Route de la Corniche, 20110* **Tel** *04 95 76 06 13* **Fax** *04 95 76 13 14* **Rooms** *26* *Map B5*

The most exclusive hotel in the area. Accommodation here spans the range from deluxe to absolute seclusion. Rent a suite in the private Villa Miramar, sunbathe beside the pool, or indulge in the island's freshest fish. Alternatively, grab one of the hotel's picnic baskets and head off for a romantic afternoon. **www.miramarboutiquehotel.com**

**Key to Price Guide** *see p158* **Key to Symbols** *see back cover flap*

## QUENZA Sole e Monti

☐☐☐☐  €€

*Quenza, 20122* **Tel** *04 95 78 62 53* **Fax** *04 95 78 63 88* **Rooms** *20*      **Map** *C5*

In the lovely town of Quenza, the Sole e Monti is a perfect location for hiking enthusiasts. Although beautiful during the summer (but bring a jacket: Quenza can be chilly even in August!), this area really comes into its own during the autumn season. Excellent meals are served around an open fire. **www.solemonti.com**

## SARTÈNE Hôtel des Roches

☐☐☐☐☐  €€

*Rue Jean Jaurès, 20100* **Tel** *04 95 77 07 61* **Fax** *04 95 77 19 93* **Rooms** *60*      **Map** *C5*

At the edge of Sartène's old town, the Hôtel des Roches' most beautiful feature is its breathtaking panoramic restaurant, which overlooks the lush valley below. While the hotel itself is a relatively modern building, rooms with balconies and views over the valley are a peaceful choice for your holiday. **www.sartenehotel.fr**

## SARTÈNE Hôtel Rossi

☐☐☐  €€€

*Quai Casabianca, Route de Propriano, 20100* **Tel** *04 95 77 01 80* **Fax** *04 95 73 46 67* **Rooms** *25*      **Map** *C5*

A petit and pretty establishment just 1 km (0.6 mile) outside of Sartène's old town, this hotel offers its guests a private garden and swimming pool, both overlooking the surrounding valley and the nearby medieval town. Although the Rossi is just off the main road, guests are immersed in nature. **www.hotelfiordiribba.com**

## SARTÈNE Hôtel St Damianu

☐☐☐☐  €€€€

*Quartier San Damien, 20100* **Tel** *04 95 70 55 41* **Rooms** *28*      **Map** *C5*

This winning hotel has large airy rooms and terraces with fabulous views of either the Golfe de Valinco or the mountains. Facilities include a huge swimming pool surrounded by decking, as well as a garden, hammam, disabled access, secure parking and an excellent dining room. **www.sandamianu.fr**

# CORTE AND THE INTERIOR

## CALACUCCIA L'Acqua Viva

☐☐  €€

*Lieu-dit Scardacciole, 20224* **Tel** *04 95 48 06 90* **Fax** *04 95 48 08 82* **Rooms** *14*      **Map** *C3*

A family-run hotel in the Corsican mountains, L'Acqua Viva is an ideal base for hikers and nature enthusiasts. Rooms are simple but bright and airy, and the private balconies are perfect for breakfast with a view. In the summer heat, you can head from here to the nearby Radulle waterfalls. **www.acquaviva-fr.com**

## CORTE Hôtel de la Paix

☐☐  €€

*9 Avenue Général de Gaulle, 20250* **Tel** *04 95 46 06 72* **Fax** *04 95 46 23 84* **Rooms** *64*      **Map** *C3*

The interior of this pleasant family hotel, built in 1932 in a quiet street in the town centre, has been renovated, with parquet floors throughout. Some rooms have terraces, and those at the back enjoy views over the gardens and mountains. Parking is available nearby. Closed 10 days at Christmas.

## CORTE Hôtel Les Jardins de la Glaciere

☐☐☐☐  €€

*Gorges de la Restonica, 20250* **Tel** *04 95 45 27 00* **Fax** *04 95 45 27 01* **Rooms** *20*      **Map** *C3*

Take advantage of Corte's close proximity to the gorgeous Vallée de la Restonica by staying at this pretty little hotel, located just 1 km (0.6 mile) out of town. The river pools at the garden's edge, and breakfast can be had on the terrace overlooking its banks. Closed Jan–Mar. **www.lesjardinsdelaglaciere.com**

## CORTE Hôtel du Nord et de l'Europe

☐☐  €€

*22 Cours Paoli, 20250* **Tel** *04 95 46 00 68* **Fax** *04 95 46 03 40* **Rooms** *15*      **Map** *C3*

Located right on Corte's main street, the Hôtel du Nord et de l'Europe is the oldest hotel in town. Persevere past its somewhat gloomy entrance, and you will find simple but clean rooms. The ample one-euro breakfast (not included) makes this spot more than worth the price. Free WiFi connection. **www.hoteldunord-corte.com**

## CORTE Hôtel Dominique Colonna

☐☐☐☐  €€€

*Vallée de la Restonica, BP 83, 20250* **Tel** *04 95 45 25 65* **Fax** *04 95 61 03 91* **Rooms** *29*      **Map** *C3*

A short drive from the town centre, the Dominique Colonna was named after the former goalkeeper of the French football team. Currently owned and run by his grandson, the hotel is positioned on the cool riverbanks in the Vallée de la Restonica. Don't miss a meal at the Auberge de la Restonica next door. **www.dominique-colonna.com**

## VENACO Paesotel e Caselle

☐☐☐☐  €€€€

*Lieu-dit Agniudipino, 20231* **Tel** *04 95 47 39 00* **Fax** *04 95 47 06 65* **Rooms** *47*      **Map** *C3*

The spacious and quiet rooms here are designed to evoke the feel of a traditional shepherd's hut. Choose between the main building or bungalows built mainly from river rocks. Visit in May to enjoy the local cheese festival, along with great views over the Vallée du Tavignano. Obligatory half-board in July and August. Closed Oct. **www.e-caselle.com**

## VIZZAVONA Hotel du Monte D'Oro

☐  €

*Col de Vizzavona RN 193, 20219* **Tel** *04 95 47 21 06* **Fax** *04 95 47 22 05* **Rooms** *45*      **Map** *C3*

You'll feel as though you are in an Agatha Christie novel as you walk into this charming hotel, built in 1880 and located in the forest, on the road between Ajaccio and Bastia. Wood-panelled corridors and an elegant dining room are some of the features. A *gîte* is also available for rent. Closed Nov–Mar. **www.monte-oro.com**

# WHERE TO EAT

An apéritif at sunset in front of the small harbour in Ajaccio, or fresh grilled fish on a small beach in Cap Corse, cannelloni stuffed with *brocciu* cheese at a *ferme-auberge* or the elegant refinement of a restaurant in a large hotel – Corsica offers many options when it comes to eating and drinking. The beauty of a trip to this island also depends on its rich cuisine, which blends the flavours of the sea with those of the land. In Corsica the food is generally good and not

**Tearoom sign in Ajaccio**

overpriced. Cafés and bistros are ideal for a quick snack and, if you want to economize, there are pizza parlours, especially in seaside resorts. Even inland, where tourism is less hectic, you can find nice places offering typically Corsican specialities. Indeed, if you are staying along the coast, it is still worthwhile making a trip inland to have a fine meal. At country inns, good regional food is often accompanied by interesting conversations with the locals.

**A small beach restaurant in Bussaglia, near Porto**

## RESTAURANTS

In Corsica, restaurants in the coastal towns offer fresh fish, grilled shrimp, lobsters, sardines with fresh *brocciu* cheese, *aziminu* (an elaborate seafood stew) and other seafood specialities. These establishments often have verandas or tables outdoors, along the promenades or in the harbour area.

The more exclusive restaurants in the tourist resorts include Le Floride *(see p176)* in Ajaccio and the Jardin d'A Cheda *(see p177)* in Bonifacio. Among the best fish restaurants in Corsica are Chez Huguette *(see p173)* in Bastia and Le Bout du Monde *(see p173)* in Calvi.

There are also high-quality hotel restaurants, including the Centre Nautique *(see p177)* in Bonifacio, the Grand Hôtel de Cala Rossa *(see p177)* in Lecci and the refined Le Belvédère *(see*

*p178)* in Porto-Vecchio. Other types of hotel, such as Casa Musicale *(see p174)* in Pigna, have fine restaurants that successfully combine tradition and innovation.

The restaurants known as *tables gastronomiques* are a guarantee of quality for the variety of their menu, the careful preparation of the dishes and the excellent service, while the places called *tables du terroir* offer typical Corsican dishes, such as game, charcuterie and home-made cheeses.

Seaside resorts also have bistros, which are ideal for a simple meal, a slice of quiche or a plate of cheese or cold cuts, and pizza parlours, which also offer *crêpes* and local specialities at low prices.

In the villages inland, it is possible to eat at typical restaurants with genuine products such as ham, pork neck salami and *figatellu* (liver sausage).

The restaurants recommended on pages 172–9 are among the best in Corsica.

### FERME-AUBERGES

An excellent option when it comes to eating consists of the *ferme-auberges* ("farm-inns"). They offer genuine Corsican dishes made with products from the farm itself, such as cheese, vegetables and charcuterie. Among the best, A Pignata *(see p177)*, in Levie, features specialities based on chestnut flour, while La Bergerie d'Acciola *(see p178)*, near Sartène, serves different cheeses made on the premises.

Most *ferme-auberges* offer half-board accommodation. During the summer, guests can stay on a weekly basis only.

**Outdoor dining at a typical small restaurant**

Outdoor café in a shaded esplanade

## BARS AND CAFES

Many bars and cafés, especially those in coastal towns, have tables outdoors. They become particularly crowded during the apéritif hour, when people gather at their local bar or café to have a glass of *pastis*, Cap Corse or Corsican beer, accompanied by olives.

These cafés also serve breakfast, and in many pastry shops there are small tables where you can enjoy croissants, biscuits, pastries, cakes and tarts, some of which are made with chestnuts or fruit.

The most characteristic Corsican cafés are located in Place St-Nicolas in Bastia, along the Quai Landry in Calvi, on the main square in Porto-Vecchio and along the yacht harbour in Ajaccio.

## BREAKFAST

In Corsica, breakfast *(petit déjeuner)* is an important ritual. The day begins with coffee *(café au lait* or *café crème)*, accompanied by fresh bread *(baguette)*, eaten with honey or preserves. There are also croissants and *pains au chocolat*. The large hotels serve continental breakfasts, while on the farms breakfast consists of the farm's own products, such as honey, milk and preserves.

## PRICES AND PAYING

Besides the à la carte menu, almost all restaurants in Corsica have fixed-price menus *(formule)*, the prices of which differ according to the dishes. These menus offer regional or fish and seafood specialities and sometimes give you the opportunity to try typical dishes that would otherwise be hard to find.

In general, a complete meal in an average-level restaurant costs €20–€25, while in bistros and simple restaurants it is €13–€15. If you do not want to spend much, try the pizzerias – a meal here never costs more than €10–€12.

Restaurants usually accept the most common credit cards used in Europe; smaller establishments in less frequented areas prefer cash.

## OPENING HOURS AND RESERVATIONS

Opening hours in Corsica are similar to those in mainland France. Lunch is usually served from 12:30 to 2:30pm and dinner from 7:30 to 10pm, but in tourist resorts many places close later in summer. The villages inland have shorter opening hours. Most establishments close once a week and for their holidays, which usually coincide with the low season.

In the summer, especially in the evening, it is always advisable to book a table.

## VEGETARIAN FOOD AND WHEELCHAIR ACCESS

Vegetarians will not have too hard a time ordering a meat- or fish-free meal in Corsica. Among the options are omelettes, cheese, pizzas and *cannelloni al brocciu*.

Wheelchair access and other facilities for the disabled may be hard to find, especially in the old historic centres and villages, although many places have conformed to the new regulations. Holiday Care *(see p197)* publishes a guide listing all the establishments with wheelchair access in France and Corsica.

## DRESS AND SMOKING

There is no need to dress elegantly in restaurants, unless they are exclusive. However, avoid going to the opposite extreme: it is best not to dine in your bathing costume, even in places along the seaside.

Smoking is no longer permitted in Corsican restaurants.

The elegant dining room in La Caravelle *(see p177)*, in Bonifacio

# The Flavours of Corsica

Corsican cuisine reflects centuries of outside influences, while still proudly maintaining its own identity. The Greeks and Phoenicians introduced olives and vines; chestnuts arrived with the Genoese in the 16th century; clementines were first planted in the 20th. All now play a key role in local dishes, along with semi-wild pigs, game, seafood and herbs. Climate, terrain, coastline and history all contribute to the wonderful produce found here, and its island status means that many Corsican specialities are unique and seldom found beyond its shores. In particular, Corsicans are rightly proud of their superb charcuterie *(see p97)* and cheeses.

**Clementines**

**Donkey saucisson on sale in Bastia's colourful market**

### MEAT & SEAFOOD

Goat kid is a favourite meat in Corsica, while pigs are raised for fresh meat and charcuterie. There is also abundant game, including wild boar, rabbit, hare, pigeon and partridge. The semi-wild black pigs that roam the uplands often end up in a distinctive range of hams and sausages that has more in common with Italian

than French charcuterie. *Prisuttu* is a cured ham that is hung to dry for one to two years; *salsiccia* and *salamu* are air-dried sausages made of minced pork. Marbled red *coppa* is made from pork shoulder, and the dark red, peppery *lonzu* from cured pork fillet. Both are lightly smoked. The most unusual product is *figatelli*, a dark, U-shaped, smoked liver sausage which can be grilled or dried and eaten cold.

Corsican seafood includes mullet, bass, swordfish, monkfish, sardines and anchovies, as well as lobster, squid, sea urchins and crabs. Oysters and mussels are cultivated in the Etang de Diane on the eastern side of the island.

### CHEESES

A cheese you're sure to come across in one form or another on the island is Brocciu or Brucciu, a mild,

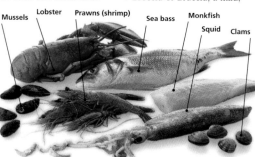

**Mussels**   **Lobster**   **Prawns (shrimp)**   **Sea bass**   **Monkfish**   **Squid**   **Clams**

**Selection of seafood found in the clear waters off the Corsican coast**

---

### CORSICAN DISHES AND SPECIALITIES

**Olives and their oil**

Numerous pasta dishes testify to Corsica's Italian past: macaroni with *stufatu* stew; ravioli or cannelloni stuffed with Brocciu; or wild boar lasagne. Fresh fish is often simply grilled over charcoal but there is also a *bouillabaisse*-style fish soup called *aziminu*. Sea urchins *(oursins)* scooped out with a spoon or bread are a winter treat. Wild boar and kid are stewed or roasted with herbs and garlic; suckling pig is roasted with herbs; lamb, rabbit or veal may be cooked with olives and tomato. Vegetable gratins feature, and bean dishes encompass thick soups, a *cassoulet*-style stew, and broad (fava) beans with bacon *(fèves au lard)*. The best-known dessert is *fiadone*; others feature figs or clementines; fritters *(fritelli)* are made from chestnut flour.

**Soupe corse** *simmers white beans, onions, cabbage and other vegetables. Ham and pasta are added at the end.*

**Cheese stall in Ajaccio's open-air market**

white, fresh cheese similar to Italian Ricotta or the Brousse of Provence. It is made from whey and usually eaten fresh – within 48 hours – sprinkled with sugar or in many cooked dishes, although it can be left to mature into a hard, dry ball. The island's other cheeses mostly get their names, including Niolo, Venaco, Sartène and Bastelicaccia, from the area where they were first made; others are simply called by the generic name of Tome or Tomme. They vary from mild semi-soft cheeses with washed rinds to hard, pressed cheeses which gain in strength as they age and may be matured until they are hard and crumbly. Newer varieties include Brin d'Amour, which is rolled in herbs, and Bleu de Corse, a Roquefort-like blue ewes' milk cheese.

## FRUIT & VEGETABLES

Corsica grows all types of citrus fruit, including kumquats. Clementines are one of the island's main crops, most of the harvest being exported to the mainland.

**Chestnuts ripening on the tree in the Corsican sunshine**

The Corsican clementine is small and firm with a sharp, tangy flavour and a thin, tightly-fitting skin. You'll also find exotic species such as Barbary figs and the *arbousier* or strawberry tree. Vegetables include aubergines (eggplants), courgettes (zucchini), beans, chard, tomatoes and peppers. Some of the olive trees in the south of the island are over 1,000 years old. The chestnut tree was dubbed *l'arbre à pain* (the bread tree) because it gave islanders a form of flour to supplement that from the limited cereals on the island. Today, chestnuts are found in many recipes, and they are still ground into flour.

### ON THE MENU

**Canistrelli** Chestnut cookies

**Civet de sanglier aux châtaignes** Wild boar stewed in red wine with chestnuts

**Courgettes farcies** Courgettes (zucchini) stuffed with meat, cheese and vegetables and then baked

**Pulenda** Type of polenta, made with chestnut flour

**Ragoût de cabri** Kid stewed in red wine with onions

**Stufatu** Pork, beef, lamb and ham cooked in red wine and served with pasta

**Tianu d'agneau aux olives** Neck of lamb stewed with herbs and olives

**Cabri roti**, *roast kid, is a celebratory feast, studded with rosemary and garlic, crisp outside and succulent within.*

**Rouget aux anchois** *is red mullet fillets with a piquant anchovy stuffing, fried until crisp and golden.*

**Fiadone** *is a baked cheesecake made from drained Brocciu along with eggs, sugar and lemon zest.*

# What to Drink in Corsica

Corsican wines date back to the period when the ancient Greeks and Romans colonized the island, as revealed by the amphoras of wine found in galleys that sank off the east coast. Full-bodied, fruity and strong, Corsican wines are made from three local grapes, Sciaccarellu, Niellucciu and Vermentinu, which, over the years, have been combined with others from the Continent that have flourished on the island. The wines are made in nine zones that have the AOC (*Appellation d'Origine Controlée*) designation, which is a guarantee of superior quality and authenticity. In addition, Corsica produces various liqueurs and brandies that are made from maquis plants such as myrtle and strawberry tree and that reflect the strong flavours of the island. There are also local mineral water springs and aromatized beers.

**The tables of the Café Napoléon, in Place St-Nicolas, Bastia**

## LIQUEURS AND APERITIFS

As an apéritif, Corsicans drink *pastis*, an aniseed liqueur that in the summer is enjoyed with ice. Other liqueurs are made from myrtle, strawberry tree and citrus fruits like tangerines, oranges and citrons. Castagniccia also produces a chestnut liqueur.

*Cap Corse is a real institution also known abroad. Its inimitable bitter and acidulous taste derives from quinine. This Corsican apéritif can be purchased at the Maison Mattei (see p63), the historic house founded in Bastia in 1872.*

**Citron liqueur**

**Tangerines**

**Citrons**

## WATER AND BEER

Cool mineral water flows from springs in the mountains and is then bottled and sold throughout the island. Beer is also produced on the island. Corsican beer is known for its strong aromas.

**Zilia mineral water**

**Orezza mineral water**

**St-Georges mineral water**

**Three brands of beer** *are produced in Corsica. Pietra is amber-coloured and includes chestnuts among its ingredients; Serena is pale and light; Colomba is a Belgian/German-style wheat beer with a strong taste thanks to the addition of myrtle.*

**The best-known** *sparkling (pétillante) mineral water is Orezza, from the Castagniccia area, which is bottled and distributed throughout Corsica and even to fine restaurants in Paris. Other mineral water comes from the Zilia springs, in the Balagne area, and from St-Georges, near Ajaccio.*

## WINE

Corsican wines usually bear the name of the AOC zone in which they are made on their labels. These zones are: Ajaccio, Calvi, Coteaux du Cap Corse, Figari, Patrimonio, Porto-Vecchio and Sartène. Two other AOCs are called Muscat du Cap Corse and Vins de Corse. Wines also bear the name of the winemaker, preceded by the words *Clos* or *Domaine*, to guarantee the fact that they are made in the winery or estate on the label.

An AOC Cap Corse wine label

**Among the best** *Corsican white wines, there is a good, fruity Malvasia made from grapes grown on the terraced vineyards of Cap Corse. The AOC Patrimonio is famous for its Niellucciu, a dry wine made from a local grape. Other first-rate white wines are those from AOC Muscat du Cap Corse.*

AOC Coteaux du Cap Corse

AOC Vins de Corse

**Rosé** *is a common wine and the Porto-Vecchio, Patrimonio and Vins de Corse AOCs are among the best. The basic grapes used are the local Niellucciu and Sciaccarellu, which are mixed with many other grapes to produce a tasty wine with a fine bouquet that is ideal for summer consumption.*

AOC Patrimonio

AOC Vins de Corse

### RECOMMENDED AOC WINERIES

The best wines can be purchased directly from the wineries.

**AOC Ajaccio**
A Cantina, Les Marines, Porticcio.
*Tel 04 95 25 08 90. Fax 04 95 24 38 07.*
Clos Capitoro, Ajaccio.
*Tel 04 95 25 19 61. www.clos-capitoro.com*

**AOC Calvi**
Domaine Balaninu Nobile, Calvi. *Tel 04 95 65 37 10.*

**AOC Figari**
Olmu di Cagna, Coopérative de Figari. *Tel 04 95 71 87 42.* Domaine de Tanella, Figari. *Tel 04 95 71 00 25.*

**AOC Muscat du Cap Corse**
Clos Nicrosi, Rogliano.
*Tel 04 95 35 41 17. Fax 04 95 35 47 94.*
Domaine de Pietri, Morsiglia (for Rappu).
*Tel 04 95 35 64 79.*

**AOC Patrimonio**
Domaine Gentile, St-Florent.
*Tel 04 95 37 20 20. www.domaine-gentile.com*

**AOC Porto-Vecchio**
Domaine de Torraccia, Lecci, Porto-Vecchio.
*Tel 04 95 71 43 50.*

**AOC Sartène**
Domaine San Michele.
*Tel 04 95 77 06 38.*

**AOC Vins de Corse**
Le Clos Lea, Aléria. *Tel 04 95 57 13 60.*

**Red wines**, *which are full-bodied and have a good bouquet, are mostly made from local grapes. The best reds in Corsica belong to the AOC Patrimonio, thanks to the mild climate and the soil, which is particularly suitable for grape cultivation. Connoisseurs will also enjoy reds from AOC Ajaccio, made from Sciaccarellu grapes, which are every bit as good as Beaujolais. Also worth a try are the reds from Coteaux du Cap Corse, Figari, Porto-Vecchio and Sartène AOCs, the last of which is particularly robust.*

AOC Patrimonio

**Dessert wines** *are mostly made in the Cap Corse and Patrimonio areas, and among the best are the white muscat and red aleatico. A rare white dessert wine from Cap Corse is Rappu, which can be purchased only from the wineries that produce it. Rappu makes a perfect accompaniment for all dry desserts.*

The label of a wine originating from the AOC Muscat du Cap Corse

# Choosing a Restaurant

These restaurants have been selected across a wide range of price categories for their exceptional food, good value for money and interesting location. The chart lists the restaurants by area, and by ascending price order. For map references refer to the road map of Corsica on the back endpaper.

**PRICE CATEGORIES**
Price categories for a three-course meal for one, including half a bottle of house wine, tax and service:

€ Under €25
€€ €25–€40
€€€ €40–€55
€€€€ Over €55

## BASTIA AND THE NORTH

### ALGAJOLA La Vieille Cave
€€

*9 Place de l'Olmo* **Tel** *04 95 60 70 09*          **Map** *C2*

Follow the locals in Algajola and you'll end up at La Vieille Cave, a traditional Corsican restaurant just steps from the beach. The atmospheric background is provided by Algajola's castle walls and the sea beyond. Enjoy lunch on the flowering terrace, or stop by for dinner; daily specials are tailored to suit both meat and fish fanatics.

### ALGAJOLA U Castellu
€€

*10 Place Château* **Tel** *04 95 60 78 75*          **Map** *C2*

There are few places as picturesque as U Castellu in the evening, with its wooden seats and tables adorning a terrace nestled below Algajola's castle walls. On the menu are modern variations of classic Corsican recipes; the main courses, such as anchovy, red pepper and pine-nut tart, are particularly delicious.

### BASTIA Cocovert
€

*4 Cours Pierangeli, 20200* **Tel** *04 95 32 79 54*          **Map** *D2*

A cross between a delicatessen and a restaurant, Cocovert offers the best local ingredients, whether in their raw or cooked forms. Stop by for an amazing lunch, and then take home the ingredients necessary to re-create it. An interesting selection of sandwiches is also available.

### BASTIA Chez Anna
€€

*3 Rue Jean Casale, 20200* **Tel** *04 95 31 83 84*          **Map** *D2*

Standing in Place Saint-Nicholas, you might catch a glimpse of Chez Anna, at the end of an alleyway: it's the building covered in climbing ivy and decorated with fairy lights. The arched stone ceiling and white tablecloths set the mood, whether you choose a simple (but outstanding) pizza or a daily special, like the Fisherman's Plate.

### BASTIA L'Algua
€€

*Le Vieux Port, 20200* **Tel** *04 95 38 43 71*          **Map** *D2*

Located in the Vieux Port, l'Algua is the perfect place to visit after a day out at sea. The decor marries black walls with leopard-print fabrics, but the effect is clean and simple, rather than garish. Try summery dishes such as roasted cherry tomatoes with mozzarella, or the salad of red mullet and citrus fruits – a successful and interesting contrast of textures.

### BASTIA Le 10 Rue Napoléon
€€

*10 Rue Napoléon, 20200* **Tel** *04 95 36 46 87*          **Map** *D2*

This tiny restaurant behind the Chapelle Saint-Roch is run by an entirely female staff. Blending sophistication (the decor) and simplicity (the food), the team offers ten seasonal specials each day. Try mains like Swiss chard and goat's cheese tart, but make sure to leave enough space for the phenomenal desserts (€5.50–€6.50).

### BASTIA Le Caveau de Marin
€€

*14 Quai des Martyrs de la Libération, 20200* **Tel** *04 95 31 62 31*          **Map** *D2*

Situated on the esplanade in close proximity to the Vieux Port, this superior restaurant offers regional specialities and fresh seafood. On the menu are dishes such as pasta with *boutargue* (silver-mullet roe), grilled meats or piles of langoustines fished from the nearby lagoons. Dine in the small quiet terrace or in the elegant dining room.

### BASTIA U Tianu
€€

*4 Rue Monseigneur Rigo, 20200* **Tel** *04 95 31 36 67*          **Map** *D2*

Stroll past this hole-in-the-wall establishment on any weekend night and you're likely to see hordes of locals squeezing their way up the staircase to the dining room. At €23 for a starter and a main course, the prices are unbeatable – and so is the quality of the food. Menu options often include dishes like chickpea salad and stuffed sardines. Closed Nov–Jan.

### BASTIA Au Café des Intimes
€€€

*9 Place Hôtel de Ville, 20200* **Tel** *04 95 31 87 23*          **Map** *D2*

Specializing in Middle Eastern food, this animated restaurant in the bustling marketplace serves fresh fish in tagines and couscous. If you are very hungry, try the Royal Couscous, a feast of chicken, lamb, spicy meatballs and vegetables. Desserts include iced crème caramel with hot chocolate sauce.

**Key to Symbols** *see back cover flap*

### BASTIA Le Bouchon €€€
*4 bis Rue Saint-Jean (Le Vieux Port), 20200* **Tel** 04 95 58 14 22

Map D2

High-end, classy and more traditionally French than Corsican, Le Bouchon is both an exquisite wine bar and a bistro of note. Specialities include seared *foie gras* and suckling pig braised in wine. Finish your meal with an outstanding plate of mixed Corsican cheeses, served with locally produced jams. Closed Feb.

### BASTIA Chez Huguette €€€€
*Le Vieux Port, 20200* **Tel** 04 95 31 37 60

Map D2

In the corner of Bastia's Vieux Port, Chez Huguette may not immediately catch your eye, but understated elegance is the policy at this exclusive restaurant boasting two Michelin stars. Chez Huguette offers swish but simple delicacies, like Cap Corse crayfish (charged per 100g). The wine list, as expected, is top notch. Closed 2 wks at Christmas.

### BASTIA Le Table du Marché Saint-Jean €€€€
*Place du Marché, 20200* **Tel** 04 95 31 64 25

Map D2

A seafood restaurant in the true French fashion, Le Table du Marché Saint-Jean offers its patrons a vast array of succulent delicacies from the sea. If you're watching your budget, visit at lunch time to take advantage of their €25 menu. Traditional Corsican meat dishes are also available.

### CALVI L'Abri Côtier €€
*Rue Joffre, 20260* **Tel** 04 95 46 00 04

Map B2

Enjoy the panoramic views from the huge windows in this port-side restaurant, which offers a cosmopolitan menu of sushi with ginger, carpaccio of fish, breast of duck, sea bass with citrus fruit or grilled Corsican veal, all beautifully presented. Finish your meal with spiced bananas or chestnut macaroon with ice cream. Closed mid-Nov–mid-Mar.

### CALVI U Casanu €€
*18 Boulevard Wilson, 20260* **Tel** 04 95 65 00 10

Map B2

High-backed mint-green booths and funky 1920s posters line the walls of this tiny Corsican establishment. The menu features primarily traditional, hearty dishes such as Corsican-style tripe, and octopus cooked in tomatoes and red wine. It is best to book a table in advance, since U Casanu tends to fill up quickly in the high season.

### CALVI U Fornu €€
*Impasse du Boulevard Wilson, 20260* **Tel** 04 95 65 27 60

Map B2

Located just off Boulevard Wilson, one of Calvi's main shopping streets, U Fornu boasts both generous portions and traditional recipes. Try the wild-boar stew, or the fresh squid served in its own ink. *Fiadone*, or Corsican cheesecake, is one of the house specials, and the shady terrace is an ideal place to enjoy it.

### CALVI Le Bout du Monde €€€
*Plage du Calvi, 20260* **Tel** 04 95 65 15 41

Map B2

Excellent food awaits at this friendly but classy beach spot. You will be spoiled for choice between seafood platters, langoustine ravioli, scallops in orange butter, grilled rib of beef or huge salads, followed by caramelized apple tart or chestnut cream for dessert. Closed lunch in winter; Feb.

### CALVI U Minellu €€€
*Traverse de l'Église, 20260* **Tel** 04 95 65 05 52

Map B2

One of the best spots in Calvi to taste regional specialities and mingle with the locals. Dine alfresco on the colourful terrace, illuminated by glowing glass lanterns, and try the menu of the day for the best of what's on offer. Seasonal recipes, such as cannelloni stuffed with Swiss chard and *brocciu* cheese, or wild-leek tart, truly stand out.

### CALVI L'Emile's Restaurant €€€€
*Quai Landry, 20260* **Tel** 04 95 65 09 60

Map B2

For Michelin-starred French dining in Calvi, head to L'Emile's Restaurant, overlooking the port. The terrace is a perfect spot for watching the incredibly wealthy glide in on their majestic yachts, while letting Iranian caviar (charged per 50g portion) slide down your throat. Most wines are served by the glass, so each course may be perfectly paired.

### CALVI U Callelu €€€€
*Quai Landry, 20260* **Tel** 04 95 65 22 18

Map B2

Although U Callelu may look like just any other terraced restaurant on the lively Quai Landry promenade, this establishment serves up some of the freshest fish available on the port. Try the swordfish tartare, simply dressed in olive oil and lemon, or splurge on the catch of the day. Closed Oct–Apr.

### CENTURI Le Vieux Moulin €€
*Centuri Port, 20238* **Tel** 04 95 35 60 15

Map D1

The most luxurious place to dine in the tiny fishing village of Centuri, Le Vieux Moulin is located in the former Palais Olivari, built at the end of the 19th century. As would be expected, any and all of the fresh fish and seafood dishes (especially the crayfish) are truly mouth-watering.

### ERBALUNGA A Piazzetta €€
*Place du Village, 20222* **Tel** 04 95 33 28 69

Map D1

Packed by 12:30pm on most weekdays, A Piazzetta's terrace spills out on to Erbalunga's main square, tempting locals and tourists alike. Fresh takes on classic Mediterranean dishes – such as grilled vegetables with breaded mozzarella, or creamy spaghetti with *boutargue* (silver-mullet roe) – are served up with a smile. An excellent spot for lunch.

### ERBALUNGA Le Pirate

🖼️📧🍴🅿️ €€€€

*Place Marc Barobu, 20222* **Tel** *04 95 33 24 20*
**Map** *D1*

For pure indulgence, Michelin-starred Le Pirate will not disappoint. The food is exquisite, and the wine list equally high-end. The "Menu Découverte" (€65) offers a sampling of the restaurant's more innovative recipes. Add an extra €25, and the sommelier will recommend four wines (one glass per course) to accompany your meal. Closed Jan–Feb.

### L'ÎLE ROUSSE A Siesta

📧♿🖼️🅿️ €

*Promenade à Marinella, 20220* **Tel** *04 95 60 28 74*
**Map** *C2*

Fresh seafood is the pride of this trendy beach restaurant. On hot nights they move the tables directly on to the beach, so you can dine under the stars and with your feet in the sand. Enjoy spidercrabs, lobster, *bouillabaisse* or other delicious choices such as seafood ravioli and carpaccio of fish. Excellent desserts and wine list. Closed Jan–Mar.

### L'ÎLE ROUSSE Les Gourmands… dissent

📝🖼️📧🍴🆅 €

*Rue Notre-Dame, 20220* **Tel** *04 95 34 20 74*
**Map** *C2*

From *fougasse* (a soft bread) stuffed with salmon and cherry tomatoes, to pastries and pots of chocolate fondue, Les Gourmands… dissent makes everything that is for sale in the little bakery and restaurant. Stop in for breakfast (which includes juice, a hot beverage, a pastry, bread and jams) or to indulge in an delicious afternoon treat.

### L'ÎLE ROUSSE L'Île d'Or

🖼️📧🍴 €

*Place Paoli, 20220* **Tel** *04 95 60 12 05*
**Map** *C2*

The perfect place for a leisurely lunch on a hot afternoon, L'Île d'Or's terraced area occupies a corner of the town's main square. Open every day for lunch and dinner, the restaurant serves a wide range of dishes, from pizza to salads, as well as the usual regional plates, to suit all tastes and budgets.

### L'ÎLE ROUSSE A Quadrera

🖼️🔽🍴 €€

*6 Rue Napoléon, 20220* **Tel** *04 95 60 44 52*
**Map** *C2*

A Quadrera is literally a hole in the wall on one of Île Rousse's backstreets, but don't let the minuscule size put you off. The owners are fun and friendly, and the regional specialities on offer are delicious. Try My Wife's Soup (traditional Corsican) or Mr Jojo's Salad (goat's cheese, honey and *panzetta*, a type of cured ham).

### L'ÎLE ROUSSE U Spuntinu

🖼️📧🔽🍴 €€

*1 Rue Napoléon, 20220* **Tel** *04 95 60 00 05*
**Map** *C2*

The chefs at U Spuntinu (literally "a snack" in Corsican) proudly create only what they consider to be genuine Corsican dishes, using the freshest local ingredients. Try the courgette dumplings, or the wild-herb and *brocciu* tart, both truly out of the ordinary. Don't miss the very affordable three-course lunchtime menu.

### MACINAGGIO U Lampione

🖼️📧🍴 €€

*Marina, 20248* **Tel** *04 95 35 45 55*
**Map** *D1*

A down-to-earth restaurant on Macinaggio's port, U Lampione offers its patrons a wide range of fresh fish and crispy pizzas, as well as lobsters (in season). While away the afternoon watching the boats drift in and out of the marina, sitting in the shade of the restaurant's breezy terrace.

### MACINAGGIO Maison Bellini

🖼️📧🍴 €€€

*Marina, 20248* **Tel** *04 95 35 40 37*
**Map** *D1*

Fairly isolated at the north end of Macinaggio's port, Maison Bellini sports crisp white tablecloths and fine table settings on its rustic wooden terrace. The restaurant is renowned for its fish soup (a variation of Marseille's *bouillabaisse*), and it tends to be frequented by well-heeled tourists hopping off their yachts.

### OLMI CAPPELLA La Tornadia

🖼️🔽🍴 €€

*Route de la Forêt de Tartagines, Pioggiola, 20259* **Tel** *04 95 61 90 93*
**Map** *C2*

Enjoy traditional Corsican cooking at La Tornadia, while sitting outside under the chestnut trees. The unusual mountain specialities on the menu, such as the braised veal in blueberry sauce, are difficult to find anywhere else on the island. The highest village in the Giussani region, Pioggiola boasts spectacular views over the verdant valleys below.

### PIGNA A Casarella

📝🖼️🔽🆅 €€

*Pigna, 20220* **Tel** *04 95 61 78 08*
**Map** *C2*

Fancy lunch overlooking the Mediterranean, listening to local guitar music, maybe enjoying a glass or two of organic juice? A Casarella adds a modern edge to classical Corsican dishes. Try seasonal mixes like their *brocciu* cheese and courgette salad with grated carrots, mint and bell-pepper confit. Tapas-style portions are also available to share.

### PIGNA Casa Musicale

🖼️ €€

*Pigna, 20220* **Tel** *04 95 61 77 31*
**Map** *C2*

Set in the white-stone, pedestrianized village of Pigna, this is the place to stop at if you are interested in trying unadulterated Corsican dishes. With its aim to preserve the cultural and gastronomic heritage of the area, Casa Musicale has gained island-wide renown. Be sure to reserve, if only for a platter of cured meats. Closed Jan–mid-Feb.

### SAINT-FLORENT César

🖼️🍴🆅 €€

*Saint-Florent Port, 20217* **Tel** *04 95 37 15 33*
**Map** *D2*

César, on Saint-Florent's port, is a buzzing spot to dine any evening of the week. Try one of the eight types of mussels on offer, or sip a glass of local Patrimonio wine as you indulge in one of the restaurant's many home-made pasta dishes. An excellent place to visit with kids, since the menu includes a wide range of children's dishes.

**Key to Price Guide** *see p172* **Key to Symbols** *see back cover flap*

### SAINT-FLORENT L'Arriere Cour 🖼️🚪🍴Ⓥ €€
*Place Doria, 20217* **Tel** *04 95 35 33 62*                                   ***Map*** *D2*

Just off Place Doria, L'Arriere Cou is both a *crêperie*, offering myriad sweet and savoury pancakes, and a restaurant with a menu of more traditional Corsican dishes. The plant-covered terrace affords a welcome respite from the unrelenting summer sun. Try the crispy *beignets de fromage frais*, a kind of fried soft-cheese dumpling. Closed Jan–Feb.

### SAINT-FLORENT L'Auberge de l'Europe 🖼️📋🍴Ⓥ €€
*Saint-Florent Port, 20217* **Tel** *04 95 35 32 91*                            ***Map*** *D2*

This is without a doubt Saint-Florent's finest restaurant. Owned by the Hôtel de l'Europe, and boasting splendid views over the port, L'Auberge offers a three-course menu for €28. Specialities include thinly sliced smoked swordfish in a caper, lemon and tomato dressing, and *brocciu* ravioli doused in a creamy spinach sauce.

### SAINT-FLORENT La Rascasse ♿🖼️📋 €€€
*Rue Strada Nova, 20217* **Tel** *04 95 37 06 99*                               ***Map*** *D2*

Inventive cooking is the norm at this upscale fish restaurant in a prime position on the port. Ensconce yourself on the terrace and study the yachts as you wait for your order of fish soup, seafood risotto or grilled squid. Try the classic *bouillabaisse* or a grilled lobster, and be sure to leave enough room for one of the sublime desserts.

## AJACCIO AND THE WEST COAST

### AJACCIO Auberge Colomba 🖼️📋🍴 €€
*3 Rue Trois Marie, 20000* **Tel** *04 95 51 30 55*                            ***Map*** *B4*

Under an awning, on the side of a staircase leading down to Ajaccio's port, the Auberge Colomba is an excellent little restaurant that dabbles in high-end French cuisine, with dishes like pan-fried *foie gras*, as well as offering more traditional regional fare. The salads are exceptionally fresh and varied.

### AJACCIO Auberge du Cheval Blanc 🖼️🚪 €€
*18 Rue Bonaparte, 20000* **Tel** *04 95 21 17 98*                            ***Map*** *B4*

This pizzeria and restaurant is consistently rated as a top spot by Ajaccio's youth population. Rustic decor and varied budget options make the Auberge du Cheval Blanc a prime location for a simple yet tasty dinner based on Mediterranean cuisine covering various regions, from Italy to the South of France and Corsica itself. Closed Jan.

### AJACCIO Chez Paulo 🖼️📋🚪🍴Ⓥ €€
*7 Rue Roi de Rome, 20000* **Tel** *04 95 51 16 47*                           ***Map*** *B4*

Large wooden tables and a young and friendly staff set the scene at Chez Paulo, a laid-back spot where you can grab a quick pizza or a full meal. Visit after 10pm to catch the traditional Corsican cabaret of folk songs and guitar music. If you haven't had your fill of wild boar yet, you can try the typically Corsican "Menu Maquis" (€19).

### AJACCIO Da Mamma ♿🖼️📋🍴Ⓥ €€
*3 Passage Guingette, 20000* **Tel** *04 95 21 39 44*                         ***Map*** *B4*

Although Da Mamma may be difficult to find, hidden away in Ajaccio's back allies, it is one of the most exceptional eateries in the city, using products entirely sourced from the island. Choose one of the three outdoor tables, under hanging vines and a huge rubber tree, or opt for a more traditional setting in the vaulted interior. Closed Jan–Feb.

### AJACCIO Le Spago 🖼️📋🚪🍴Ⓥ €€
*Rue Emmanuel Aréne, 20000* **Tel** *04 95 21 15 71*                          ***Map*** *B4*

Everything about ultra-contemporary Le Spago emanates cutting-edge cool, especially the acid-green tabletops and white garden furniture, which present a striking contrast to the ancient surroundings. Young patrons and loud music make this a lively but worthy pit stop.

### AJACCIO Pampasgiolu 🖼️📋🍴 €€
*15 Rue de la Porta, 20000* **Tel** *04 95 50 71 52*                          ***Map*** *B4*

Reserve ahead at this popular eating place in the old city, with its attractive, rustic dining rooms and small terrace. Try the *spuntini* (snack) platters of local fish or meat specialities, or opt for dishes such as the duck breast with pears. A good selection of desserts includes a deep, rich chestnut fondant. Closed Mon lunch; Sun.

### AJACCIO Restaurant des Halles 🖼️📋🍴Ⓥ €€
*4 Rue des Halles, 20000* **Tel** *04 95 21 42 68*                            ***Map*** *B4*

Open since 1933, the Restaurant des Halles has changed hands a few times over the years but remains a firm local favourite. In the evening, live music is often served up along with the daily specials such as oven-baked sea bass. The restaurant is famed for its *aïoli*, a delicious garlicky mayonnaise served with fish and vegetables. Closed last 2 wks Jan.

### AJACCIO Le 20123 📋♿🖼️📋🍴 €€€
*2 Rue Roi de Rome, 20000* **Tel** *04 95 21 50 05*                           ***Map*** *B4*

Originally opened in 1987 in the town of Pila Canale (postcode 20123), this gourmet Corsican restaurant moved to Ajaccio in 1998 but retained its original name. Forget ordering à la carte: Le 20123 offers one set menu (with choices), which changes daily. The result is a fabulous selection of dishes you may not have tried. Closed mid-Jan–mid-Feb.

## AJACCIO Le Floride 🖼️▤    €€€
*Route Amirauté, Port Charles Ornano, 20090* **Tel** *04 95 22 67 48*     **Map** *B4*

Situated on Ajaccio's port, Le Floride is a charming restaurant renowned for its ultra-fresh sea urchins, giant shrimp and locally caught fish. Right next door is the Bistro Le Floride, which offers more budget-friendly options, like the famous *bruschette* (toasted bread smothered in chopped tomatoes, creamy cheese and seasonal vegetables).

## AJACCIO Le Grand Café Napoléon 🖼️🖼️🖼️🖼️    €€€
*10 Cours Napoléon, 20000* **Tel** *04 95 21 42 54*     **Map** *B4*

Island dining is mostly associated with basking on sun-filled terraces, but Le Grand Café Napoléon, the oldest spot in town, is one place that offers indoor dining steeped in character. The café's chairs are decorated in beautiful upholstered fabrics, and the walls are adorned with photos of Ajaccio in times gone by. Ideal for a pre-dinner aperitif.

## AJACCIO Palm Beach 🖼️    €€€
*Route des Sanguinaires, 20000* **Tel** *04 95 52 01 03*     **Map** *B4*

This excellent restaurant in a beach setting on the road to the Îles Sanguinaires offers an elegant dining room and a terrace with splendid views over the bay. The English chef prepares impeccably cooked dishes such as line-caught sea bass in salt, saddle of lamb in a herb crust, or fillet of beef with wild garlic. Sumptuous desserts complete the picture.

## CUTTOLI CORTICHIATTO A Casetta 🖼️🖼️    €€€
*Lieu-dit Cantege Canale, 20167* **Tel** *04 95 25 66 59*     **Map** *B4*

Serving modern French/Corsican fare, A Casetta mixes local mountain- and sea-sourced ingredients for dishes like giant shrimp wrapped in cured ham, or filet of duck on orange-infused, caramelized porcini mushrooms. Outstanding and beautifully presented desserts round out your dining experience at this eminent little restaurant.

## OTA Chez Felix 🖼️▤🖼️    €€
*Ota, 20150* **Tel** *04 95 26 12 92*     **Map** *B3*

Known to cook up some of the best food in the Ota-Porto region, this restaurant serves traditional Corsican dishes based on Felix Ceccaldi's family recipes, which have been handed down through the generations. Those with a sweet tooth can choose from no fewer than 13 divine desserts every day.

## PIANA Hôtel Les Roches Rouges 🖼️🖼️    €€€
*Piana, 20115* **Tel** *04 95 27 81 81*     **Map** *B3*

The delightful terrace of the Hôtel Les Roches Rouges *(see p162)* is one of Corsica's premium spots for a sunset cocktail. After that, you can move inside to the Art Deco dining room, with its airy high ceilings and frescoes, for a gourmet meal. Owner Madame Mady's outgoing character adds to the overall charm.

## PISCIATELLO Auberge du Prunelli 🖼️🖼️Ⓥ    €€
*Bastelicaccia, 20129* **Tel** *04 95 20 02 75*     **Map** *B4*

This outstanding *auberge* just south of Ajaccio has fed a wide range of notable patrons, including French film star Alain Delon. Dine on regional specialities, many of which are made with ingredients gathered locally by owner René Orlandazzi. The atmospheric open fire is especially enjoyable during the chilly winter months.

## PORTICCIO L'Arbousier 🖼️▤🖼️🖼️    €€€€
*Hôtel Le Maquis, 20166* **Tel** *04 95 25 05 55*     **Map** *B4*

Head waiters Georges and Antoine, have been seamlessly orchestrating the fine dining here for the past 27 years, and the service is top-notch. On the menu, try the twice-cooked baby pigeon in a myrtle-wine sauce, or the roasted lamb with rosemary. There is a pretty west facing terrace from which to watch the sun set.

## PORTO Mini-Golfe ▤🖼️    €€
*Porto Marina, 20150* **Tel** *04 95 26 17 55*     **Map** *B3*

Leave Porto's main complex of restaurants and shops behind, and cross over the Japanese-style wooden bridge to reach this eucalyptus-shaded beach hideaway. On the menu, you will find a wide choice of grilled meats, fish salads and pasta dishes, with an accent of Oriental spices courtesy of the Antillaise chef. Closed Oct–Apr.

## PORTO Le Maquis 🖼️🖼️Ⓥ    €€€
*Porto par Ota, 20150* **Tel** *04 95 26 12 19*     **Map** *B3*

For gourmet dining, plus fabulous views over Porto, head to Le Maquis, on the north side of town. A terraced eating area offers tables both indoors and out, and the menu serves up delicacies such as ravioli stuffed with scallops in a marinated vegetable sauce. The home-made desserts are sinfully indulgent.

## SAGONE A Sponda 🖼️▶    €€
*Sagone, 20118* **Tel** *04 95 28 01 66*     **Map** *B4*

Set just across the street from the waterfront, on the edge of Sagone, A Sponda is one of the most popular restaurants in the region. Enjoy local meats and freshly caught fish, as well as cooling sea breezes, on the huge wooden terrace. In winter, the friendly staff serve up traditional specialities from Corsica's mountain regions.

## SAGONE L'Ancura 🖼️Ⓥ    €€€
*Port de Sagone, 20118* **Tel** *04 95 28 04 93*     **Map** *B4*

A tiny restaurant on Sagone's port, L'Ancura's specialities are pizza and fish, both cooked in a flaming wood-fired oven. Two separate terraces overlook the fishing boats, hauling ingredients directly from the sea to the restaurant's kitchen. Don't miss the chargrilled sea kebabs and the heavenly *bouillabaisse*, both local favourites. Closed Nov–Mar.

**Key to Price Guide** *see p172* **Key to Symbols** *see back cover flap*

# BONIFACIO AND THE SOUTH

### BONIFACIO A Manichella
€€  Map C6

*Place du Marché, Haute Ville, 20169* **Tel** *04 95 73 12 75*

A Manichella offers bargain eats in a glamorous setting. Dine on the southeast terrace to enjoy magnificent views of Sardinia on a clear day. House specialities include large salads and crêpes, but it is also wise to try the daily specials, or the *assiette degustation*, or tasting plate (around €12), for a little mix of whatever is seasonal.

### BONIFACIO Cantina Doria
€€  Map C6

*27 Rue Doria, 20169* **Tel** *04 95 73 50 49*

Smooth, dark, wooden tables, bench seating and a tiny interior give Cantina Doria somewhat of a pub-like feel. Favoured by the young and trendy, this little eatery is a great spot to try local specialities, or partake in a light dinner of simple Corsican soup and dessert (€13). The cuisine focuses on recipes from the island's interior. Closed Oct–Mar.

### BONIFACIO The Kissing Pigs
€€  Map C6

*15 Quai Banda del Ferro, 20169* **Tel** *04 95 73 56 09*

Who could resist popping into an establishment called The Kissing Pigs? At this wine bar and restaurant on Bonifacio's port, all of the many beverages on offer can be ordered by the bottle or by the glass. Dine on plates of grilled meats, or salads that combine mountain cheeses and the ever-present cured pork.

### BONIFACIO Hôtel Restaurant du Centre Nautique
€€€  Map C6

*Quai Nord, BP 65, 20169* **Tel** *04 95 73 50 44*

For a culinary experience that will leave you whirling with delight, this is the place to go in Bonifacio. Recipes herald from the south of the island, and the emphasis is on the merging of sea ingredients with influences from the nearby mountains, in dishes such as grilled giant shrimp marinated in wild fennel.

### BONIFACIO Les 4 Vents
€€€  Map C6

*29 Quai Banda del Ferro, 20169* **Tel** *04 95 73 07 50*

Although the decor may be a little on the kitsch side (think a wealth of tiny flags hanging from the ceiling), during the summertime, Les 4 Vents serves up some of the freshest fish in Bonifacio. In keeping with the seasons, the winter months witness this restaurant's focus shift to typically Alsatian specialities.

### BONIFACIO Au Jardin d'A Cheda
€€€€  Map C6

*Cavallo Morto, BP 3, 20169* **Tel** *04 95 73 03 82*

The gardens of A Cheda seamlessly blend Mediterranean wilderness and Asian decor. The gentle sound of tumbling fountains creates an appropriately exotic backdrop for chef Sebastien Mortet's contemporary Corsican cuisine. Choose one of the surprise menus (four or five courses, €68–€79) to try Mortet's latest gourmet creations.

### BONIFACIO La Caravelle
€€€€  Map C6

*37 Quai Camparetti, 20169* **Tel** *04 95 73 00 03*

The most elegant place to eat on the bustling quayside serves glistening fresh seafood in dishes such as lobster risotto, seafood platter and langoustine in basil butter. Cheese is served with walnuts and dried pears, and desserts include old favourites like Crêpes Suzette. Dress up for this upscale restaurant, and be sure to reserve a table. Closed winter.

### BONIFACIO Stella d'Oro "Chez Jules"
€€€€  Map C6

*7 Rue Doria, 20169* **Tel** *04 95 73 03 63*

A high-end, traditional tavern in Bonifacio's old town, the Stella d'Oro offers gourmet adaptations of traditional Corsican recipes. Try the rabbit with sage and lemon confit, or the house speciality, aubergines *à la bonifacienne* (cooked with egg and breadcrumbs). This is a favourite spot of French celebrities, including Johnny Hallyday.

### CAMPOMORO Hôtel Restaurant le Ressac
€€  Map B5

*Belvedere, 20110* **Tel** *04 95 74 22 25*

Located on the long beach in Campomoro, the family-run restaurant at the Hôtel le Ressac is your best bet for a delicious meal on the Golfe de Valinco. Dine on traditional Corsican dishes, primarily based around freshly caught fish. The pizzas cooked in the wood-fired oven are also exceptional.

### LECCI Grand Hôtel de Cala Rossa
€€€€  Map D5

*Lecci, 20137* **Tel** *04 95 71 61 51*

One Michelin star, garden dining and a path straight to a private beach make a meal at this exclusive restaurant one to savour. Although not cheap, the outstanding cuisine has been created using the freshest ingredients, all sourced locally. A truly special place for a romantic evening meal, when the outdoor area twinkles by candlelight.

### LEVIE A Pignata
€€€  Map C5

*Route du Pianu, 20170* **Tel** *04 95 78 41 90*

Dining at A Pignata, one of the oldest farm-restaurants in the south of Corsica, is by advance reservation only, but it is worth the effort. The restaurant specializes in regional dishes, such as wild-boar stew. For a blast of local history, note that this *auberge* is located just 3 km (2 miles) from the archeological sites of Cucuruzzu and Capula. Closed Nov–Dec.

### PINARELLO La Fleur de Sel  🖼️🍴  €€€
*Pinarello, 20144 **Tel** 04 95 71 06 49*          **Map** D5

Terraced seating huddles around a central olive tree, just steps from the gorgeous white Pinarello beach. The menu may not be extensive, but gourmet dining at La Fleur de Sel offers enough dishes to suit most tastes. Try the grouper cooked in a salt crust and served with a pear and Muscat-wine fondue.

### PORTO-VECCHIO A Cantina di l'Orriu  🖼️📋  €€
*5 Cours Napoléon, 20137 **Tel** 04 95 70 26 21*          **Map** C6

The outdoor seating at A Cantina di l'Orriu, just off the Place de la République, entices you to stop for a glass of chilled wine. Savour one of the fantastic aperitif combos, such as a glass of AOC Calvi white served with toasted bread and olive pâté. Then nip next door to the restaurant shop to pick up local treats for your friends back home.

### PORTO-VECCHIO L'Endroit  🖼️V  €€
*3 Rue Général de Gaulle **Tel** 04 95 70 63 63*          **Map** C6

Beige, angular and, above all, contemporary, this tiny café on the edge of Porto-Vecchio's old town definitely lives up to its name – "The Place". This is an excellent spot for a quick and healthy lunch, always prepared with the freshest ingredients available. Make sure to try one of their many coffee-based drinks.

### PORTO-VECCHIO Le Tourisme  ♿🖼️📋  €€
*Cours Napoléon, 20137 **Tel** 04 95 70 06 45*          **Map** C6

This popular establishment is situated in the upper town, facing the church. A friendly place decorated in a brasserie style, Le Tourisme serves Provençal and Corsican specialities, including a large choice of fish dishes, as well as veal and game in season. The owner will source lobster for you if you give him 24 hours' notice. Closed Sun lunch.

### PORTO-VECCHIO Chez Anna  🖼️V  €€€
*16 Rue Camille de Rocca Serra, 20137 **Tel** 04 95 70 19 97*          **Map** C6

Modern and minimalist, Chez Anna blends Corsican regional recipes with rustic Italian cooking. Home-made pasta dishes and fresh seafood, like gnocchi with mussels, are exceptional, as are the desserts. Although the indoor eating area tends to be a little cramped, the spacious outdoor terrace more than makes up for it. Closed mid-Oct–mid-Apr.

### PORTO-VECCHIO Le Bistro  ♿🖼️  €€€
*4 Quai Paoli, 20137 **Tel** 04 95 70 22 96*          **Map** C6

This lively eating spot in the yachting harbour in the lower town has a pretty dining room and a large terrace. On the menu you will find fresh seafood, including red mullet with anchovies and tomatoes, sea bream, and grilled spiny lobster. There is also excellent *tartare* of beef or stew of wild boar, in season. Good choice of desserts. Closed Feb.

### PORTO-VECCHIO Le Belvedere  🖼️📋🍷  €€€€
*Route de Palombaggia, 20137 **Tel** 04 95 70 54 13*          **Map** C6

As you pass by, the arched, flowered entrance to this Michelin-starred restaurant, is eye-catching enough to make you slow down, even if you didn't know about the gourmet restaurant inside. For a romantic dinner, you can dine by candlelight on the terrace perched above the sea, while enjoying views of Porto-Vecchio's old town across the bay.

### PROPRIANO Le Cabanon  🖼️  €€
*26 Avenue Napoléon, 20110 **Tel** 04 95 76 06 76*          **Map** B5

Skewered tiger prawns and scallops are among the most popular dishes at this charming quayside restaurant. Start with fish soup or aubergine (eggplant) caviar, and follow with grilled red mullet or sea bream in a white-wine sauce. Alternatively, try the oysters from the east-coast lagoons. End your meal with the excellent cheese selection.

### PROPRIANO U Pescadori  🖼️📋🔌🍴  €€
*13 Avenue Napoléon, 20110 **Tel** 04 95 76 42 95*          **Map** B5

Owned, and supplied, by a family of fishermen, U Pescadori provides delicious freshly caught seafood. The decor is nautical, and there are a few tables crammed on the sidewalk outside the door. As expected from members of the Marmite d'Or (a gastronomic association that promotes traditional local foods), the cuisine is absolutely sublime.

### ROCCAPINA Auberge Coralli  🖼️  €€
*Roccapina beach, 20100 **Tel** 04 95 77 05 94*          **Map** B5

Enjoy fabulous views of Roccapina's Lion's Rock, a natural rock formation, while dining on seafood in its many forms at the Auberge Coralli. After lunch, head down to the beach: its white sands and crystal-clear water make it one of the island's most beautiful places to spend a lazy afternoon.

### SARTÈNE La Bergerie d'Acciola  🖼️  €
*Giuncheto, 20100 **Tel** 04 95 77 14 00*          **Map** C5

This outstanding, relaxed restaurant with views over the surrounding valleys offers a fabulous opportunity to taste local specialities, and take your favourites home with you afterwards. All the raw ingredients at La Bergerie d'Acciola, as well as the dishes, are home-picked or home-made. Don't miss the amazing chestnut ice cream (seasonal). Closed winter.

### SARTÈNE Auberge Santa Barbara  🖼️🍷  €€
*Alzone 3 km/2miles out of Sartène on the road to Propriano, 20100 **Tel** 04 95 77 09 06*          **Map** C5

Owned by Gisèle Lovichi, Corsica's foremost female chef, this outdoor eatery is set in lovely gardens. Choose between home-made charcuterie, country soup with a vegetable salad, stuffed leg of lamb, or saddle of lamb with a herb crust. Finish with *fiadone*, a dessert made with Corsican cheese, lemons and eggs. Closed mid-Oct–Feb.

## SOLLACARO Le Moulin Farellacci      🖼 🔽 🍴    €€€
*Hameau de Calvese, 20140*  **Tel** *04 95 74 62 28*     **Map** *B5*

An ancient restored oil mill, Le Moulin Farellacci offers alfresco dining in the garden, with views over the valley all the way to the sea. True country cooking dominates the menu: try the chicken roasted in a sage-infused salt crust. Evenings are livened up by traditional Corsican folk songs. Open during the summer months only.

## ZONZA Auberge du Col de Bavella      🖼 🍴    €€
*Col de Bavella, 20124*  **Tel** *04 95 72 09 87*     **Map** *C5*

Known locally for its charcuterie, or cured meats, the Auberge du Col de Bavella also draws crowds with its renowned chestnut tart. Its ample and filling portions have made it a favourite of GR20 hikers. Head to the natural pool 2.5 km (1.5 miles) out of town on the D420 for a refreshing post-prandial swim.

# CORTE AND THE INTERIOR

## CORTE A Scudella      🖼 🍴    €
*Place Paoli, 20250*  **Tel** *04 95 46 25 31*     **Map** *C3*

Specializing in traditional recipes from the Corte region, this unassuming little eatery in a corner of Place Paoli has reasonable prices. Its daily changing specials, such as filet of perch or three-fish terrine, are outstanding. For a lighter meal, try the Menu Fraîcheur (€10): a double portion of any starter, followed by dessert.

## CORTE La Rivière à Vins      🍷 🖼 🔽 🍴 V    €
*5 Rampe Sainte-Croix, 20250*  **Tel** *04 95 46 37 04*     **Map** *C3*

Truly a dream come true for avid carnivores. All of the many types of meat on offer at La Rivière à Vins are cooked in a large wood-fired oven, and even the salads tend to be based around locally cured meats, such as hams and salamis. Try the Plateau Gourmand (€16) for a small sampling of everything.

## CORTE Osteria di u Castellu      🖼 🍴    €
*5 Quartier Calanches, 20250*  **Tel** *04 95 46 32 50*     **Map** *C3*

Open only during the sweltering summer months, the Osteria di u Castellu is located just below the Belvedere lookout point and the Citadel in Corte's old town. Stop in for abundant salads, pizzas or a simple set menu. Set among nearby trees, the tables offer shady respite for pleasant dining. Closed Nov–Apr.

## CORTE U Museu      🖼 📋    €
*Rue St-Joseph, 20260*  **Tel** *04 95 61 08 36*     **Map** *C3*

At the foot of the citadel, in the old town, this large restaurant has several dining rooms, as well as a tree-shaded terrace. There is a wide choice of dishes, ranging from pizzas, pastas and salads to traditional Corsican specialities of white beans and lamb, *brocciu*-stuffed lasagne, and grilled meats with herbs.

## CORTE A Casa d'Orsu      🍷 🖼 🍴    €€
*4 Rue Scoliscia, 20250*  **Tel** *06 80 60 70 42*     **Map** *C3*

Friendly staff serve up traditional Corsican specialities on the sunny terrace of A Casa d'Orsu ("The Bear's House"), in Corte's old town. Popular with hikers returning from the mountains there is hearty wild-boar terrine and fantastic home-made pasta dishes to help restore energy levels.

## CORTE L'Osteria di l'Orta      ♿ 🍷 🖼 🔽 V    €€
*Villa Guelfucci, Pont de l'Orta, 20250*  **Tel** *04 95 61 06 41 or 06 81 87 83 20*     **Map** *C3*

Personally restored by owners Antoine and Marina Guelfucci, a 19th-century former family home is now the site of this wonderful restaurant. Try one of the set menus (€25–€32), which include produce grown by the couple, as well as hams and meats raised (and cured) directly on the property.

## CORTE U Paglia Orba      🖼 📋 🍴 V    €€
*1 Avenue Xavier Luciani, 20250*  **Tel** *04 95 61 07 89*     **Map** *C3*

U Paglia Orba prides itself on researching and re-creating regional recipes, in order to ensure that the local gastronomic traditions are not lost over time. Unique menus for special occasions can also be developed with advance notice. One of the best restaurants in town, this relaxed spot is well worth a visit.

## PONTE LECCIA Chez Jacqueline      🍷 🖼 🍴    €€
*Pont-de-Castirla, 20218*  **Tel** *04 95 47 42 04*     **Map** *C3*

If you have your own transport, head 14 km (8.5 miles) north of Corte to the intimate Chez Jacqueline for a tasty meal. Whether you choose to eat on the shady terrace in summer, or in one of the rustic interior rooms during the winter, make sure you save room for the unique dessert, a *brocciu* cheese and brandy pudding.

## VIZZAVONA Hôtel-Restaurant du Monte d'Oro      🖼 V    €
*Col de Vizzavona, 20219*  **Tel** *04 95 47 21 06*     **Map** *C4*

With just 50 permanent residents, it's a surprise that Vizzavona is even known outside of its immediate environs. But for hikers of the GR20, this village is a favourite stop, not least for a meal at the rustic 19th-century Hôtel-Restaurant du Monte d'Oro. Enjoy delicious traditional Corsican cuisine on the scenic terrace. Closed Oct–Apr.

# SHOPPING IN CORSICA

Corsica offers a great variety of locally produced foods – from honey and a wide range of chestnut-based products, to charcuterie, sausages and cheeses prepared by shepherds with maquis herbs. The best places to buy this produce are the lively, colourful food markets in the main towns. It is also interesting to visit the centres of production, including the alpine *bergeries* and the many wineries throughout the northern part of the island. Handicraft production is quite varied and efforts to revive the ancient arts of knife-making, pottery and stoneware, basket-weaving and glass-blowing are proving increasingly popular. There are handicraft centres in the cities, but it is more enjoyable to go directly to the workshops to see how these objects are made. The most active region for handicraft production is Balagne.

Shepherd's leather bag

## OPENING HOURS

In Corsica, shops operate from Tuesday to Saturday (9am to noon; 3 to 6pm). Food shops are open from 8am to noon and from 2 to 6pm, and also on Sunday morning. In the summer, especially in tourist resorts, opening hours are usually extended, and some shops are also open on Monday.

## CREDIT CARDS

Credit cards are accepted almost everywhere, but some shop owners might set a minimum purchase of about €15. Workshops and smaller shops inland tend to prefer cash payment.

## SHOPPING CENTRES

On the outskirts of Bastia and Ajaccio there are shopping centres and supermarkets. They are usually open from 9am to 8pm, except for Monday morning and Sunday. On sale are clothes, shoes, sports accessories, perfumes, books and food, at reasonable prices. These centres also have restaurants and cafés.

## HANDICRAFTS

For quality products, try any of the craftsmen's workshops belonging to the Casa di l'Artigiani, a network of about 50 artisans who guarantee the authenticity of their products. You can also try shops that display the sign Association d'Artisans de Corse or Corsic'Arte. The best option, however, may be to go directly to the workshops, such as those in Balagne *(see pp76–7)*.

Among the best souvenirs are objects made of olive and chestnut wood, straw and wicker baskets, handmade scarves and rugs, Orezza's myrtle-wood pipes, blown-glass objects from Feliceto, and wooden music boxes from Pigna.

One of the many wine producers in the Cap Corse area

The most famous Corsican handicraft products are knives, and the leading makers are Jean-Pierre Caggiari and Laurent Bellini of **Atelier du Couteau** in Ajaccio and **Pol Demongeot** in Calvi.

Pottery and stoneware are also widespread, with workshops throughout the island. Of particular interest are the ateliers of **Jacques Quilichini** in Pigna and **Fely (Terraghja)** in Corte.

Among the now-scarce luthiers is Christian Magdeleine at **Guitare et Cetera** in Bastia *(see p61)*, who specializes in guitars, and **Ugo Casalonga** in Pigna.

Other interesting shops are **Maison du Coral** in Ajaccio, which sells cut minerals (diorite, porphyry and rhyolite) and coral, and **Cyrnarom** in Bastia *(see p62)*, which distils flowers and plants to create typically Corsican perfumes. Wild-flower essences are also sold in the markets.

**A stall with an array of tempting products at an Ajaccio market**

Browsing at the Sunday market in Bastia

## MARKETS AND FAIRS

The lively, colourful markets are a must for visitors to Corsica. The one in Bastia is held in the Place de l'Hôtel-de-Ville every morning (except Monday), with stalls that sell vegetables, fish, Corsican specialities and even clothes. There are also vendors who make *crêpes* and local snacks. The bric-à-brac market is held in Place St-Nicolas, in front of the outdoor cafés.

The daily food market in Ajaccio, in Place Campinchi, features mostly regional products, such as charcuterie and sausages, wines, sweets, cheese, oil and honey.

In Calvi, greengrocers and vendors of typical products sell their wares under the roof of the covered market, which can be reached by going up a stairway from Rue Clemenceau.

In nearby L'Île Rousse, the covered market facing Place Paoli dates from the 19th century and is classified as an historic building.

In the second week of September a handicraft fair takes place at Porto-Vecchio. On the first weekend of July there is a wine fair at Luri and on the first weekend after 14 July there is an olive fair in Balagne.

## REGIONAL SPECIALITIES

There are many Corsican gastronomic delights, first of all honey, which boasts six AOC designations. A range of honeys from different plants can be found at **Franck Dupré** in Calenzana and **U Stazzu** in Ajaccio.

Corsica's famous *canistrelli* (almond, hazelnut, lemon or aniseed biscuits) are for sale at these recommended shops: **Boulangerie A Viletta** and **Mathieu Carlotti** in Ajaccio and **E Fritelle** in Calenzana.

Local charcuterie and cheeses can be found in all food shops, the best of which are **Charcuterie Pantalacci** in Ajaccio and **U Muntagnolu** and **U Paese** in Bastia.

Local wines (*see p171*) are sold at the **Enoteca** in Ajaccio. For apéritifs try the **Maison Mattei** in Bastia (*see p63*).

The only surviving artisan who makes lobster nets at Cap Corse

# DIRECTORY

## SHOPPING CENTRES

**Carrefour**
Cours Prince Impérial, Ajaccio.

**Centre Commercial La Rocade**
Ajaccio.

**Centre Commercial de Santa Devota**
Airport Rotunda, Borgo, Bastia.

**Centre Commercial de Toga**
Port de Toga, Bastia.

**Champion**
Mezzavia, Ajaccio.

**Galerie Marchande de l'Hypermarché**
Avenue Sampiero Corso, Bastia.

**La Rocade**
Route Nationale 193, Furiani. Géant Casino.

## HANDICRAFTS

**Atelier du Couteau**
2 Rue Bonaparte, Ajaccio. *Tel* 04 95 52 05 92. *Knives.*

**Cyrnarom**
9 Ave Monseigneur Rigo, Bastia. *Tel 04 95 31 70 60. Perfumes.*

**Fely (Terraghja)**
Corte. *Tel 04 95 46 28 74. Pottery.*

**Guitare et Cetera**
2 Place Guasco, Bastia. *Tel 04 95 31 78 99. Stringed instruments.*

**Jacques Quilichini**
Pigna. *Tel 04 95 61 77 25. Pottery.*

**Maison du Coral**
1 Rue Fesch, Ajaccio. *Tel 04 95 21 47 94 . Coral.*

**Pol Demongeot**
Fort Mozello, Calvi. *Tel 04 95 65 32 54. Knives.*

**Ugo Casalonga**
Pigna. *Tel 04 95 61 79 18. Stringed instruments and wooden music boxes.*

**Verrerie Corse**
Feliceto. *Tel 04 95 61 73 05. Blown-glass objects.*

## REGIONAL SPECIALITIES

**Boulangerie A Viletta**
Avenue Beverini, Ajaccio. *Cakes and croissants.*

**Charcuterie Pantalacci**
Boulevard Pugliesi Conti, Ajaccio. *Charcuterie.*

**Confiserie Saint Sylvestre**
Soveria. *Tel 04 95 47 42 27. Preserves.*

**E Fritelle**
Tiassu Longu, Calenzana. *Tel 04 95 62 78 17. Biscuits.*

**Enoteca**
Rue Maréchal Ornano, Ajaccio. *Wines & liqueurs.*

**Franck Dupré**
Hameau de Pellicciani, Calenzana. *Tel 04 95 65 07 74. Honey and by-products.*

**Maison Mattei**
Place St-Nicolas, Bastia. *Tel 04 95 32 44 38. Corsican wines & liqueurs.*

**Mathieu Carlotti**
Place Vincetti, Bastia. *Tel 04 95 31 09 93. Preserves, chocolate.*

**U Muntagnolu**
15 Rue César Campinchi, Bastia. *Tel 04 95 32 78 04. Charcuterie and cheese.*

**U Paese**
4 Rue Napoléon, Bastia. *Tel 04 95 32 33 18. Charcuterie and cheese.*

**U Stazzu**
1 Rue Bonaparte, Ajaccio. *Tel 04 95 51 10 80. Honey, wines, charcuterie.*

# What to Buy in Corsica

The flavours and scents of Corsica can be enjoyed in the island's gastronomic delicacies – from honey and sweets, to cheese and charcuterie. The result of an age-old tradition, these products are available in all the large towns, especially in the markets, where they can be purchased directly from the producers. There is also a great variety of typical handicraft products that Corsican artisans have adapted to more modern tastes. The Strada di l'Artigiani in Balagne *(see pp76–7)* is where most of their workshops are located.

**Terracotta mask**

**Corsican knife-making** *has evolved from old shepherds' tools to elegant knives with manta ray-skin handles and damask-steel blades. Artisans now produce collector's items.*

## HANDICRAFTS

Wood, sandstone, animal horns and glass are the basic materials for Corsican handicrafts, and indeed are among the earliest ever used by man. Corsican artisans have given free rein to their creativity, without ever losing sight of local traditions. Their craft perfectly combines past and present, making every object unique for visitors from all over the world.

**Coral necklaces** *and pendants are crafted in keeping with the age-old art of the Ajaccio coral carvers. The fresh creativity of young local artisans has produced fine necklaces, earrings, bracelets and pendants.*

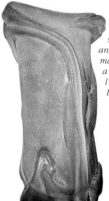

**The art of glass-blowing** *has produced vases, sculptures, glasses, jugs and many other objects. A master glass-blower in Feliceto, a village on the Strada di l'Artigiani, in the heart of Balagne, makes these items.*

**Ceramic ashtray**

**Enamelled shell**

**Ceramic wares,** *such as plates, vases, jugs and tiles, are made with a potter's wheel, fired in the oven and enamelled with typical Mediterranean colours. The stoneware and* raku *ceramics (see p76) are also worth purchasing.*

**Hand-crafted** *music boxes are made mostly in Pigna. They are brightly coloured and come in the shapes of donkeys and dancing figures. The musical pieces, such as A Muresca and Ciucciarella, are typical Corsican melodies.*

**Wooden objects** *are also a common product of Corsican handicraft. They include pipes made from olive, myrtle and heather wood, musical instruments and small pieces of furniture, often with unusual inlay work.*

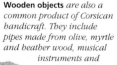

**The essences** *of lavender, Corsican pine, myrtle and orange blossoms are used to produce perfumes with the scent of the maquis and Corsican forests.*

### PERFUMES

The fragrant oils extracted from Mediterranean maquis vegetation, including juniper, myrtle, lavender, cistus and mastic, can be found in many essences that bring to mind the land of Corsica. The woods also yield the balsamic essence of pine resins.

**Lavender, one of the components of perfumes**

### GASTRONOMIC DELICACIES

Like all other regions in the Mediterranean, Corsica produces many gastronomic specialities that visitors can take back home as a reminder of their time on the island. These varied local delicacies will satisfy anyone's palate.

**Corsican pâtés,** *charcuterie and sausages are wonderfully tasty. The best ones hail from Bastelica, Castagniccia and Niolo. Boar pâté is also delicious.*

**Corsican cheeses** *include the famous brocciu, a sort of ricotta, as well as goat's-milk cheeses and others that are aged and flavoured with maquis herbs.*

**Liqueurs** *are among the typical products of the island. Some of the best are the Maison Mattei apéritifs, which are famous throughout the world, and products made from myrtle and other maquis herbs. These liqueurs are distilled by artisans in various regions of Corsica.*

**Aromatic vinegars** *made from herbs, apples and honey, and extracts of fruit such as hydromel, which are like the old-fashioned sweet syrups, are other typical Corsican products.*

**Chestnut cake,** *typical of Castagniccia, is among Corsica's best-known sweets. Fiadone is a traditional cake made of* brocciu *cheese scented with orange blossoms. The aromatized nougat is also special.*

**Citron and honey nougat**

**Home-made** *preserves are a speciality. They are made from melon, myrtle, peach, citron, clementine and figs. The fig-with-walnut preserve makes for a superb accompaniment to cheese.*

**The local honey** *is another product bearing the flavours and scents of the island. It can be strong and bitter (chestnut), delicate (asphodel) or aromatic (lavender or strawberry tree) and is sold in the markets.*

# ENTERTAINMENT IN CORSICA

Although Corsica's main attractions are the sea and natural scenery, there is no lack of cultural activity and entertainment, especially in the seaside resorts and the main cities, such as Ajaccio and Bastia. For up-to-date information about concerts, theatre productions and cinemas, consult the local newspaper, *Corse-Matin*. In the summer, in addition to the

**Passing the time with old friends at a café**

numerous traditional festivals *(see pp32–5)*, many outdoor nightspots, discos and concerts ensure an entertaining evening. During the day, there are many organized excursions by boat and a wide range of sports and outdoor activities available *(see pp188–93)*, as well attractions related to the sea, such as an aquatic park and thalassotherapy centres.

**Excursion boat moored near the bastions of Bonifacio**

## EXCURSIONS BY BOAT

Like all islands, Corsica offers a wide variety of interesting activities related to the sea. For those who do not have their own boat, there are many companies that hire them out *(see p207)*, with a skipper, or even a crew, if necessary. Also, in the summer months, there are numerous organized excursions or cruises along the coast that will allow you to admire the natural marvels of the island from the sea and stop in a secluded cove for a swim.

Among the best-known and most highly recommendable cruises is the one that takes visitors to the beautiful red cliffs of the Scandola Nature Reserve *(see pp104–5)*. The boats depart from various towns, including Ajaccio, Calvi, Porto, Cargèse, Tiuccia, Porticcio and other nearby harbours.

Do not fail to take the excursions from Ajaccio to the solitary Îles Sanguinaires *(see p92)*, and those departing from Propriano *(see p128)* to the Golfe de Valinco and the southwest coast.

The tours of the cliffs of Bonifacio and the Îles Lavezzi and Cavallo *(see pp116–17)* start from Bonifacio, which is also the departure point for trips across the Straits of Bonifacio *(see p113)* to the coast of Sardinia.

In the northern part of Corsica, most of the excursions to the beaches of Lodo, Cap Corse and the Désert des Agriates depart from the port of St-Florent.

Diving cruises on motorboats are organized more or less anywhere in Corsica, even for an entire weekend. Further information on diving sites and organizers can be found on page 191.

## TRAVELLING ON THE PETIT TRAIN

A typical Corsican attraction consists of the small, fairytale-style trains that take visitors on a leisurely tour of the main towns on the island. These vehicles are called *Petits Trains* because they are reminiscent of the train rides in children's amusement parks.

The *Petits Trains* operate in Ajaccio, Bonifacio, Corte and L'Île Rousse, generally departing from the centre of town – at Corte, for example, from the Citadelle – and following itineraries through the streets to show you the main sights and monuments. *Petits Trains* move quite slowly so that you can take photographs and enjoy the views while comfortably seated on the colourful little carriages.

**The delightful *Petit Train* in Corte, at the entrance to the Citadelle**

A group performing during the Calvi Jazz Festival

## AQUATIC PARKS

Although popular in many seaside resorts all over Europe, amusement parks featuring aquatic activities are still uncommon in Corsica. The only park of this sort on the island is **Aqua Cyrne Gliss** in Porticcio. With its slides, water chutes, boat rides, swimming pools of all kinds and fountains, Porticcio's aquatic park will delight youngsters and adults alike.

## THALASSOTHERAPY

Those who feel that holidays are the perfect opportunity to regenerate the body and relax will not be disappointed by what Corsica has to offer.

Like many other French maritime resorts, the island allows the opportunity to undergo sea-water therapy, also known as "thalassotherapy". This consists of a series of completely natural cures that, through the use of sea water, help the body to eliminate the toxins caused by stress and too much work. As a result of these cures, the body feels considerably reinvigorated.

In Corsica, thalassotherapy is provided by the prestigious **Sofitel**, near Ajaccio, and by **Riva Bella**, a nature resort and spa in Aléria. The packages on offer usually include both board and cures.

Alternatively, you can go to the first-rate spas scattered in the interior of the island.

## MUSIC AND DANCE

The programme of cultural events, in particular music, is especially full during the summer months, even though there are concerts and performances in the low season as well.

In the last week of June, Calvi resounds with the notes of the Jazz Festival (*see p33*), one of the best-known musical events in Corsica, which features some of the leading names on the international jazz scene.

In early July, the Estivoce (*see p33*) in Pigna is dedicated to traditional Corsican polyphonic music, and many choirs and groups offer a glimpse into authentic island culture.

In Ajaccio, the first two weeks of July are given over to the Blues Festival "Nuits du Blues" (*see p33*), which features music performed by famous international artists and groups.

In Patrimonio, during the third week of July, folk, jazz and gipsy musicians give exciting performances for the Guitar Nights festival (*see p33*), while from July to September Ajaccio plays host to Les Estivales (*see p33*), with concerts and dance performances.

One of the most popular festivals among Corsicans themselves, though relatively unknown to foreign visitors, is Les Musicales de Bastia (*see p35*), held in October. This is a festival of folk music, jazz and dance.

In late May, the **Kallisté Theatre** and other venues in Ajaccio host Île Danse (*see p32*), a festival exploring the art of dance featuring leading European companies.

Local tourist offices offer information regarding the programmes of these various festivals and sell tickets. You can alternatively log on to www.visit-corsica.com.

## CINEMA AND THEATRE

During the summer, in the main seaside resorts there are many outdoor cinemas that show the latest films every evening, including the one at Porto, which is situated in the eucalyptus grove of the Marina. A film marked *VO* in listings is in its original language.

The main cinemas are in Bastia (**Le Regent** and **Le Studio**) and Ajaccio (**Empire**, **L'Aiglon**, **Bonaparte** and **Laetitia**).

March sees the Bastia Film Festival (*see p32*), which features international film productions. During the first week of October the city hosts a British Film Festival; in November the Mediterranean Cultures Film Festival (*see p35*) is staged here; and in January the Italian Film Festival (*see p35*) organizes screenings of Italian films, retrospectives of Italian actors and directors, and lectures. Ajaccio is another centre for film, with Italian, Spanish and Asian festivals.

In the winter, there is an important theatre and opera season in Bastia.

A show performed in a Bastia theatre during the winter

## NIGHTLIFE

Discotheques in Corsica are few and far between compared to other European seaside resorts, and they are mostly concentrated in the larger coastal towns.

One of the best-known clubs on the island is **La Via Notte**, on the south edge of Porto-Vecchio. A favourite with teenagers, this club hosts famous international DJs in July and August.

Among the most famous clubs in Bastia are **Le Velvet**, frequented by people in their early 20s, and **L'Apocalypse**, in Biguglia. Another good club is **Noche de Cuba**, which attracts older crowds into Cuban music.

The biggest club in Ajaccio is **L'Entracte**. Popular spots in Porticcio are **Le Blue Moon**, which has a large terrace, and **Atlantids**, which features both disco music and techno. There is a healthy choice of nightlife in Calvi, **La Camargue** has an outdoor dance floor and a swimming pool. About 5 km (3 miles) from the centre of town is **L'Acapulco**, also renowned for its restaurant. Lastly, in Propriano there are two venues for late-night

Calvi's promenade, illuminated by the neon signs of the nightspots

dancing: the discotheques **Le King** and **Le Midnight**.

If clubbing is not your scene and you would rather drink a cocktail or listen to music, Corsican towns have many bars of every kind. In Bastia the most popular spots are concentrated around the Vieux Port area and the Port Toga quarter, which in the summer becomes a huge pedestrian precinct with shows and entertainment. Here the tables of the disco bars and restaurants almost touch the water. Among the most popular places are **Le Bounty**, **Le Café de la Place**, **Le Cézanne Café**, **Le Zanzibar**, **La Rhumerie**, **Café Wha!** and

**Le Bouchon**, a wine bar with live music and a fine wine list where you can drink by the glass or the bottle while having salad or canapés.

In Ajaccio the great variety of nightspots includes **Le Pavillon Bleu**, **Le Son des Guitares**, **Le Privilège** piano bar and **Le Temple du Jeu**.

Calvi has **Chez Tao**, an historic piano bar in the Citadelle, and **Le Rocher**, a piano bar open till 3am.

Among the best spots in Porto-Vecchio are **La Canne à Sucre**, ideal for an ice cream or a drink, and **La Taverne du Roi**, a popular venue that often hosts jazz and cabaret singers.

Café Wha!, one of the best-known nightspots in Bastia, popular with people of all ages

# DIRECTORY

## EXCURSIONS BY BOAT

**A Dieu Vat**
Porto-Vecchio.
*Tel 04 95 70 27 58.*

**Centre Nautique Valinco**
Port de Plaisance,
BP67, Propriano.
*Tel 06 12 54 99 28.*

**Colombo Line**
Port de Plaisance,
Calvi.
*Tel 04 95 65 32 10.*

**Croisières Grand Bleu**
Cargèse.
*Tel 04 95 26 40 24.*

**Le Djinn**
Porto-Vecchio.
*Tel 04 95 70 56 61.*

**Nave Va**
2 Rue Jean-Baptiste
Marcaggio, Ajaccio.
*Tel 04 95 21 83 97.*
Porticcio.
*Tel 04 95 25 94 14.*

**Rocca Croisières**
Rue Fred Scamaroni,
Bonifacio.
*Tel 04 95 73 13 96.*

**Thalassa Croisières**
Marina, Bonifacio.
*Tel 06 86 34 00 49, 04
95 73 05 43.*

**U San Paulu**
Macinaggio.
*Tel 04 95 35 07 09.*

## PETITS TRAINS COMPANIES

**ITT**
Imm. Beau site,
Pietralba, Ajaccio
(departure: Place Foch).
*Tel 04 95 51 13 69.*

**Le Petit Train**
Col de Fogata,
L'Île Rousse
(departure: Place Paoli).
*Tel 04 95 60 26 79.*

**TTB**
Via Simoni/Sennola,
Bonifacio (departure:
the port).
*Tel 04 95 73 15 07.*

**U Trenu**
Corte (departure:
municipal car park,
behind the train station).
*Tel 06 09 95 70 36.*

## AQUATIC PARKS

**Aqua Cyrne Gliss**
Porticcio.
*Tel 04 95 25 17 48.*

## THALASSOTHERAPY

**Hotel Sofitel**
Golfe d'Ajaccio, Porticcio.
*Tel 04 95 29 40 40.*

**Riva Bella**
Aléria.
*Tel 04 95 38 81 10.*
**www**.rivabella-inf.com

## CINEMAS

**L'Aiglon**
Cours Grandval, Ajaccio.
*Tel 04 95 70 35 02.*

**Bonaparte**
10 Cours Napoléon,
Ajaccio.
*Tel 04 95 51 29 46.*

**La Cinémathèque de Corse**
Espace Jean-Paul de Rocca
Serra, Porto-Vecchio.
*Tel 04 95 70 35 02.*

**Empire**
30 Cours Napoléon,
Ajaccio.
*Tel 04 95 21 21 00.*

**Laetitia**
24 Cours Napoléon,
Ajaccio.
*Tel 04 95 21 07 24.*

**Le Regent**
5 Rue César Campinchi,
Bastia.
*Tel 04 95 31 03 08.*

**Le Studio**
1 Rue Miséricorde, Bastia.
*Tel 04 95 31 12 94.*

## THEATRES

**Aghja**
6 Chemin de Biancarello,
Ajaccio.
*Tel 04 95 20 41 15.*

**Kallisté**
6 Rue Colonel
Colonna d'Ornano,
Ajaccio.
*Tel 04 95 22 43 03.*

## DISCOTHEQUES

**L'Acapulco**
Calvi.
*Tel 04 95 65 08 03.*

**L'An 200**
3 Rue Deux Villas, Corte.
*Tel 04 95 46 17 04.*

**L'Apocalypse**
Biguglia, Bastia.
*Tel 04 95 33 36 83.*

**Atlantids**
Porticcio.
*Tel 04 95 25 03 98.*

**Le Blue Moon**
Les Marines, Porticcio.
*Tel 04 95 25 07 70.*

**La Camargue**
Calvi.
*Tel 04 95 65 08 70.*

**L'Entracte**
Casino Municipal,
Ajaccio.
*Tel 04 95 50 40 65.*

**Le King**
Blvd du Général
de Gaulle, Propriano.
*Tel 04 95 20 45 60.*

**Le Midnight Express**
Blvd du Général
de Gaulle, Propriano.
*Tel 04 95 76 05 21.*

**Noche de Cuba**
5 Rue Chanoine Leschi,
Bastia.
*Tel 04 95 31 02 83.*

**Le Velvet**
15 Maison Romieu,
Bastia.
*Tel 04 95 31 01 00.*

**La Via Notte**
Porto-Vecchio.
*Tel 04 95 72 02 12.*

## NIGHTSPOTS

**Le Bouchon**
4 bis Rue St-Jean,
Vieux Port, Bastia.
*Tel 04 95 58 14 22.*

**Le Bounty**
Port de Toga, Bastia.
*Tel 04 95 34 20 34.*

**Le Café de la Place**
Blvd Général de
Gaulle, Bastia.
*Tel 04 95 32 06 51.*

**Café Wha!**
Bastia.
*Tel 04 95 34 25 79.*

**La Canne à Sucre**
Porto-Vecchio.
*Tel 04 95 70 35 25.*

**Le Cézanne Café**
Port de Plaisance,
Toga, Bastia.
*Tel 04 95 34 16 60.*

**Chez Tao**
Rue St-François, Calvi.
*Tel 04 95 65 00 73.*

**Le Pavillon Bleu**
Cabaret, 26 Cours du
Général Leclerc, Ajaccio.
*Tel 04 95 51 12 90.*

**Le Privilège**
7 Rue Eugène
Macchini, Ajaccio.
*Tel 04 95 50 11 80.*

**La Rhumerie**
Place Galetta, Bastia.
*Tel 04 95 37 19 53.*

**Le Rocher**
Sant'Ambroggio,
Lumio, Calvi.
*Tel 04 95 60 68 74.*

**Le Son des Guitares**
Rue du Roi de Rome,
Ajaccio.
*Tel 04 95 51 16 47.*

**La Taverne du Roi**
43 Rue Borgo,
Porto-Vecchio.
*Tel 04 95 70 41 31.*

**Le Temple du Jeu**
2 Avenue de la Grande
Armée, Ajaccio.
*Tel 04 95 10 19 39.*

**Le Zanzibar**
2 Rue Favalelli, Bastia.
*Tel 04 95 34 01 27.*

# SPORTS AND OUTDOOR ACTIVITIES

Corsica is an ideal destination for sports and outdoor enthusiasts. Along the coast, those who love the sea will find beaches with fine sand and coves among craggy cliffs that can often be reached only by boat, as well as splendid sea floors. For hiking or trekking buffs, there is no end of possibilities, with hills, mountains and trails of varying degrees of difficulty. Even the best cyclists will have their work cut out for them along the steep hairpin turns

Mountain
hiker

of the inland roads that lead to the passes in the central mountain range. Canoeing, kayaking and rafting aficionados will love the swiftly flowing torrents. And horse riding is a fascinating way of visiting the hills of Corsica. In keeping with the French passion for the great outdoors, all sports and other activities in Corsica are organized efficiently and thoroughly. The Directory on page 193 lists a selection of useful addresses.

## HIKING

More than 25 years ago, Corsica inaugurated its longest hiking route, the GR20 *(see pp22–7)*, which crosses the entire island along a northwest–southeast axis. Annually, more than 17,000 hikers from all over the world walk through woods, forests and rugged ridges following this long-distance path.

Because the GR20 is now overflowing with hikers, other paths have been created to ease congestion. These are less difficult than the GR20 and are called *Mare e Monti* ("sea and mountains"; *see p27*) if the paths start out from the sea and go inland to the peaks, and *Mare a Mare* ("sea to sea"; *see p27*) if they go from coast to coast via the interior.

Among the latter, there are three main routes from west to east: Cargèse to the beach

**Amazing rock formations along a hiking trail**

at Cervione, in Castagniccia; Ajaccio to Ghisonaccia; and Propriano to Porto-Vecchio. These paths are usually at a low altitude and tend to run on flatter terrain. They also go through villages where it is possible to buy food and drink, so one can hike with a lighter backpack.

Among the most interesting *Mare e Monti* hikes is the one that goes from Cargèse to Calenzana, in Balagne, via Evisa and Galéria.

Besides these long routes, there are many areas that are of interest to hikers. Among these are the Vallée de l'Asco *(see p150)*, at the foot of Monte Cinto, the Calacuccia zone *(see p151)*, the upper Vallée de la Restonica *(see p139)*, the Col de Vizzavona *(see p142)* and the splendid Col de Bavella area *(see pp122–3)*.

**Hikers on their way through Corsica's wild landscape**

There are many useful hiking guide books, such as *Trekking in Corsica*, by David Abram, published by Trailblazer Guides, which covers all the island's best routes (including the GR20), or Robin G Collomb's *Corsica Mountains*, published by West Co, UK. The *Guide de la Randonnée en Corse* ("Guide to Long Hikes in Corsica"), published by Didier Richard, provides many hiking suggestions, as does *Corse*, a guide published by the Institut Géographique National. The topographical maps produced by the same institute are vitally important for difficult hikes.

Before setting off with your backpack, bear in mind that, although the Corsican mountains in summer seem to be hiker-friendly and sunny, bad weather and storms are

An exciting canoeing experience on a rushing torrent

quite common at high altitudes and may easily cause sudden sharp drops in temperature. Furthermore, remember that the food- and water-supply stations are not always well-stocked.

## CLIMBING

Although there are no internationally famous rock-climbing areas in Corsica, there are plenty of challenging and attractive cliffs and walls.

There are basically two types of rock here – granite and limestone – and they require different climbing techniques and styles.

Among the climbers' favourite sites are Ponte Leccia and Solenzara, the Nebbio region, with the cliffs of Caporalino and Pietralba, the Col de Bavella *(see pp122–3)*, with routes of varying difficulty, and the longest routes in the Teghje Liscie and Balagne areas.

## RAFTING

One of the main features of Corsica consists of the watercourses, both large and small, in the valleys of the interior. Rafters love these rivers because of the wild scenery they pass through. Rafting is a very technical sport for experts only, and in Corsica there are agencies and specialized guides that organize the descents down the rivers, from the easiest to the most difficult. The easiest gorges are along the course of the Vecchio, Aïtone and Tavignano rivers. More difficult routes are some stretches of the Taravo and the Vacca (near Bavella) rivers, and the long descents of torrents such as the Negretto (near Ponte Leccia), the Sportellu (Porto) and the Polischello (Levie).

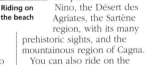

Riding on the beach

## CANOEING AND KAYAKING

Corsica has a lot of rainfall, and in the mountains this becomes rather heavy snow-fall, sometimes as much as 2 m (6 ft). Consequently, in spring, when the temperatures rise and the thawing season begins, the island welcomes many canoeists who come from all over Europe, eager to take advantage of the abundance of gushing water, as well as beautiful gorges and mountain scenery.

Corsican rivers tend to be technical and spectacular. The Taravo, Rizzanese and Fium'Orbo rivers offer splendid descents. The most famous and difficult are the Tavignano, Golo and Prunelli rivers, as well as the Liamone.

## HORSE RIDING

Corsica offers many opportunities for horse riding. The most interesting areas for this activity are the green hills of the Castagniccia area, the divide between the Bozio and Corte regions, the Tavignano river as far as the plateaus of Lac de Nino, the Désert des Agriates, the Sartène region, with its many prehistoric sights, and the mountainous region of Cagna.

You can also ride on the sandy shores of the east coast or on the grassy top of the white cliffs of Bonifacio.

A departure point for canoe or kayak excursions

## SAILING

With its rugged coasts, small rocky islands and the Scandola and Lavezzi marine reserves, Corsica is a favourite with yachting buffs from all over the world. This appeal is compounded by the constant presence of wind.

The voyage from the ports in southern France is rather long (Cap Corse is 119 nautical miles from St-Tropez, 100 from Nice and 83 from Menton), but it sails over a zone famous for frequent sightings of fin whales. The stretch of the sea 45 nautical miles north-west of Calvi is where you are most likely to find these marvellous sea mammals.

Departing from the Italian coast, the crossing to Corsica is shorter and one can make a stopover at the islands of the Tuscan archipelago. Cap Corse is 49 nautical miles from Livorno, while the distance from Bastia to the island of Elba is 40 nautical miles.

The circumnavigation of Corsica is also popular with yachtsmen *(see p206)*. This route passes by various types of coastline: sandy and filled with pools on the eastern sides; craggy and indented at Cap Corse; and varied, with tall rock faces on the west side. The strongest wind is around the Straits

**Sailing lessons at Marina de Meria, Cap Corse**

of Bonifacio, between Corsica and Sardinia. Be careful when sailing here, because the wind is often violent and there are numerous large ships that navigate this part of the sea.

If you do not have a boat of your own, it is possible to hire one in all the ports and tourist resorts, where there are also agencies that offer boat tours of the coast with the skipper and crew included in the price.

Navigating along the coasts of Corsica, you will come across two very important marine reserves: the Scandola Nature Reserve *(see pp104–5)* and the Réserve de Lavezzi *(see p117)*, which, in turn, is part of the Parc Marin de Bonifacio *(see p113)*, an initiative of the French and Italian governments that has succeeded in protecting and improving this major stretch of sea, where numerous regattas are held.

### THE DISTANCE IN NAUTICAL MILES BETWEEN PORTS

| | |
|---|---|
| Bastia–St-Florent | 48 |
| St-Florent–Calvi | 30 |
| Calvi–Girolata | 21 |
| Girolata–Porto | 6 |
| Porto–Cargèse | 12 |
| Cargèse–Ajaccio | 21 |
| Ajaccio–Propriano | 22 |
| Propriano–Roccapina | 15 |
| Roccapina–Bonifacio | 12 |
| Bonifacio–Lavezzi | 6 |
| Lavezzi–Porto-Vecchio | 18 |
| Porto-Vecchio–Bastia | 67 |

**Boats anchored at one of the many fabulous coves on Îles Lavezzi**

## WINDSURFING

The areas and resorts where sailing is common and nautical clubs are based also tend to have facilities for windsurfing. All the tourist towns along the coast offer the possibility to practise this sport, which is an exciting combination of surfing and sailing. There are many small schools that rent windsurfing equipment and offer courses at different levels of ability.

Corsica, like most islands, is blessed with good breezes, especially along the west coast and the cliffs in the south. However, in the south the wind is perhaps too strong and potentially dangerous, so windsurfing in this area should be practised by experts only.

**A windsurfer in search of wind at Îles Lavezzi**

## DIVING

The sea floors in Corsica are rich in fauna and natural beauty. There are about 60 clubs on the island that have ideal sites for diving. Among these, the **Station Recherches Sousmarines et Océanographiques**, which is situated at the Pointe Revellata promontory, not far from Calvi, offers courses for beginners and short courses on marine biology. It is also possible to stay here and organize your own dives.

Among the most famous diving sites are the beautiful Mérouville zone, northeast of Îles Lavezzi, and the islet

**A diver about to surface with a fine day's catch**

of Sperduto, which is part of the Réserve de Lavezzi. As is the case with all protected areas, diving here is subject to strict regulations and limits, so it is best to make enquiries at the Réserve offices or in one of the diving clubs in the area beforehand.

In southeast Corsica, not far from the Golfe de Porto-Vecchio, the small Îles Cerbicale have interesting diving sites in the Île du Toro area, where there are many shipwrecks.

In southwest Corsica, in the Golfe de Valinco, facing Propriano, the most popular sites are those around the rocks of the so-called *cathédrales* ("cathedrals"), off the coast of Porto-Pollo, and the Secche di Belvedere. Near the Pointe de la Parata, which, together with the Îles Sanguinaires, closes off the Golfe d'Ajaccio to the north, is a diving site called Tabernacle, while in the southern part of the gulf is the shipwreck of the *Meulère*.

Further north, in the Golfe de Sagone are the sandbanks of the Provençale and the wreck of a Canadair aeroplane. In the Golfe de Porto, the Punta Mucchilina sand bar offers a great variety of fauna and flora, as well as the wreck of a coal ship.

Divers in the Calvi area often visit the Pointe Revellata canyon, at the northernmost confines of the Scandola Nature Reserve *(see pp104–5)*, and the wreck of a Boeing B-17 bomber that lies 28 m (90 ft) below sea level.

Further north, in the Golfe de St-Florent, there are the sea floors of Punta Vecchiara and the sand bar of Saleccia, while the Île de Giraglia, at the northern tip of Cap Corse, is famous for a wonderful dive west of the lighthouse.

## CYCLING

Corsica offers several opportunities for cyclists. Many routes follow paths on the hills through the central mountain range, and they are generally located in very beautiful forest areas.

In spring and summer, there is an abundance of cyclists at the Col de Vizzavona, Col de Verghio, Col de Verde and Col de Bavella. The coastal roads are also lovely, but be aware that they tend to be very windy and congested.

Whatever your choice, bear in mind that the roads are narrow, mostly on hills with steep rises, and have many curves. There are few places for food and drinks along the way. Furthermore, the road surface is not always good, so it is advisable to bring along a spare inner tube and the tools needed for repairs.

Cycling fans normally have their own bicycles, but there are agencies that offer bicycle tours of a week or more. The advantage of these tours is that a van is available to carry your luggage from one stop to another. In case of fatigue, cyclists are taken into the van or to a doctor.

**Consulting a map for the next leg of a bicycle journey**

## MOUNTAIN BIKING

One of the most ecologically friendly ways to discover the interior of Corsica is by mountain bike. The rises are generally steep and the paths quite rough, so make sure you are well equipped and that you take plenty of water with you.

Among the areas suggested by experts for their beauty are the forests of Ospédale, Bavella and Cagna, and the entire central Alta Rocca zone. Except for the summer months, the paths through the maquis in the Désert des Agriates, in the northern part of the island, are splendid, as are some stretches of the *Mare a Mare* and *Mare e Monti (see p27)* paths and the long route from Propriano to Ajaccio.

It is easy to find a bike for hire in the summer.

## GOLF

The ultimate golf course in Corsica is without a doubt the one at Pointe de Sperone *(see p117)*, a short distance from Capo Pertusato. The course lies on the soft hills bordered by maquis facing the Îles Lavezzi and Cavallo. This 18-hole, par-72 golf course is more than 6 km (4 miles) long.

The other golf courses and golf schools on the island are at Ajaccio (school), Bastia (9 holes), Lezza (6 holes) and Reginu (6 holes).

Information concerning the golf courses and the various tournaments held on the island is available on the **Ligue Corse de Golf** website (www.liguecorsedegolf.org).

## WINTER SPORTS

The tourists who throng to Corsica in the summer may find it hard to believe, but in winter there is a considerable amount of snow on the mountain peaks of the central range. So, from December to March, four small ski resorts inland offer fine downhill runs and even circular cross-country courses to skiing aficionados.

But the real attraction of Corsica, which does not have many ski-lift facilities,

**Snow-capped peaks in the Monte Cinto region**

**Alpine cross-country skiing**

are the routes for alpine cross-country skiing (*ski de randonnée*), for which there are various possibilities in spring as well. First of all, there is the difficult route that follows the central divide and runs more or less along the routes marked out in summer by the GR20 long-distance path. There are also many other possible routes starting off from the locality of Ghisoni (towards Monte Renoso), from the upper Vallée de la Restonica, from Haut-Asco and from the Campotile plateau.

Between Quenza and Zicavo, on the Coscione plateau, there are several courses for those who love adventurous cross-country skiing or long walks with snowshoes. Here the utmost caution is necessary, since the weather can be treacherous. Be sure to have plenty of supplies with you, because supply stations are few and far between. Spring alpine skiing requires the same precautions adopted on other mountains.

**The prestigious golf club on the Pointe de Sperone, near Bonifacio**

# DIRECTORY

## HIKING

**Compagnie Régionale des Guides et Accompagnateurs de Montagne de Corse**
Tel 04 95 48 10 43.

**Corse Odyssée**
Quenza.
Tel 04 95 78 64 05.
www.gite-corse-odyssee.com

**Corsica Raid Aventure (race)**
Tel 04 95 25 16 16.
www.corsicaraid.com

**In Terra Corsa**
Train station,
Ponte Leccia.
Tel 04 95 47 69 48.
www.interracorsa.fr

**Parc Naturel Régional de la Corse**
Ajaccio.
Tel 04 95 51 79 10.
www.parc-corse.org

## CLIMBING AND MOUNTAINEERING

**Corsica Madness**
(alpine guides).
Tel 04 95 78 61 76,
06 13 22 95 06.
www.corsica madness.com

**In Terra Corsa**
Train station,
Ponte Leccia.
Tel 04 95 47 69 48.
www.interracorsa.fr

**Jean-Paul Quilici**
(alpine guides).
Tel 04 95 78 64 33.

**Marc Gambotti**
(alpine guides).
Tel 06 20 90 18 05.

**Pierre Pietri**
(alpine guides).
Tel 04 95 32 62 76.

**René Eymerie**
(alpine guides).
Tel 06 27 21 66 60.

**Vallecime**
(alpine guides).
Casamacioli &
Sant'Andrea di Bozio.
Tel 04 95 48 69 33 or
06 14 74 44 98.
www.vallecime.com

## RAFTING

**Corse Aventure**
Route de Sartène,
Corri Bianchi,
Eccica-Suarella.
Tel 04 95 25 91 19.
www.corse-aventure.com

**In Terra Corsa**
Train station,
Ponte Leccia.
Tel 04 95 47 69 48.
www.interracorsa.fr

## CANOEING AND KAYAKING

**Altore**
St-Florent.
Tel 04 95 37 19 30.
www.altore.com
info@altore.com

**Commission Nager en Eau Vive**
Bastia. c/o Jean Pierre
Vergnon.
Tel 04 95 31 51 12.

## HORSE RIDING

**Equiloisirs (FAE)**
N200, Corte.
Tel 04 95 61 09 88.

**In Terra Corsa**
Train station,
Ponte Leccia.
Tel 04 95 47 69 48.
www.interracorsa.fr

## SAILING AND WINDSURFING

**Calvi Marine**
Calvi.
Tel 04 95 65 01 12.

**Calvi Nautique Club**
Calvi.
Tel 04 95 65 10 65.

**Centre Nautique des Fauvettes**
Porto-Vecchio.
Tel 04 95 70 93 00.

**Centre Nautique des Glénans**
Bonifacio.
Tel 04 95 73 03 85.
www.glenans.asso.fr

**Centre Nautique de Porticcio**
Porticcio.
Tel 04 95 25 01 06.
www.le-cnp.fr

**Corsica Voile**
Macinaggio.
Tel 04 95 35 48 20.
www.corsica-voile.com

**L'Île Bleue – Boni-Ship**
Bonifacio.
Tel 04 95 73 04 12.

**Multi Service Plaisance**
Porto-Vecchio.
Tel 04 95 70 29 13.

**Soleil Rouge Yachting**
Ajaccio.
Tel 04 95 21 89 21.

## DIVING

**Fédération Française Études et Sports Sousmarins**
Solenzara.
(List of 83 Corsican clubs.)
Tel 04 95 57 48 31.

**Station Recherches Sousmarines et Océanographiques**
Pointe Revellata, Calvi.
Tel 04 95 65 06 18.
Fax 04 95 65 01 34.
stareso@stareso.com
www.stareso.com

## CYCLING AND MOUNTAIN BIKES

**Corsica Moto Rent**
Ajaccio.
Tel 04 95 51 34 45.
Porto-Vecchio.
Tel 04 95 70 03 40.
www.rent-car-corsica.com

**Europe Active**
Tel 04 95 44 49 67.
www.velo-corse.com

**Garage d'Angeli**
Place Christophe Colomb,
Calvi.
Tel 04 95 65 02 13.
www.garagedangeli.com

**Rout'evasion**
Ajaccio.
Tel 04 95 22 72 87.
www.routevasion.com

**TTC Moto**
Propriano.
Tel 04 95 76 15 32.
www.ttcmoto.fr

## GOLF

**Bastia Golf Club**
Castellarese, Borgo.
Tel 04 95 38 33 99.
www.golfborgo.fr

**Golf Club Sperone**
Domaine de Sperone,
Bonifacio.
Tel 04 95 73 17 13.
Fax 04 95 73 17 85.
www.sperone.com

**Ligue Corse de Golf**
Tel 04 95 32 54 53.
www.liguecorse degolf.org

## WINTER SPORTS

**Bergeries de Capannelle**
Ghisoni.
Tel 04 95 57 01 81.

**Calacuccia Skiing Resort (cross-country skiing)**
Calacuccia tourist office.
Tel 04 95 48 05 22.
http://asniolu.club.fr

**Col de Verghio Skiing Resort**
Tel 04 95 48 00 01.

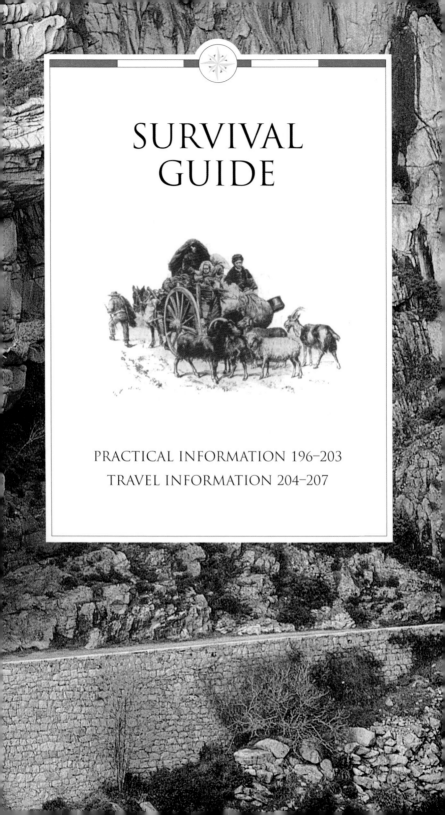

# SURVIVAL
# GUIDE

# PRACTICAL INFORMATION

In Corsica, tourism is an important industry – and not only in summer, when visitors come to enjoy the sea. Spring and autumn are ideal for tours inland, for hikes in the mountains and visits to the archaeological sites. Travelling within Corsica is easy: the hotels, restaurants and camp sites are of a high quality and visitors can rely on the wide-ranging network of assistance from the Agence de Tourisme de la

**Sign for tourist information**

Corse and the local tourist offices. When planning a trip to Corsica, it is best not to have a heavy schedule, and to avoid long trips, despite the apparently short distances: the roads may be extremely scenic, but they are not very fast because of the numerous bends and the sometimes rough surfaces. Furthermore, each village has surprises in store, be they historic, scenic or gastronomic, and it would be a pity to miss them.

**The Corsican coastline in the spring**

In the tourist offices you may find brochures and maps of the area, lists of the local hotels and restaurants, and information on the museums and archaeological sites.

The larger cities, such as Ajaccio and Bastia, also print pamphlets every year concerning festivals and other cultural activities, including music, dance, cinema and theatre.

If you want to plan your vacation from home, make enquiries at a French tourist organization, such as the **Maison de la France**, which has much material on Corsica and can also provide information over the telephone.

## WHEN TO GO

Corsica offers varied natural scenery and many different environments.

July and August are the best months for seaside holidays, but beware: the resorts will be crowded and it will be very warm.

The best period for hiking and climbing is from May to September, but even October can be quite pleasant if you limit your hikes to the foothills.

In order to enjoy the tranquil beauty of the island to the full, it is advisable not to visit Corsica between mid-July and mid-August.

## VISAS AND PASSPORTS

Corsica is a region of France and follows the same laws and regulations. European Union citizens are not subject to customs controls, but it is a good idea to have your documents handy.

For stays of three months or less, no visa is required for citizens of other European countries and for US, Canada and New Zealand nationals. However, visitors from other parts of the world, including Australia, must have a visa, which can be obtained from a French consulate in the country of departure.

## TOURIST INFORMATION

All the main cities on the island have a tourist office, which may be called either Office de Tourisme or Syndicat d'Initiative. Smaller Corsican towns have centres that provide information on that particular area, including nearby villages. Sometimes the town hall itself (*mairie*) is used as a visitors' centre.

## TICKETS AND OPENING HOURS

As a general rule, archaeological sites and museums in Corsica charge an admission fee. Most of them, however, have reduced prices for visitors aged under 18 and over 60. In some cases, discounted tickets are available for students with international student cards.

The opening hours of museums and archaeological sites vary: generally speaking,

**Logo of Bastia tourist office**

◁ One of the most fascinating stretches of the D81 highway, cut out of the marvellous Calanques de Piana

**A road sign indicating an historic monument**

the main museums stay open all day, while digs are closed one day a week (either Sunday or Monday). If you want to visit churches and chapels, it is best to find out the opening hours from the town halls or tourist offices before embarking on your trip. Likewise, if you are planning to take a special tour to minor localities, it is advisable to contact the relevant tourist offices first.

Bear in mind that opening hours differ in high and low season. Detailed information is provided in the central section of this guide, which has the individual descriptions of the resorts, as well as in this section and the *Travellers' Needs* section (*see pp152–93*).

## DISABLED TRAVELLERS

In terms of providing for the disabled, Corsica is still a long way behind mainland France. Only a relatively small number of establishments – bars, restaurants, hotels and pensions – supply adequate facilities for wheelchair access.

The French guidebook *Guide Rousseau H comme Handicapés*, published by La Route Robert, contains detailed lists of the places with wheelchair access and other facilities. **Tourism For All** publishes an English-language brochure with information on all the establishments in France and Corsica in which architectural barriers have been eliminated to allow for easier access for the disabled.

## SERVICES FOR STUDENTS

Full-time students who own an **International Student Identity Card** (ISIC) are entitled to reductions in

the price of tickets and for numerous tourist initiatives. The ISIC card is an internationally recognized document that can be purchased from student travel agents or via the ISIC website.

## LANGUAGES

Although the official language in Corsica is French, the local language has also always been in use there, making the island a bilingual area.

In 1974 Corsican was officially recognized as a regional tongue. After the reopening of the University of Corte in 1981, written Corsican was codified and old literary texts re-evaluated (*see pp30–31*).

Corsican is more like Italian than French – it is reminiscent of Ligurian dialect spoken with a Sardinian accent. As a result, many Corsicans understand and speak Italian. Road signs are in Corsican and French, although the French is often obscured by nationalist graffiti.

**International Student Identity Card**

## FRENCH TIME

Corsica is one hour ahead of Greenwich Mean Time (GMT) and summer (daylight saving) time operates from spring to early autumn. Postmeridian time is indicated in two ways: either "8pm" or "20:00" (20 heures), for example.

## ELECTRICAL ADAPTORS

Electrical current in Corsica is 220v AC. Except for some small villages inland, the central hole of the sockets is generally earthed. It is wise to purchase a suitable adaptor, if necessary, before leaving for Corsica.

---

# DIRECTORY

## EMBASSIES & CONSULATES

**Australian Consulate**
Paris. *Tel* 01 40 59 33 00.

**British Consulate**
Marseille. *Tel* 04 91 15 72 10.

**Canadian Consulate**
Paris. *Tel* 01 44 43 29 00.

**Irish Embassy**
Paris. *Tel* 01 44 17 67 00.

**US Consulate**
Marseille. *Tel* 04 91 54 92 00.

## TOURIST ORGANIZATIONS

**Agence de Tourisme de la Corse**
17 Blvd du Roi Jérôme, Ajaccio.
*Tel* 04 95 51 00 00.
**www.**visit-corsica.com

**Maison de la France**
*Tel* 09068 244 123 (UK only).
**www.**franceguide.com
**www.**francetourism.com
(US-based).

## TOURIST OFFICES

**Bastia**
Place St-Nicolas.
*Tel* 04 95 54 20 40.

**Bonifacio**
2 Rue Fred Scamaroni.
*Tel* 04 95 73 11 88.

**Calvi**
97 Port de Plaisance.
*Tel* 04 95 65 16 67.

**Corte**
La Citadelle.
*Tel* 04 95 46 26 70.

## USEFUL NUMBERS

**International Student Identity Card (ISIC)**
**www.**isiccard.com

**Parc Naturel Régional de la Corse**
2 Rue Major Lambroschini, Ajaccio.
*Tel* 04 95 51 79 10.
**www.**parc-corse.org

**Tourism For All**
*Tel* 0845 124 99 71.
**www.**tourismforall.org.uk

# Personal Security and Health

**Fire Brigade insignia**

Corsica is a tranquil and safe region for travellers. The locals welcome foreign visitors, being well aware that they are a positive factor for the island's life and economy. Generally speaking, personal security is not really a problem, for either men or women. The disorders that sometimes make the news are the work of a handful of extremists of the Corsican independence movement and do not represent a danger for foreign visitors. Health standards on the island are high: as well as the hospitals in the main cities, there are physicians on 24-hour duty and medical facilities in all the resorts, especially those popular with tourists.

## PERSONAL SECURITY

On the whole, dangerous or harmful incidents in Corsica rarely take place. Visitors, including lone women travellers, are unlikely to come across any problems of personal security.

Anyone walking along the streets on the island cannot help noticing the large amount of graffiti everywhere calling for Corsican independence from France. In recent decades, some violent incidents have been linked to the independence movement. But even though the extremist fringe of this movement has sometimes made recourse to acts of terrorism, this tension is on the wane, and tourists have never been targeted by these factions. It is, however, a good rule to avoid entering into heated arguments or taking part in public demonstrations while in Corsica, as they might have unpleasant consequences.

## CORSICAN POLICE

In France there is a police corps called *Gendarmerie Nationale*, which deals with major crimes and operates mainly outside the large cities, although it might intervene should serious incidents occur.

In the cities, those responsible for maintaining law and order act both as traffic wardens and as policemen, also taking care of minor problems. In case of need, go to the nearest police station *(gendarmerie)*. If you are in a small, isolated village, you can go to the local town hall *(mairie)* during office hours.

## ROAD HAZARDS

The roads in Corsica are not the best maintained in Europe. The road surface is not always in good condition, the lanes are often narrow and there are a great many bends, especially in the mountainous interior.

When travelling by car *(see p205)*, it is therefore a good idea to bring along a spare tyre and tools for minor repairs or problems. You are also required by law to carry reflective safety jackets for yourself and all passengers, and a warning triangle, for use in case of an accident. In the event of a breakdown, get everyone out of the car before attempting a repair or calling the emergency services.

## FIRE HAZARDS

Since a large part of the island is covered with luxuriant forests, Corsica appears as a verdant paradise compared to other islands in the Mediterranean.

In the extensive woods in the interior and in the coastal areas with thick maquis vegetation, fire prevention is of vital importance. In these areas the wind blows almost constantly, the climate is hot and there is abundant vegetation – all factors that favour outbreaks of fire. Furthermore, because of the many steep ridges, canyons and rough terrain on the island, fires can be hard to control and put out. A case in point is the huge fire in the Vallée de la Restonica, which occurred in the summer of 2000, and in July 2009 around 6,000 ha (15,000 acres) were ravaged by fire in the area around the village of Aullène in southern Corsica.

Firemen intervene both on the ground, and, as soon as possible, with firefighting aeroplanes known as Canadair, and smaller, more manageable helicopters that get their water supply from the artificial lakes inland.

Not only is common sense called for, but European regulations must be obeyed as well. It is strictly forbidden to light fires outdoors, except in rigorously controlled areas. Smokers must never throw lighted cigarette butts on the roads or in the brush. You must also keep an eye out for any fire or smoke

**A vehicle used by the fire brigade suitable for rough terrain**

A Canadair dumping tons of water on to a brush fire

and make sure you report it to the fire brigade as soon as possible.

If you are planning to take a long hike on terrain that is a potential fire risk, it is best to inform the local authorities of this before you start off. This way they will know how many people may be in danger should a fire break out in that area.

## LEGAL ASSISTANCE

As with any destination, for your own security take out a travel insurance policy.

In case of particular difficulties or serious incidents that require police intervention, the best thing to do is to contact your consulate (see p197) as soon as possible, since it will be able to provide all the necessary assistance in your language.

**Pharmacy sign**

## PERSONAL BELONGINGS

Although Corsica, like so many other tourist areas, is a peaceful region, travellers should take all the necessary precautions dictated by common sense.

Always take out insurance on your personal belongings, do not leave your luggage unattended and visible in a car, and do not travel with a lot of cash.

All cases of theft should be reported at the nearest police station immediately. Should you lose your documents, it is best to ask for help at your country's consulate in France (see p197).

## MEDICAL TREATMENT

When visiting Corsica, citizens of European Union countries who are entitled to medical treatment from their own national health service have the right to the same assistance they would receive in their own country. Before leaving the UK, British tourists must get a European Health Insurance Card (EHIC) from a post office or online; it allows complete medical treatment and reimbursement of most of the expenses (which have to be paid on the spot) on the part of the Caisse Primarie d'Assurance-Maladie. Non-EU citizens must obtain medical insurance from their own countries prior to departure. The number to call for the emergency service is 15.

## HOSPITALS AND PHARMACIES

Hospitals in Corsica are well organized and efficient. They are situated in the four main cities and in the largest tourist resorts, where there are also 24-hour duty physicians for foreign visitors.

Almost all the towns have pharmacies. They can be recognized by the neon sign in the form of a green cross outside. If a pharmacy is closed, the address of the nearest open one is always listed outside, as are the opening hours.

# DIRECTORY

## EMERGENCY NUMBERS

**Police**
*Tel 17.*

**Fire Brigade**
*Tel 18.*

**Ambulance**
*Tel 15.*

**Med Cross**
*Tel 1616 (emergencies at sea).*

**Night-duty Physician/24-hour Pharmacies**
*Tel 17.*

**Road Emergencies**
*Tel 112.*
Touring Club *Tel 08 00 08 92 22.*
AA Europe *Tel 04 72 17 12 00.*

## HOSPITALS

**Hôpital d'Ajaccio**
27 Avenue Impératrice Eugénie.
*Tel 04 95 29 90 90* or
04 95 29 91 49 (emergencies).

**Hôpital de Bastia**
Route Royale. *Tel 04 95 59 11 11*
or 04 95 59 10 51 (emergencies).

**Hôpital de Bonifacio**
Route Santa Manza.
*Tel 04 95 73 95 73.*

**Hôpital de Corte**
Avenue 9 Septembre.
*Tel 04 95 45 05 00.*

**Hôpital "Cacciabello"**
D48 outside Sartène.
*Tel 04 95 77 95 00.*

## MINOR RISKS

Take precautions to avoid sunburn, which is as much a risk for those hiking in the mountains as for those holidaying on the coast.

If you suffer from allergies, take along insect repellent.

**Sign for a Corsican hospital with the building in the background**

# Banking and Local Currency

Since 2002, most European tourists in Corsica no longer have to deal with the issue of currency exchange, since France is a member of the European Monetary Union and the currency in circulation within the Union is the euro. For visitors from other countries, however, exchanging currency is an easy and rapid procedure, both in banks and at the reception desks of hotels and pensions. The exchange rate of the euro and other non-European Union currencies is established daily and the rates can be found in all newspapers.

**A cash dispenser (ATM) outside a bank**

## BANKS

Banks in Corsica have the same opening hours as those in the south of France (8.30am to noon; 1:30 to 4:30pm) and are closed on Saturday and Sunday. Over public holidays, they are often closed from Friday noon to Tuesday morning.

Most European visitors no longer need to exchange currency, since the euro became the common currency of many EU countries in January 2002.

Although documents are not normally necessary when exchanging currency, your identification card or passport may sometimes be requested.

The main foreign currencies can be exchanged in banks, as can traveller's cheques, the rates of which are slightly different (they tend to be less advantageous). Banks also offer other services for foreign visitors; relevant information is provided on the spot.

For security reasons, many banks have double electronically operated doors. You must first push the button outside to open the door leading off the street. Once you are in the area between the two doors, you must wait for the green light to come on (which it does when the outside door is closed) and then the inside door opens automatically.

## CASH DISPENSERS (ATMS)

Cash dispensers (ATMs) can be found in and outside of almost all the banks in Corsica and they operate around the clock. Cash withdrawals can be made by means of bank cash-dispenser cards or credit cards, such as Visa, MasterCard, Diners Club and American Express.

Be aware of your surroundings and make sure that no one sees your personal identity number (PIN) when you withdraw cash from an ATM.

## CREDIT CARDS

Even if the amount is small, payment with credit or debit cards in all kinds of shop and in hotels and restaurants is quite widespread and normal in Corsica. However, be aware that small shops and eateries inland might prefer cash.

The most widely accepted cards in Corsica are Visa and MasterCard. You may find it difficult at times to use American Express and Diners Club credit cards.

An alternative to credit cards is Visa TravelMoney, which works as a pre-paid ATM card. This service can be arranged with Visa or Travelex before your departure, creating an account that will hold your pre-determined holiday funds. The Visa TravelMoney card can then be used to withdraw cash from any Visa ATM by means of a PIN number.

## DIRECTORY

### BANKS

**Banque de France**
8 Rue Sergent Casalonga, Ajaccio.
**Tel** 04 95 51 72 40; 2 Crs Pierangeli, Bastia. **Tel** 08 11 90 18 01.

**Crédit Lyonnais**
22 Rue César Campinchi, Bastia.
**Tel** 08 20 82 31 40.

**Travelex**
www.travelex.com

### LOST CREDIT CARDS

**American Express**
**Tel** 01 47 77 72 00 (Paris).

**Visa/MasterCard**
**Tel** 0800 901 179/0892 705 705.

When the funds in the holiday account are exhausted, the card can be thrown away.

## BUREAUX DE CHANGE

The largest tourist resorts have exchange offices where the exchange rates are quite close to the official ones. Before you exchange your money, check the official rate that day and the commissions charged for every single currency-exchange operation.

Many hotels also have currency-exchange services for their clients. Again, it is best to know what the rates and commissions are beforehand, since these operations are usually expensive. There is no limit to the amount of money you may take into France, but if you bring more than €7,500 into the UK you need to declare it on arrival.

**One of the very few bureaux de change in Corsica**

## LOCAL CURRENCY

The Euro (€) is the common currency of the European Union. It went into general circulation on 1 January 2002, initially for twelve participating countries. France was one of those twelve countries taking the Euro in 2002, with francs phased out by March 2002. EU members using the Euro as sole official currency are known as the Eurozone. Several EU members have opted out of joining this common currency. Euro notes are identical throughout the Eurozone countries, each one including designs of fictional architectural structures. The coins, however, have one side identical (the value side) and one side with an image unique to each country. Both notes and coins are exchangeable in each participating country.

### Bank Notes

*Euro bank notes have seven denominations. The €5 note (grey in colour) is the smallest, followed by the €10 note (pink), €20 note (blue), €50 note (orange), €100 note (green), €200 note (yellow) and €500 note (purple). All notes show the stars of the European Union.*

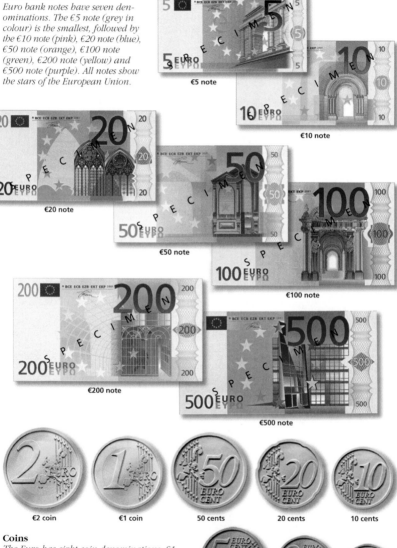

€5 note

€10 note

€20 note

€50 note

€100 note

€200 note

€500 note

€2 coin    €1 coin    50 cents    20 cents    10 cents

### Coins

*The Euro has eight coin denominations: €1 and €2; 50 cents, 20 cents, 10 cents, 5 cents, 2 cents and 1 cent. The €2 and €1 coins are both silver and gold in colour. The 50- 20- and 10-cent coins are gold. The 5-, 2- and 1-cent coins are bronze.*

5 cents    2 cents    1 cent

# Communications

**Public telephone sign**

The French national telephone company is *France Telecom*, now rebranded as *Orange*, while the postal service is called *La Poste*. Both are quite efficient and there are phone booths and post offices throughout Corsica. Internet access is less widespread, even though all the public offices and tourist bureaus have e-mail and there are various websites for visitors looking for information on the island. There are also three networks for mobile phones. In the summer, some foreign newspapers can be found in the main towns, but they usually arrive a day after publication.

**Two examples of telephone cards used in France and Corsica**

## POSTAL SERVICE

The French postal service is efficient and punctual. In the post office *(bureau de poste)* it is possible to purchase stamps *(timbres)*, either singly or in sheets *(carnets)* with ten stamps, and to post letters and parcels in various ways (priority, special delivery and so on). Here you can also consult telephone directories *(annuaires)*, purchase pre-paid telephone cards *(télécartes)*, receive or send money by means of postal money orders *(mandats)*, and cash postal giros. The main post office of every city or town also offers *poste restante*, or a post-office box service. In addition, French post offices feature a variety of financial services.

The main post offices are open from 8am to 7pm, sometimes with an hour's break for lunch. In smaller towns, and everywhere on Saturday, they are open only in the morning.

There are eight different postal rates for international post. The least expensive is for items destined for European Union countries, which is the same as the domestic rate. The most expensive is for items sent to Asia and

Australia. Sending bulky parcels is usually rather expensive.

**Corsican postbox**

Corsican postboxes are yellow, with the blue logo of *La Poste* on them, and in larger towns and cities they may have up to three different holes: for local post; post for another *département*; and international post.

## THE DÉPARTEMENTS

The administrative system in France dates back to the time of the French Revolution, when the nation was divided into administrative units with equal authority and value. These were the 96 *départements* that are still operative; they are grouped into *régions* and subdivided into 35,000 local *communes*.

Corsica is a region with two *départements*: 2A Corse-du-Sud and 2B Haute-Corse, which correspond more or less to the old separation into the *Delà des monts* and *Deça des monts* areas *(see p40)*.

Addresses in France always have a five-digit postcode. The first two digits correspond to the *département*, the third indicates the city, and the last two are for the quarters or minor localities.

## PUBLIC TELEPHONES

Most public telephones in Corsica are touch-tone and function with pre-paid telephone cards, which come in various denominations, measured in units *(unités)*. For local calls, a *unité* lasts about six minutes; this time progressively decreases as the distance increases (for example, for a call to Australia a unit lasts four seconds).

Bars and restaurants have a different type of phone, coin- or token-operated, while post offices have booths where you pay after the call.

The international-calls service is called *pays direct*. With this system you call the operator and then pay either with your credit card or by making a collect call.

## PHONING IN CORSICA

All phone numbers in France have ten digits and they include the former area codes. The first two figures indicate the four zones into which France is divided – in Corsica these digits are 04, which stand for the southeast zone. The next two figures, which, in the case of Corsica, are 95, indicate the *région*. For police emergencies, dial 17; for local directory enquiries, dial 118 followed by 000, 008 or 218. Be aware that you will be charged for this service.

## INTERNATIONAL CALLS

If you want to make an international call, you must dial 00 and then the international number for the country you're phoning (44 in the case of the UK), followed by the area code

**LA POSTE**

**Logo of the French postal and telecommunications service**

and the number you want to reach. Other country codes are 1 for Canada and the USA, 353 for Ireland, 61 for Australia, and 64 for New Zealand.

To call Corsica from abroad, dial 0033 followed by the number of the person or business you want to contact, leaving out the initial 0.

If you want the operator for information on international numbers, you should dial 3200.

**A telephone booth with the logo of France Telecom**

## MOBILE PHONES AND INTERNATIONAL CALLS

Corsica has three companies that manage mobile-phone services: *Orange, Bouygues* and *SFR*. Mobile phones from all European countries work perfectly well along the coast of the island, but less so in the interior, where both coverage and reception can be patchy.

It is also worth bearing in mind that, should you make a call from Corsica to a foreign country, added to the cost of the call is the price of the international portion. Likewise, when you receive a call, the price of the international part of the call is charged to the mobile phone that was called. For more detailed information on the fees charged by the various mobile-phone companies and the best rates available,

contact your mobile-phone company in your own country. For long phone calls it is usually cheaper to use one of the many telephone booths throughout the island.

## RADIO AND TV

As well as the national television networks, Corsica has local TV and radio stations, some of which broadcast in Corsican.

Due to the proximity to Sardinia and Tuscany, many private homes and hotels in Corsica also receive the main Italian TV channels.

Hotels tend to offer the leading European and American satellite channels, such as Sky News, BBC World and CNN.

The France Arte channel shows foreign films in their original language every night.

## NEWSPAPERS

As in the other regions in France, there are two kinds of newspapers in Corsica: those distributed on a nationwide scale, such as *Le Monde, Le Figaro* and *Libération*, and the local, regional ones, such as *Corse-Matin*. Local papers provide useful information regarding cultural events, cinema, theatre and sports, but they do not leave much space for foreign news.

In the summer, in the main cities it is easy to find foreign newspapers, which usually arrive one day late.

**The daily newspaper *Corse-Matin*, with its weekly insert**

## DIRECTORY

### POST OFFICES

**Ajaccio**
13 Cours Napoléon.
*Tel 04 95 51 84 75.*

**Aléria**
Cateraggio.
*Tel 04 95 56 55 00.*

**Bastia**
Avenue Maréchal Sebastiani.
*Tel 04 95 32 80 70.*

**Bonifacio**
Place Carrega, Rue St Dominique.
*Tel 04 95 73 73 73.*

**Calvi**
1 Boulevard Wilson.
*Tel 04 95 65 90 90.*

**Cargèse**
Traverse Stéphanopoli de Comène.
*Tel 04 95 26 41 97.*

**Corte**
Avenue Baron Mariani.
*Tel 04 95 46 80 00.*

**Porto-Vecchio**
Route Nationale 198.
*Tel 04 95 70 95 00.*

**Zonza**
Au Bourg.
*Tel 04 95 78 67 67.*

### INTERNET

In the main cities, there are Internet cafés where customers can surf the Web for a small charge.

The website of the central Agence de Tourisme is **www.visit-corsica.com**. Among the most useful websites is **www.corsica-guide.com**, with information on local events, geography, culture and museums. For accommodation, you can also visit **www.destination-corse.com**.

The site of the Parc Naturel Régional de la Corse is **www.parc-corse.org**; and if you are interested in the local wineries, the website is **www.vinsdecorse.com**.

Information on current events in Corsica is at **www.corsica-info.com**, while **www.u-corsu.com** is a good search engine for all things Corsican and has an English version.

# TRAVEL INFORMATION

Corsica has excellent connections with the rest of Europe and there are regularly scheduled flights linking the airports in Ajaccio, Bastia, Figari Sud Corse (near Bonifacio) and Calvi with others in Provence and southern France, as well as Paris. There are also several charter flights in the high season. Another popular means of transport to the island from both southern France and Italy is the ferry. To get around the

**Bus for tourist excursions**

island there are few alternatives to a car. The only railway line connects Bastia to Ajaccio and Calvi. There is a network of public buses, but they do not go to all the inland resorts and you may have to wait a long time for connections. When driving, bear in mind that the roads are often winding and panoramic, and the average speed limit is rather low; be very careful when the traffic is heavy, especially if the weather is bad.

## ARRIVING BY AIR

In the summer Corsica is well served by charter flights departing from Gatwick (Calvi, Ajaccio, Figari and Bastia), Heathrow (Ajaccio), Stansted and Manchester (Figari and Calvi), Birmingham (Bastia) and Edinburgh (Calvi). **Holiday Options** offers flights at good prices, as well as package holidays.

Direct scheduled flights from the UK to Corsica are offered by **easyJet**. **British Airways**, **Corse-Mediterranée** and **Air France** also have flights to Corsica, but via Paris, Marseille or Nice.

US visitors often travel via France, which is served by Air France, **United Airlines** and **Delta** among others. From France, Corsica can be reached with a regional carrier (such as **Nouvelles Frontières/ Corse Air International**).

**One of the large car ferries serving Corsica**

**AIRFRANCE /**
Logo of the French national airline Air France

## AIR FARES

Generally speaking, air fares to Corsica are fairly expensive during the summer season. However, for those willing to shop around, there are also good-value last-minute deals to be had, as well as various combinations, with a minimum and maximum number of days,

that allow you to stay in Corsica without spending too much. In the low season the offers are cheaper.

## PACKAGE HOLIDAYS

There are several package-tour operators dealing with Corsica. A package holiday includes at the very least air fare and accommodation; some also include food, car rental and activities.

One of the most reputable package-tour operators is **Club Med**. Renowned for the high level of service and excellent facilities, Club Med has a holiday village *(see p155)* near Cargèse. Childcare and all activities are included in the price.

Package tours are also handled by **Simply Corsica**, the UK's largest operator on the island, and **Corsican Places**, both of which offer hotel rooms and a variety of self-catering accommodation.

## ARRIVING BY FERRY

Ferries are a popular means of transportation for visitors travelling to Corsica from France or Italy. Because of the large number of visitors, if you plan to go to the island by car in the summer it is best to book well ahead, especially if you are towing a caravan or travelling in a camper.

In the summer there are fast car ferries that save you a lot of time in the crossing, but they cost more than the normal ferries.

The port of Bastia has many routes, with links to Marseille, Nice, Toulon, Genoa and Savona, La Spezia, Livorno, and Piombino. Ajaccio is accessed via ferries departing from southern France and from Genoa, and there is also a line that goes from Ajaccio to Porto Torres, in Sardinia. Bonifacio can be reached by ferry only from Sardinia. The **Societé Nationale Mari-**

**On the train from Ajaccio to Bastia**

time **Corse Mediterranée** (SNCM) and **Compagnie Méridionale de Navigation** (CMN) are the French shipping lines. If you leave from Italy or France, **Corsica Ferries** offers several links with the island, including departures from Civitavecchia (only in summer) and Livorno and Savona (all year round), as well as Toulon and Nice. **Moby Lines** connects Bastia and Piombino (July and August), Livorno and Genoa for about the same price.

In the summer there is also a frequent ferry service from France and Italy to Calvi, L'Île Rousse and Porto-Vecchio.

### FERRY FARES

The highest fare for two people and a car 4–5 m (13–16 ft) long on the Livorno–Bastia ferry is about €260 return, but there are special rates and discount tickets (up to a minimum of €105).

### TRAVELLING BY TRAIN

Investment in a modern auto-rail system in Corsica aims to improve journey times and passenger comfort. The Bastia–Corte–Ajaccio railway affords magnificent views and has five trains per day in each direction.

One of the most frequented train stations is Vizzavona, which many visitors use as a departure point for the GR20 long-distance hiking path (*see pp22–7*). To get to Calvi by train from Ajaccio (and vice versa), change trains at Ponte Leccia.

Information about timetables can be found at main railway stations, and at **www.train-corse.com**, where information on service upgrades can also be found.

### TRAVELLING BY BUS

The bus line that offers service in the area around Corte is the **Société des Autocars Cortenais**. The central-north area of Corsica is covered by **Autocars Santini**. Ajaccio, Sartène and Bonifacio are served by bus lines such as **Eurocorse**, while **Société des Autobus Bastiais** covers the area around Bastia.

Because of the seasonal variation in the schedules, it is always a good idea to make enquiries at the local tourist offices before setting off on a bus journey.

### TRAVELLING BY CAR

A regular driver's licence is the only document required to travel by car in Corsica. Naturally, the great number of minor roads is an invitation to explore the lesser-known areas on the island; these require a much lower speed and particular attention and caution. When planning a tour or excursion, you should base it on an average speed of 40–50 km/h (25–30 mph). There may be animals on the road or, in summer, large caravans and campers that go slowly on hairpin turns, so you must reduce your speed.

You can travel faster only on the Routes Nationales (Bastia–Calvi, Bastia–Corte–Ajaccio, Bastia–Porto-Vecchio and Ajaccio-Bonifacio). There are more petrol stations along the coast than inland, and in the tourist resorts near the sea it is easy to find automatic petrol pumps that will accept bank notes or credit cards.

### CAR RENTAL

The offices of the main car-rental companies are in airports and port passenger terminals. These include **Avis**, **Hertz**, **Europcar** and **Budget Rent a Car**, as well as local companies such as **Ada**, which offers very different rates according to the season. By paying a small surcharge, you can pick up your car in one place and return it in another.

### TRAVELLING BY MOTORCYCLE

Corsica is a paradise for motorcyclists. The roads are difficult but rewarding, and the dry summers are favourable for this means of transportation. Motorcycles are also advantageous in avoiding traffic jams, especially along the coast.

As is the case with cars, you must be extremely careful, especially on the mountain roads.

Motorcycles can be hired from most main cities in Corsica (Ajaccio, Porto-Vecchio, Bastia, Calvi, Porto and Propriano). You will also find centres that hire motorcycles and offer assistance for those arriving with their own bikes.

**Travelling by camper in Corsica – a simple way to enjoy the scenery**

## TRAVELLING BY BOAT

Boats of all kinds can be found in Corsican waters during the summer months. You can use your boat to travel from one resort to another within Corsica or for making the crossing from a port in Italy or France *(see p190)*. Obviously, this voyage should be made only by expert navigators whose boats are able to withstand the hazards of the open sea. Even the shortest crossing, from Sardinia in the Straits of Bonifacio *(see p113)*, is not without its pitfalls due to the strong winds that often blow in this part of the sea.

Sailing remains undoubtedly one of the best ways to explore the coasts of Corsica. Even a simple dinghy or a small sailboat, rented or brought along with your car in a ferry, are ideal for leaving in the morning and returning in the evening after a fine day's boating.

## BOAT HIRE

There are many possibilities for hiring boats in Corsica. The boat-hire companies

The harbour at Cargèse, one of the stages on a tour of the coast

have all types of craft to offer their clients, and they also provide assistance and maintenance. The rates can be by the hour or by the day, and there are even weekly rates for those who decide to make long trips. In such cases the agencies offer boats with a skipper or even a crew.

Naturally, the price varies according to the type of boat you hire, the duration of the trip and whether a skipper or crew are provided. The period of rental is also a factor, the highest rates being in July and August.

## CIRCUMNAVIGATING THE ISLAND

A classic choice of trip for experienced yachtsmen is a tour around the island. This is a fascinating adventure because the coast of Corsica is spectacular and has many secluded coves that cannot be reached by car or even on foot.

The chart below lists the ports on the island and their facilities. Although temporary berths are added in summer, ports are likely to be crowded, so phone beforehand or arrive in the early afternoon.

| PORTS | INFORMATION | BOAT BERTHS TOTAL | BOAT BERTHS TEMPORARY | FUEL STATION | MAINTENANCE AND REPAIR |
|---|---|---|---|---|---|
| Ajaccio, Ornano | 04 95 22 31 98 | 830 | 160 | ● | ● |
| Ajaccio, Tino Rossi | 04 95 21 93 28 | 260 | 140 | ● | ● |
| Bastia, Port de Toga | 04 95 34 90 70 | 357 | 50 | ● | ● |
| Bastia, Vieux Port | 04 95 31 31 10 | 260 | 40 | ● | ● |
| Bonifacio | 04 95 73 10 07 | 330 | 120 | ● | ● |
| Calvi | 04 95 65 10 60 | 480 | 100 | ● | ● |
| Campoloro | 04 95 38 07 61 | 464 | 80 | ● | ● |
| Cargèse | 04 95 26 47 24 | 235 | 25 | ● | ● |
| Lumio | 04 95 60 70 88 | 250 | 0 | ● | ● |
| Macinaggio | 04 95 35 42 57 | 585 | 240 | ● | ● |
| Pianottoli Caldarello | 04 95 71 83 57 | 160 | 80 | ● | ● |
| Porto-Vecchio | 04 95 70 17 93 | 450 | 150 | ● | ● |
| Propriano | 04 95 76 10 40 | 420 | 50 | ● | ● |
| St-Florent | 04 95 37 00 79 | 750 | 150 | ● | ● |
| Solenzara | 04 95 57 46 42 | 450 | 100 | ● | ● |

# DIRECTORY

## AIRPORTS

**Ajaccio**
Campo dell'Oro.
*Tel* 04 95 23 56 56.
www.ajaccio.aeroport.fr

**Bastia**
Poretta.
*Tel* 04 95 54 54 54.
www.ccihc.fr

**Calvi**
Ste-Catherine.
*Tel* 04 95 65 88 88.
www.ccihc.fr

**Figari-Sud-Corse**
*Tel* 04 95 71 10 10.
www.figari.aeroport.fr

## AIRLINES

**Air France**
France. *Tel* 3654.
UK. *Tel* 0871 663 3777.
www.airfrance.com

**British Airways**
UK. *Tel* 0844 493 0787.
www.britishairways.com

**Corse-Méditerranée
(CCM)**
*Marseille, Nice, Lyon.*
*Tel* 3654 or 04 95 29 05
09. www.aircorsica.com

**Delta Air Lines**
France. *Tel* 0811 640 005.
UK. *Tel* 0845 600 0950.
www.delta.com

**easyJet**
www.easyjet.com

**Holiday Options**
49 The Martlets, Burgess
Hill, West Sussex RH15
9NN. *Tel* 0844 779 999.
www.holidayoptions.co.uk

**Nouvelles
Frontières/Corse Air
International**
*Paris, Marseille, Bordeaux,
Strasbourg, Lyon,
Lille, Nice, Toulouse,
Brussels.* Bastia.
*Tel* 04 95 32 01 62.
www.nouvelles-
frontieres.fr

**United Airlines**
France.
*Tel* 0810 72 72 72.
UK. *Tel* 0845 844 4777.
www.ual.com

## PACKAGE HOLIDAYS

**Club Med**
*Tel* 0871 424 4044.
www.clubmed.co.uk

**Corsican Places**
*Tel* 0845 330 2059.
www.corsica.co.uk

**Simply Corsica**
*Tel* 020 8541 2205.
www.simply-travel.co.uk

## FERRY PORTS

**Ajaccio**
*Tel* 04 95 51 21 80.

**Bastia**
*Tel* 04 95 55 25 00.

**Bonifacio**
*Tel* 04 95 73 06 75.

**Calvi**
*Tel* 04 95 65 10 60.

**L'Île Rousse**
*Tel* 04 95 60 45 54.

**Porto-Vecchio**
*Tel* 04 95 70 43 08.

**Propriano**
*Tel* 04 95 76 04 36.

## FERRIES

**Compagnie
Méridionale
de Navigation**
Ajaccio. *Tel* 08 10 20 13
20. www.lameridionale.fr

**Corsica Ferries**
*Livorno, Savona, Toulon,
Nice.* Bastia.
*Tel* 04 95 32 95 95.
www.corsicaferries.com

**Moby Lines**
*Genoa, Livorno, Piombino.*
Bastia. *Tel* 04 95 34 84 94.
Bonifacio. *Tel* 04 95 73
00 29. www.mobylines.it

**Societé Nationale
Maritime Corse
Mediterranée
(SNCM)**
*Marseille, Toulon, Livorno,
Nice.* Ajaccio.
*Tel* 04 95 29 66 65.
Bastia. *Tel* 04 95 54 66 99.
Calvi. *Tel* 04 95 65 01 38.
L'Île Rousse.
*Tel* 04 95 60 09 56.
Livorno. *Tel* 0586 21 05
07. www.sncm.fr

## RAILWAY STATIONS

**Ajaccio**
*Tel* 04 95 23 11 03.

**Bastia**
*Tel* 04 95 32 80 61.

**Calvi**
*Tel* 04 95 65 00 61.

**Corte**
*Tel* 04 95 46 00 97.

**L'Île Rousse**
*Tel* 04 95 60 00 50.

**Ponte Leccia**
*Tel* 04 95 47 61 29.

**Vizzavona**
*Tel* 04 95 47 21 02.

## BUS COMPANIES

**Autocars Santini**
*Tel* 04 95 37 02 98.

**Eurocorse**
*Tel* 04 95 21 06 30.

**Société des
Autobus Bastiais**
www.bastiabus.com

**Société des
Autocars Cortenais**
*Tel* 04 95 46 02 12.
www.autocars-
cortenais.com

## CAR RENTAL

**Ada**
Ajaccio. *Tel* 04 95 23 56
57. Bastia. *Tel* 04 95 54
55 44. www.ada.fr

**Avis**
Ajaccio.
*Tel* 04 95 23 56 90.
Bastia. *Tel* 04 95 54 55 46.
Calvi. *Tel* 04 95 65 88 38.
Figari. *Tel* 04 95 71 00 01.
www.avis.com

**Budget Rent a Car**
Ajaccio.
*Tel* 04 95 23 57 21.
Bastia. *Tel* 04 95 30 05 04.
Calvi. *Tel* 04 95 65 88 34.
www.budget.fr

**Europcar**
Ajaccio.
*Tel* 04 95 23 57 01.
Bastia. *Tel* 04 95 30 09 50.
Bonifacio.
*Tel* 04 95 73 10 99.
Calvi. *Tel* 04 95 65 10 19.
Corte. *Tel* 04 95 46 06 02.
www.europcar.co.uk

**Hertz**
Ajaccio. *Tel* 04 95 23 57
04. Bastia. *Tel* 04 95 30
05 00. www.hertz.com

## MOTORCYCLE HIRE

**Corse Motos Service**
U Centru, Porto-Vecchio.
*Tel* 04 95 70 12 88.

**Rout'Evasion**
2 Avenue Franchini, Ajaccio.
*Tel* 04 95 22 72 87.

## BOAT HIRE

**Aubert Gaston**
Route Cala Rossa,
Porto-Vecchio.
*Tel* 04 95 70 23 97.

**Balagne Sports**
Rue Napoléon, L'Île Rousse.
*Tel* 04 95 60 05 17.

**Cap Evasion**
Macinaggio.
*Tel* 06 81 70 38 48.

**Centre Nautique**
Porticcio. *Tel* 04 95 25 01
06. www.le-cnp.fr

**Corsica Voile**
Macinaggio.
*Tel* 04 95 35 48 20.
www.corsica-voile.com

**Dominique Plaisance**
St-Florent.
*Tel* 04 95 37 07 08.

**Leader Boat**
Quai Paoli, Porto-Vecchio.
*Tel* 04 95 72 03 61.
www.leaderboat.fr

**Locamarine**
Propriano. *Tel* 04 95 76 18
54. www.locamarine.com

**Marine Location**
Porto-Vecchio.
*Tel* 04 95 70 58 92.

**Multi-Service**
Santa Giulia, Porto-Vecchio.
*Tel* 04 95 70 29 13.

**Toga Loca Nautique**
Port de Toga, Bastia.
*Tel* 04 95 34 14 14.

**Tra Mare e Monti**
Port de Plaisance, Calvi.
*Tel* 04 95 65 21 26.

**Union Nautique
Insulaire**
Port de l'Amirautée, Ajaccio.
*Tel* 04 95 20 66 31.

# General Index

# Acknowledgments

Fabio Ratti Editoria would like to thank the following staff at Dorling Kindersley:

**Publishing Manager**
Anna Streiffert.

**Senior Art Editor**
Marisa Renzullo.

**Publisher**
Douglas Amrine.

**Senior DTP Designer**
Jason Little.

**Cartographers**
Casper Morris, Dave Pugh.

Dorling Kindersley would also like to thank all those whose contribution and assistance have made the preparation of this book possible.

**Main Contributors**
FABRIZIO ARDITO, a journalist and photographer born in Rome in 1957. Among his publications are several books on hiking. In the Dorling Kindersley Eyewitness Travel Guides series he has contributed to *Sardinia, Sicily* and *Jerusalem & the Holy Land*, as well as the following (so far published in Italian only, by Guide Visuali Mondadori): *The Dolomites, Northeast Italy, Central Italy, South Italy*. He has written texts and articles for various Italian publishers, periodicals and newpapers on the environment, geography and travelling in general. These include *Nuova Ecologia, Espresso,* Gambero Rosso-De Agostini, Touring Club, Giorgio Mondadori and *Unità*. He has also worked for the Italian State Television (RAI), producing various films and documentaries on nature, sports and the subterranean areas of cities.

CRISTINA GAMBARO is a journalist who has contributed articles to the leading Italian periodicals. For Gambero Rosso-De Agostini she wrote *Guide to Italian Hotels*; for Clupguide she wrote *Sardinia* and *Pakistan*; for Airplane, *Scotland* and *Ireland*; for White Star, *The Castles of Scotland*. She was also a main contributor to the following Dorling Kindersley Eyewitness Travel Guides: *Sardinia, Sicily* and *Jerusalem & the Holy Land*, as well as *Northeast Italy, Central Italy, South Italy* and *The Dolomites* (published in Italian by Guide Visuali Mondadori).

**Additional contributions**
Kathryn Tomasetti, Roger Williams.

**Design and Editorial**
Cayetana Muriel Aguado, Thierry Combret, Géraldine Gonard, Marina Dragoni. For Dorling Kindersley: Julie Bond, Lisa Fox-Mullen, Anna Freiberger, Laura Jones, Delphine Lawrance, Cathrine Lehmann, Sonal Modha, Helen Partington, Karen Villabona, Dora Whitaker.

**Editors, UK Edition**
Sylvia and David Tombesi-Walton at Sands Publishing Solutions, Lauren Robertson.

**Additional Picture Research**
Rachel Barber.

**Additional DTP**
Vinod Harish, Vincent Kurien, Azeem Siddiqui.

**Additional Cartography**
Uma Bhattacharya, Mohammad Hassan, Jasneet Kaur.

**Factchecker**
Irina Zarb.

**Consultant**
David Abram.

**Proof-Reader**
Jane Simmonds.

**Indexers**
Hilary Bird, Helen Peters.

**Additional Photography**
Max Alexander, Ian O'Leary.

## Special Thanks

We would like to thank the following persons for their contribution to this guide:

Messieurs Xavier Olivieri and Jean-Philippe di Grazia, Agence de Tourisme de la Corse, Ajaccio; Madame Marie-Eugénie Poli-Mordiconi, Musée de la Corse, Corte; Monsieur Pascal Rinaldi, Parc Naturel Régional de Corse, Ajaccio; Madame Viviane Gentile, Domaine Gentile, St-Florent; Monsieur Jean-Noël Luigi, Clos Nicrosi, Rogliano; Ms Marina della Rosa, expert sailor; the chef Carlo Romito and his assistants Giorgio Brignone and Marco Fanti, of the Palazzo Granaio restaurant in Settimo Milanese, specializing in cuisine of the upper Tyrrhenian Sea; Mrs Delphine Jaillot, Sopexa Italia, Milan; Ms Charlotte Grant, Christie's, London; Dr Biondi, Scientific Committee, Palazzo Ducale, Genoa; Dr Campodonico, curator, Museo Navale di Pegli, Genoa; Dr Alessandro Avanzino, Palazzo San Giorgio, Genoa; the Associazione Amici di Palazzo Ducale, Genoa; the Museo di Sant'Agostino, Genoa; Gabriele Reina and Roberto Bosi, Franco Maria Ricci Publishers, Milan; all the Stations Touristiques in Corsica; the Musée Fesch, Ajaccio; the French Tourist Board, Milan.

## Photography Permissions

The Publisher would like to thank the local bodies, associations and firms for the authorization to take photographs, in particular Archivio Electa, Milano; Musée de la Corse, Corte; Musée d'Antropologie de la Corse, Corte; Sopexa Italia, Milan. The Publisher would also like to thank the cathedrals, churches, museums, galleries, restaurants, hotels, shops and all those who furnished material – too numerous to be mentioned here individually – for their kind assistance and valuable contribution.

Every effort has been made to trace the copyright holders. The Publisher apologizes for any unintentional omissions and would be pleased, in such cases, to add an acknowledgment in future editions.

## Key to Picture Credits

t = top; tl = top left; tlc = top left centre; tc = top centre; trc = top right centre; tr = top right; tra = top right above; cla = centre left above; ca = centre above; cra = centre right above; cl = centre left; c = centre; cr = centre right; cla = centre left above; crb = centre right below; cb = centre below; bl = bottom left; br = bottom right; b = bottom; bc = bottom centre; bcl = bottom centre left; bcr = bottom centre right; (d) = detail.

## Picture Credits

4Corners Images: SIME / Fantuz Olimpio 10cra; SIME / Giovanni Simeone 11clb, 81cl; SIME / Johanna Huber 10bl; SIME / Spila Riccardo 11tl.

Agence de Tourisme de la Corse, Ajaccio: 17bcr, 31 (all photos), 33cb, 34 (all photos), 35cra, 37ca, 38tl, 40cb, 40crb, 41cr, 41 br, 45bc, 49bc, 87tl, 90tl, 99tc, 123br, 148tc, 162br, 163br, 182br, 184cla, 189cr, 192cl, 197cl.

Alamy Images: Jon Arnold Images / Doug Pearson 168cl; Justin Kase 169tl; a la Poste 202c; Dave Watts 10tc.

Christian Andreani, Ajaccio: 99br.

Archivio Mondadori, Milan: 18clb, 18crb, 18bcl, 19clb, 19tr, 19bl, 19bc, 19crb, 20tl, 40cla, 40bl, 42–3c, 42tl, 42br, 43tl, 43cr, 47cra, 48tc, 49tl, 69ca, 73tc, 96cla, 102c, 122tl, 122cl, 139cr, 142cl, 153 (box), 166crb, 167tr, 167br, 191br, 192 (box), 199c, 204clb.

Archivio Scala, Florence: 36.

Ardea London Ltd: Stefan Meyers 26cla.

Enrico Banfi, Milan: 105tl.

CONTRASTO, Milan: 49cb, 81cla, 81clb, 97tc, 113cl, 113bcr, 169clb, 169cb, 170cla, 170ca, 184tc, 191tc, 192tr.

CORBIS: Gary Braasch 169c.

LOUIS DOAZAN, Corsica: 99cl.

XIAOYANG GALAS: *Sea, Sunshine and Village* 8–9.

HEMISPHERES IMAGES: Georges Antoni 11br.

GETTY IMAGES: Michelle Bussellle 118–19.

GÎTES DE FRANCE: 154t.

GRONCHI FOTOARTE, Pisa: 43tr.
IMAGE BANK, Milan: 2–3, 3c, 33cra, 106, 113tc, 116trc, 130, 136tl, 136tr, 186trc, 190b, 191cl.

GIANMARIA MARRAS, Milan: 185tlc, 185br, 204cra, 205tl.

MUSÉE DE LA CORSE, Corte: 9ca, 30 (all photos), 35bcl, 42clb, 44t, 44c, 45tc, 45crb, 45bl, 46–7c, 46trd 46clb, 46bc, 47tl, 49bcr, 51 (box), 137ca, 137cra, 137crb.

OFFICE DU TOURISME DE L'AGGLOMÉRATION DE BASTIA: 196br.

PARC NATUREL RÉGIONAL DE CORSE, Ajaccio: 22cla, 22clb, 23tl, 24clb, 24bcr, 25tc, 25ca, 26clb, 27tc, 27cra, 27cla, 99tc.

RMN, Paris: 90tr, 90cl, 90bl, 90br, 91tl, 91cra.

ANNA SERRANO, Barcelona: 18bcr.

SOPEXA, Italy: 171crb.

STA TRAVEL GROUP: 197c.

STUDIO AQUILINI, Milan: 94–5, 100tl, 100clb, 100bcl, 101cra, 114tr, 114bcr, 188cra, 189b.

SYNDICAT D'INITIATIVE DE PIANA: 100tr.

JACKET
Front – 4CORNERS IMAGES: SIME / Giovanni Simeone main image; DK IMAGES: Cristina Gambaro clb. Back – ALAMY IMAGES: Nordicphotos / Sven Rosenhall bl; DK IMAGES: Max Alexander clb, tl; Marco Stoppato cla. Spine – 4CORNERS IMAGES: SIME / Giovanni Simeone t; ALAMY IMAGES: David Robertson b.
All other images © Dorling Kindersley.
For further information:
www.dkimages.com

# Corsican Words and Phrases

Although French is spoken everywhere, a few Corsican phrases can come in handy. Corsican is closer to Italian, in fact to Medieval Tuscan, both in its vocabulary and its pronounciation, but also shows a few other Mediterranean influences. Geographical terms appear in many sight names, and on the bilingual signs.

## Basics

**A'ringraziavvi**: Thank you

**Fate u piacè**: Please

**Ié**: Yes

**Nò**: No

**Và bé**: OK

**Induve**: Where

**Quandu**: When

**Chì**: What, who, which

**A'vedeci**: Goodbye

**A dopu**: See you

**Buona notte**: Goodnight

**Buona sera**: Good evening

**Buonghjornu**: Hello

**Cumu sì?**: How are you?

**Me dispiace**: Sorry

**(Nò) Capiscu**: I (don't) understand

**Parla inglese?**: Do you speak English?

## Geographical Terms

**a marina**: beach

**anse/cala**: cove

**boca/foce/col**: mountain pass

**calanca**: gorge, ravine

**casa**: house

**casatorre**: stronghold

**castellu/casteddu**: fortified settlement

**fiume**: river

**fiumicellu**: stream

**lau/lavu**: lake

**licettu**: oak forest

**muntagna**: mountain

**orriu**: shelter under a large stone or boulder, sometimes bricked in

**pianu**: plateau

**piscia**: waterfall

**ponte**: bridge

**stagnu**: pool or pond

**torre**: tower

**u paese**: village

**vignale/vignetu**: vineyard

## Directions

**dritta**: right

**semprerdrittu**: straight on

**sinistra**: left

**Induv'é...?**: Where is...?

## Shopping

**aperta/apertu**: open

**Avetene...?**: Do you have...?

**basta**: enough

**buonu mercatu**: cheap

**chiusu**: closed

**grande/maio**: big

**Hè troppu caru**: It is too much.

**menu**: less

**nulla/nunda/nudda**: nothing

**piccola/chjucu**: small

**pui**: more

**Quantu costa/Quanto hè?**: How much does it cost/is it?

**Vogliu...**: I want...

## Time, Days and Months

**Chi ora hè?**: What is the time?

**oghje**: today

**ieri**: yesterday

**dumane**: tomorrow

**ghjurnu**: day

**simana**: week

**meze**: month

| | |
|---|---|
| Monday: | **luni** |
| Tuesday: | **marti** |
| Wednesday: | **mercuri** |
| Thursday: | **ghjovi** |
| Friday: | **venneri** |
| Saturday: | **sabatu** |
| Sunday: | **dumenica** |
| January: | **Ghjennaghju** |
| February: | **Febbraghju** |
| March: | **Marzu** |
| April: | **Aprile** |
| May: | **Maghjiu** |
| June: | **Ghjiugnu** |
| July: | **Ghjugliu** |
| August: | **Aostu** |
| September: | **Sittembre** |
| October: | **Ottobre** |
| November: | **Novembre** |
| December: | **Dicembre** |

## Seasons

**auturnu**: autumn

**estate**: summer

**imbernu/ingnernu**: winter

**veranu**: spring

# French Phrase Book

## In Emergency

| | | |
|---|---|---|
| Help! | **Au secours!** | oh se**koor** |
| Stop! | **Arrêtez!** | aret-**ay** |
| Call a doctor! | **Appelez un médecin!** | apuh-**lay** uñ meds**añ** |
| Call an ambulance! | **Appelez une ambulance!** | apuh-**lay** oon oñboo-**loñs** |
| Call the police! | **Appelez la police!** | apuh-**lay** lah poh-**lees** |
| Call the fire brigade! | **Appelez les pompiers!** | apuh-lay leh poñ-**peeyay** |
| Where is the nearest telephone? | **Où est le téléphone le plus proche?** | oo ay luh tehleh**fon** luh ploo prosh |
| Where is the nearest hospital? | **Où est l'hôpital le plus proche?** | oo ay l'**opee**tal luh ploo prosh |

## Communication Essentials

| | | |
|---|---|---|
| Yes | **Oui** | wee |
| No | **Non** | noñ |
| Please | **S'il vous plaît** | seel voo **play** |
| Thank you | **Merci** | mer-**see** |
| Excuse me | **Excusez-moi** | exkoo-**zay** mwah |
| Hello | **Bonjour** | boñ**zhoor** |
| Goodbye | **Au revoir** | oh ruh-**vwar** |
| Good night | **Bonsoir** | boñ-**swar** |
| Morning | **Le matin** | mat**añ** |
| Afternoon | **L'après-midi** | l'apreh-**meedee** |
| Evening | **Le soir** | swar |
| Yesterday | **Hier** | eey**ehr** |
| Today | **Aujourd'hui** | oh-zhoor-**dwee** |
| Tomorrow | **Demain** | duh**mañ** |
| Here | **Ici** | ee-**see** |
| There | **Là** | lah |
| What? | **Quel, quelle?** | kel, kel |
| When? | **Quand?** | koñ |
| Why? | **Pourquoi?** | poor-**kwah** |
| Where? | **Où?** | oo |

## Useful Phrases

| | | |
|---|---|---|
| How are you? | **Comment allez-vous?** | kom-moñ tal**ay voo** |
| Very well, thank you. | **Très bien, merci.** | treh byañ, mer-**see** |
| Pleased to meet you. | **Enchanté de faire votre connaissance.** | oñshoñ-**tay** duh fehr votr kon-ay-**sans** |
| See you soon. | **A bientôt.** | abyañ-**toh** |
| That's fine. | **Voilà qui est parfait.** | vwalah kee ay par**fay** |
| Where is/are...? | **Où est/sont...?** | oo ay/**soñ** |
| How far is it to...? | **Combien de kilomètres d'ici à...?** | kom-**byañ** duh is keelo-**metr** d'ee-**see** ah |
| Which way to...? | **Quelle est la direction pour...?** | kel ay lah deer-ek-**syoñ** poor |
| Do you speak English? | **Parlez-vous anglais?** | par-**lay** voo oñg-**lay** |
| I don't understand. | **Je ne comprends pas.** | zhuh nuh kom-**proñ** pah |

## Useful Words (right column)

| | | |
|---|---|---|
| Could you speak slowly, please? | **Pouvez-vous parler moins vite, s'il vous plaît?** | poo-**vay** voo par-lay mwañ veet seel voo play |
| I'm sorry. | **Excusez-moi.** | exkoo-**zay** mwah |

## Useful Words

| | | |
|---|---|---|
| big | **grand** | groñ |
| small | **petit** | puh-**tee** |
| hot | **chaud** | show |
| cold | **froid** | frwah |
| good | **bon** | boñ |
| bad | **mauvais** | moh-**veh** |
| enough | **assez** | as**say** |
| well | **bien** | byañ |
| open | **ouvert** | oo-**ver** |
| closed | **fermé** | fer-**meh** |
| left | **gauche** | gohsh |
| right | **droite** | drwaht |
| straight on | **tout droit** | too drwah |
| near | **près** | preh |
| far | **loin** | lwañ |
| up | **en haut** | oñ **oh** |
| down | **en bas** | oñ **bah** |
| early | **de bonne heure** | duh bon **urr** |
| late | **en retard** | oñ ruh-**tar** |
| entrance | **l'entrée** | l'on-**tray** |
| exit | **la sortie** | sor-**tee** |
| toilet | **les toilettes, les WC** | twah-let, vay-**see** |
| unoccupied | **libre** | leebr |
| no charge | **gratuit** | grah-**twee** |

## Making a Telephone Call

| | | |
|---|---|---|
| I'd like to place a long-distance call. | **Je voudrais faire un interurbain.** | zhuh voo-dreh fehr uñ añter-oorbañ |
| I'd like to make a reverse-charge call. | **Je voudrais faire une communication PCV.** | zhuh voo**dreh** fehr oon kom-oonikah-**syoñ** peh-seh-veh |
| I'll try again later. | **Je rappelerai plus tard.** | zhuh rapeler**ay** ploo tar |
| Can I leave a message? | **Est-ce que je peux laisser un message?** | es-keh zhuh puh leh-**say** uñ mehsazh |
| Hold on. | **Ne quittez pas, s'il vous plaît.** | nuh kee-**tay** pah seel voo play. |
| Could you speak up a little please? | **Pouvez-vous parler un peu plus fort?** | poo-**vay** voo par-**lay** uñ puh ploo for |
| local call | **la communication locale** | komoonikah-**syoñ** low-kal |

## Shopping

| | | |
|---|---|---|
| How much does this cost? | **C'est combien s'il vous plaît?** | say kom-**byañ** seel voo play |
| Do you take credit cards? | **Est-ce que vous acceptez les cartes de crédit?** | es-kuh voo zaksept-**ay** leh kart duh kreh-**dee** |

| | | |
|---|---|---|
| Do you take travellers' cheques? | **Est-ce que vous acceptez les chèques de voyage?** | es-**kuh** voo zaksept-**ay** leh shek duh vway**azh** |
| I would like ... | **Je voudrais...** | zhuh voo-**dray** |
| Do you have? | **Est-ce que vous avez?** | es-**kuh** voo zav**ay** |
| I'm just looking. | **Je regarde seulement.** | zhuh ruh**gar** suhl**moñ** |
| What time do you open? | **A quelle heure vous êtes ouvert?** | ah kel urr voo zet oo-**ver** |
| What time do you close? | **A quelle heure vous êtes fermé?** | ah kel urr voo zet fer-**may** |
| This one | **Celui-ci** | suhl-wee-**see** |
| That one | **Celui-là** | suhl-wee-**lah** |
| expensive | **cher** | shehr |
| cheap | **pas cher, bon marché** | pah shehr, boñ mar-**shay** |
| size, clothes | **la taille** | tye |
| size, shoes | **la pointure** | pwañ-**tur** |
| white | **blanc** | bloñ |
| black | **noir** | nwahr |
| brown | **brun** | bruñ |
| red | **rouge** | roozh |
| yellow | **jaune** | zhohwn |
| green | **vert** | vehr |
| blue | **bleu** | bluh |

## Types of Shop

| | | |
|---|---|---|
| antique shop | **le magasin d'antiquités** | maga-**zañ** d'oñteekee-**tay** |
| bakery | **la boulangerie** | booloñ-**zhuree** |
| bank | **la banque** | boñk |
| book shop | **la librairie** | lee-**brehree** |
| butcher | **la boucherie** | boo-**shehree** |
| cake shop | **la pâtisserie** | patee-**sree** |
| cheese shop | **la fromagerie** | fromazh-**ree** |
| chemist | **la pharmacie** | farmah-**see** |
| dairy | **la crémerie** | krem-**ree** |
| department store | **le grand magasin** | groñ maga-**zañ** |
| delicatessen | **la charcuterie** | sharkoot-**ree** |
| fishmonger | **la poissonnerie** | pwasson-**ree** |
| gift shop | **le magasin de cadeaux** | maga-**zañ** duh ka**doh** |
| greengrocer | **le marchand de légumes** | mar-**shoñ** duh lay-**goom** |
| grocery | **l'alimentation** | alee-moñta-**syoñ** |
| hairdresser | **le coiffeur** | kwa**fuhr** |
| market | **le marché** | marsh-**ay** |
| newsagent | **le magasin de journaux** | maga-**zañ** duh zhoor-**no** |
| post office | **la poste, le bureau de poste, les PTT** | pohst, boo**roh** duh pohst, peh-teh-teh |
| shoe shop | **le magasin de chaussures** | maga-**zañ** duh show-**soor** |
| supermarket | **le super-marché** | soo pehr-**marshay** |
| tobacconist | **le tabac** | tabah |
| travel agent | **l'agence de voyages** | l'**azhoñs** duh vway**azh** |

## Menu Decoder

| | | |
|---|---|---|
| **l'agneau** | l'an**yoh** | lamb |
| **l'ail** | l'eye | garlic |
| **la banane** | ba**nan** | banana |
| **le beurre** | burr | butter |
| **la bière** | bee-**yehr** | beer |
| **le bifteck, le steak** | beef-**tek**, stek | steak |
| **le boeuf** | buhf | beef |
| **bouilli** | boo-**yee** | boiled |
| **le café** | kah-**fay** | coffee |
| **le canard** | ka**nar** | duck |
| **le citron pressé** | see-**troñ** press-**eh** | fresh lemon juice |
| **les crevettes** | kruh-**vet** | prawns |
| **les crustacés** | **kroos**-ta-say | shellfish |
| **cuit au four** | kweet oh foor | baked |
| **le dessert** | deh-**ser** | dessert |
| **l'eau minérale** | l'oh **meeney**-ral | mineral water |
| **les escargots** | leh zes-kar-**goh** | snails |
| **les frites** | freet | chips |
| **le fromage** | from-**azh** | cheese |
| **les fruits frais** | frwee freh fresh | fruit |
| **les fruits de mer** | frwee duh mer | seafood |
| **le gâteau** | gah-**toh** | cake |
| **la glace** | glas | ice, ice cream |
| **grillé** | gree-**yay** | grilled |
| **le homard** | o**mahr** | lobster |
| **l'huile** | l'**weel** | oil |
| **le jambon** | zhoñ-**boñ** | ham |
| **le lait** | leh | milk |
| **les légumes** | lay-**goom** | vegetables |
| **la moutarde** | moo-**tard** | mustard |
| **l'oeuf** | l'uf | egg |
| **les oignons** | leh zon**yoñ** | onions |
| **les olives** | leh zo**leev** | olives |
| **l'orange pressée** | l'oroñzh press-**eh** | fresh orange juice |
| **le pain** | pan | bread |
| **le petit pain** | puh-**tee** pañ | roll |
| **poché** | posh-**ay** | poached |
| **le poisson** | pwah-**ssoñ** | fish |
| **le poivre** | pwavr | pepper |
| **la pomme** | pom | apple |
| **les pommes de terre** | pom-duh tehr | potatoes |
| **le porc** | por | pork |
| **le potage** | poh-**tazh** | soup |
| **le poulet** | poo-**lay** | chicken |
| **le riz** | ree | rice |
| **rôti** | row-**tee** | roast |
| **la sauce** | sohs | sauce |
| **la saucisse** | soh**sees** | sausage, fresh |
| **sec** | sek | dry |
| **le sel** | sel | salt |
| **le sucre** | sookr | sugar |
| **le thé** | tay | tea |
| **le toast** | toast | toast |
| **la viande** | vee-**yand** | meat |
| **le vin blanc** | vañ **bloñ** | white wine |
| **le vin rouge** | vañ **roozh** | red wine |
| **le vinaigre** | vee**naygr** | vinegar |

## Eating Out

|  |  |  |
|---|---|---|
| Have you got a table? | **Avez-vous une table libre?** | avay-**voo** oon tahbl leebr |
| I want to reserve a table. | **Je voudrais réserver une table.** | zhuh voo-**dray** rayzehr-**vay** oon tahbl |
| The bill, please. | **L'addition, s'il vous plaît.** | l'adee-**syoñ** seel voo **play** |
| I am a vegetarian. | **Je suis végétarien.** | zhuh swee vezhay-**tehryañ** |
| Waitress/ waiter | **Madame, Mademoiselle/ Monsieur** | mah-**dam**, mah-dem wah zel/**muh-syuh** |
| menu | **le menu, la carte** | men-**oo**, kart |
| fixed-price menu | **le menu à prix fixe** | men-**oo** ah pree feeks |
| cover charge | **le couvert** | koo-**vehr** |
| wine list | **la carte des vins** | kart-deh vañ |
| glass | **le verre** | vehr |
| bottle | **la bouteille** | boo-**tay** |
| knife | **le couteau** | koo-**toh** |
| fork | **la fourchette** | for-**shet** |
| spoon | **la cuillère** | kwee-**yehr** |
| breakfast | **le petit déjeuner** | puh-**tee** deh-**zhuh**-nay |
| lunch | **le déjeuner** | deh-**zhuh**-nay |
| dinner | **le dîner** | dee-**nay** |
| main course | **le plat principal** | plah prañsee-**pal** |
| starter, first course | **l'entrée, le hors d'oeuvre** | l'oñ-**tray**, or-duhvr |
| dish of the day | **le plat du jour** | plah doo zhoor |
| wine bar | **le bar à vin** | bar ah vañ |
| café | **le café** | ka-**fay** |
| rare | **saignant** | **say**-noñ |
| medium | **à point** | ah **pwañ** |
| well done | **bien cuit** | byañ **kwee** |

## Staying in a Hotel

|  |  |  |
|---|---|---|
| Do you have a vacant room? | **Est-ce que vous avez une chambre?** | es-kuh voo-**zavay** oon shambr |
| double room | **la chambre pour deux personnes, avec un grand lit** | shambr ah duh pehr-**son**, avek un gronñ lee |
| with double bed | | |
| twin room | **la chambre à deux lits** | shambr ah duh lee |
| single room | **la chambre pour une personne** | shambr ah oon pehr-**son** |
| room with a bath, shower | **la chambre avec salle de bains, une douche** | shambr avek sal duh bañ, oon doosh |
| porter | **le garçon** | gar-**soñ** |
| key | **la clef** | klay |
| I have a reservation. | **J'ai fait une réservation.** | zhay fay oon rayzehrva-**syoñ** |

## Sightseeing

|  |  |  |
|---|---|---|
| abbey | **l'abbaye** | l'abay-**ee** |
| art gallery | **la galerie d'art** | galer-ree dart |
| cathedral | **la cathédrale** | katay-**dral** |
| church | **l'église** | l'aygleez |
| garden | **le jardin** | zhar-**dañ** |
| library | **la bibliothèque** | beeb**leeo**-tek |
| museum | **le musée** | moo-**zay** |
| railway station | **la gare (SNCF)** | gahr (es-en-say-ef) |
| bus station | **la gare routière** | gahr roo-tee-**yehr** |
| tourist information office | **les renseigne-ments touristiques, le syndicat d'initiative** | roñsayn-**moñ** too-rees-**teek**, sandee-ka d'eenee-sya**teev** |
| town hall | **l'hôtel de ville** | l'ohtel duh veel |
| private mansion | **l'hôtel particulier** | l'ohtel partikoo-**lyay** |
| closed for public holiday | **fermeture jour férié** | fehrmeh-**tur** zhoor fehree-**ay** |

## Numbers

| | | |
|---|---|---|
| 00 | **zéro** | zeh-**roh** |
| 01 | **un, une** | uñ, oon |
| 02 | **deux** | duh |
| 03 | **trois** | trwah |
| 04 | **quatre** | katr |
| 05 | **cinq** | sañk |
| 06 | **six** | sees |
| 07 | **sept** | set |
| 08 | **huit** | weet |
| 09 | **neuf** | nerf |
| 10 | **dix** | dees |
| 11 | **onze** | oñz |
| 12 | **douze** | dooz |
| 13 | **treize** | trehz |
| 14 | **quatorze** | ka**torz** |
| 15 | **quinze** | kañz |
| 16 | **seize** | sehz |
| 17 | **dix-sept** | dees-**set** |
| 18 | **dix-huit** | dees-**weet** |
| 19 | **dix-neuf** | dees-**nerf** |
| 20 | **vingt** | vañ |
| 30 | **trente** | tront |
| 40 | **quarante** | karoñt |
| 50 | **cinquante** | sañkoñt |
| 60 | **soixante** | swasoñt |
| 70 | **soixante-dix** | swasoñt-**dees** |
| 80 | **quatre-vingts** | katr-vañ |
| 90 | **quatre-vingts-dix** | katr-vañ-**dees** |
| 100 | **cent** | soñ |
| 1,000 | **mille** | meel |

## Time

| | | |
|---|---|---|
| one minute | **une minute** | oon mee-**noot** |
| one hour | **une heure** | oon urr |
| half an hour | **une demi-heure** | oon **duh-mee** urr |
| Monday | **lundi** | luñ-**dee** |
| Tuesday | **mardi** | mar-**dee** |
| Wednesday | **mercredi** | mehrkruh-**dee** |
| Thursday | **jeudi** | zhuh-**dee** |
| Friday | **vendredi** | voñdruh-**dee** |
| Saturday | **samedi** | sam-**dee** |
| Sunday | **dimanche** | dee-**moñsh** |

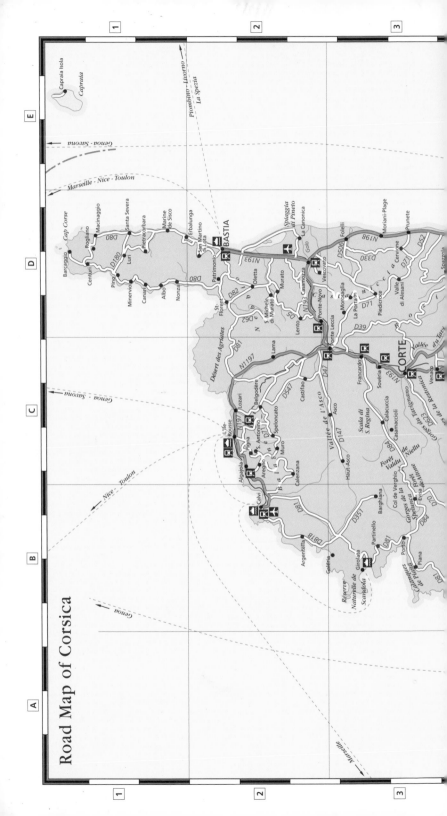

# Road Map of Corsica

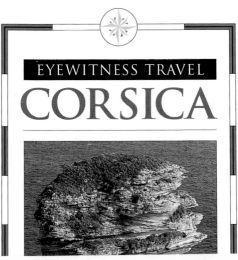

EYEWITNESS TRAVEL

# CORSICA